Managing Reputation in The Banking Industry

Stefano Dell'Atti • Annarita Trotta
Editors

Managing Reputation in The Banking Industry

Theory and Practice

Springer

Editors
Stefano Dell'Atti
University of Foggia
Foggia
Italy

Annarita Trotta
University Magna Graecia
Catanzaro
Italy

ISBN 978-3-319-28254-1 ISBN 978-3-319-28256-5 (eBook)
DOI 10.1007/978-3-319-28256-5

Library of Congress Control Number: 2016937363

Printed on acid-free paper

This Springer imprint is published by Springer Nature
The registered company is Springer International Publishing AG Switzerland

Stefano Dell'Atti dedicates this book
to Gabriella
Annarita Trotta dedicates this book
to Sabrina Maria

Preface

Reputation is a very important topic in business studies. However, it has recently become even more important, especially in the banking industry. In addition to frequent financial scandals and reputational crises, the dynamics of recent economic and financial crisis have also brought the behaviour of banks and others financial intermediaries under closer observation. Indeed, the sub-prime crisis has profoundly damaged the confidence of economic agents and their relationships with financial intermediaries. Consequently, scholars, regulators, and operators have started to devote more attention to reputational risks, especially those affecting banks.

Moreover, in the banking industry, despite the relevance of trust and relationships with stakeholders, the reputation and reputational risk research areas have until recently remained under-explored. This research field appears, therefore, extremely interesting and promising, given that some issues—such as the management of the reputational crisis and banks' reputations and the relationships between social responsibility and corporate reputation—deserve more detailed analysis.

Therefore, we find it constructive—on both the theoretical and the empirical plane—to propose a manuscript dedicated to bank reputation that develops theoretical arguments and proposes case studies regarding both the dynamic process of reputation management and certain important reputational banking crises.

The book offers an original approach to bank reputation management. Specifically, it provides a careful analysis of key aspects related to the corporate reputation, reputational risk, and reputational crises of banks. It is useful to identify the relationships among causes, mechanisms, and effects that contribute to building reputation and provide indications that will help scholars, professionals, and regulators to better manage corporate reputation and prevent reputational crises.

Indeed, bank reputation management is very important compared with other industrial sectors. It affects the stability of financial systems, the macroeconomic balances, and the propensity of financial operators to invest. As is well known, if a bank (especially a larger bank or systematic important institution) loses its reputation, it damages not only itself but the entire financial system. Public confidence is lost, financial investments collapse, and financial panic begins.

The book is organized into three parts and eight chapters. Part One offers an overview of the concepts of reputation, reputational risk, and reputational crisis in management and banking studies and proposes a model for understanding the bank reputational crisis, as well as to explore the case studies subsequently analysed.

The second part examines in detail the dynamics of both reputation management and reputational crisis, including the factors and phases of reputation management, thanks to an in-depth exploration of five interesting case studies.

Specifically, three cases are dedicated to reputational crises of important international banks. We analyse the reputational crises of Barclays, Goldman Sachs, and Lehman Brothers. We present the results of empirical analysis carried out through the observation of key variables, antecedents, and consequences of these banks' reputational crises.

By contrast, two cases are dedicated to the reputation management process implemented by the following two international banks: Intesa Sanpaolo and Unicredit Group. In these cases, interesting evidence useful for both academics and practitioners emerges.

Finally, the main findings, some concluding remarks, and guidelines for managing reputation are presented in Part Three of the book.

This work uses a qualitative research method.

The literature review uses scientific articles, books, and regulatory and supervisor reports.

Regarding the case study analyses, we draw on the multiple-case approach to posit a series of propositions that link reputation to strategic actions.

The case studies analysed were not selected randomly.

The final sample involves the following: (1) large banks with international relevance, (2) banks that suffered reputational damage in recent years or banks involved in a serious process of reputation management, and (3) banks that are developing a comprehensive approach to reputation.

These case studies cover a broad spectrum of the banking industry. More specifically, they include banks that have suffered a reputational crisis and banks that are improving their measures to prevent a reputational crisis. The wide diversity in the selected sample increases the possibility of generalizing the results and exploring patterns within the banking industry.

The book also serves a teaching function. Indeed, the reputational cases have been presented so that they can be studied in university courses.

We hope that this book not only serves the needs of practitioners engaged in the field of bank reputation but also inspires more discussion and more literature to develop the stream of inquiry regarding reputational crisis management in the banking industry.

Foggia, Italy Stefano Dell'Atti
Catanzaro, Italy Annarita Trotta

Acknowledgements

This book came to fruition through the guidance and the support of many different people. First, we offer our gratitude to the group of contributors for their hard work.

In addition, we fervently thank our publisher, Springer. We are particularly thankful to Dr Prashanth Mahagaonkar—Publishing Editor, Social Media Team Leader at Springer—and his assistants, Kay Stoll and Ruth Milewski, for their professionalism and seriousness in supporting the project and for their attention and patience devoted to the realization of the book.

Many thanks also go to the managers and staff of banks for providing the information and materials necessary to complete the case studies.

Regarding Intesa Sanpaolo, we are thankful to the following:

Dr Fabrizio Paschina, Head of Advertising and Web; Dr Valter Serrentino, Head of Corporate Social Responsibility; Dr Orio Veruska, Head of Operational and Reputational Risk; Dr Gabriella Gemo, former Head of Corporate Image; and Dr Laura Vescovo, former Head of Researches and Surveys.

Regarding the Unicredit Group, our thanks go to Dr Erika Fattori, Head of Customer Insight, and Dr Federica Paola Scardi, Strategic Analysis, Monitoring and Reporting.

Stefano Dell'Atti would also like to thank his wife, his daughter, and his parents for their unconditional support and for their patience. Additionally, thank you to the entire research team of the Chair of Banking and Finance of the University of Foggia for the continued commitment to research.

Annarita Trotta would like to thank her parents and her family for their continuing support and their tolerance of the time that this book necessitated. She would like to express gratitude to all her colleagues who provided critical insights for this project. Finally, Annarita would like to thank Father Giovanni Cananzi for his support, practical advice, and encouragement.

This book was produced with the co-financing of the following academic departments:

Department of Legal, Historical, Economic and Social Sciences, University "Magna Græcia", Campus of Germaneto, Viale Europa, 88100-Catanzaro, Italy.

Department of Economics, University of Foggia—Largo Papa Giovanni Paolo II, 1-71121 Foggia, Italy.

We want to express our gratitude to the two above academic departments.

Finally, all mistakes are ours.

Stefano Dell'Atti
Annarita Trotta

Contents

Part I
Theoretical Foundations

Reputation, Reputational Risk and Reputational Crisis in the Banking Industry: State of the Art and Concepts for Improvements

Annarita Trotta, Antonia Patrizia Iannuzzi, and Vincenzo Pacelli

Abstract The chapter introduces the relevance of reputation for the survival of banks. It discusses the state-of-the-art cornerstones regarding reputation, reputational risk and reputational crisis in the banking industry. The main concepts related to banks' reputations and reputational damage are explored in depth, focusing on reputational risk management and regulatory approaches for reputational risk. Based on these investigations, an original model for the analysis of banks' reputations and reputational crises, enriched by several variables of reputational alarm, is proposed.

1 Corporate Reputation: Definitions and Main Concepts

Reputation is a concept that is related to both individuals and organizations, and it is useful in both the public and private sectors (Booth 2000).

Over the last 30 years, scholars and practitioners have become increasingly interested in this area of study, which is the focus of a vast amount of literature. In her systematic review of corporate reputation, Walker (2010:359) identifies over 1500 articles. Nevertheless, despite the disparate and various distinct perspectives of analysis noted by researchers (Fombrun and Van Riel 1997; Chun 2005;

This chapter is the result of a collaboration between the authors. In particular, Annarita Trotta contributed to paragraphs 1, 2, and 4; Antonia Patrizia Iannuzzi contributed to paragraphs 3, 3.1, 3.2, 3.3, and 4.2; Vincenzo Pacelli contributed to paragraph 4.1.

A. Trotta (✉)
University Magna Graecia, Catanzaro, Italy
e-mail: trotta@unicz.it

A.P. Iannuzzi
Aldo Moro University of Bari, Bari, Italy
e-mail: antoniapatrizia.iannuzzi@uniba.it

V. Pacelli
University of Foggia, Foggia, Italy
e-mail: vincenzo.pacelli@unifg.it

S. Dell'Atti, A. Trotta (eds.), *Managing Reputation in The Banking Industry*,
DOI 10.1007/978-3-319-28256-5_1

Fombrun 2012), this area of study remains underexplored (Barnett et al. 2006) and chaotic due to the many, and sometimes conflicting, definitions of corporate reputations (Gotsi and Wilson 2001:24). In the 1990s, Fombrun and Van Riel (1997:128) defined the reputational landscape "*complex and multidimensional*". One decade later, Barnett et al. (2006:35) highlighted the need to achieve a "*common and more concise definition*" that is useful for practitioners. More recently, Ruiz et al. (2014:260) stated: "*In the literature regarding corporate reputation, the problems derived from the complex and intangible nature of reputation are perfectly known, making it very hard to perform a conceptual delimitation, characterization and measurement*".

These issues have urged further studies in the field, bringing order to this intriguing puzzle. It seems particularly useful to bridge the gap between academic definitions and the needs of practitioners (Bennett and Kottasz 2000).

Over the years, several academic works have discussed the definitions of reputation and related key features (Fombrun and Shanley 1990; Fombrun and Van Riel 1997; Bennett and Kottasz 2000; Barnett et al. 2006; Barnett and Pollock 2012; Helm et al. 2011), highlighting different claims and goals and providing a categorization of corporate reputation literature (Fombrun and Van Riel 1997; Barnett et al. 2006; Walker 2010; Ruiz et al. 2014).

Nonetheless, this area of study remains controversial and open to different perspectives and viewpoints. It is exceptionally promising for future explorations.

According to Fombrun (2012:95), "*three fundamental questions have been central themes of published literature: What are corporate reputations? Where do corporate reputations come from? What effects do corporate reputations have?*"

The search for the possible answers to these questions has indeed been the leitmotif of scholars and practitioners over the past 30 years.

In Table 1, we state some of the most frequently cited definitions of corporate reputation, starting from the "fundamental" definition given by Fombrun (1996) and ending with the latest definition offered by Fombrun in 2012, who notes in regard to his and other scholars' definitions the following: "*[A]lthough there are merits to such a measure, I also believe that both my own original definition, and the refinements proposed by Barnett (2006) and Walker (*2010*) may be too limiting: For one, building issue-specificity and varying standards into the construct will severely hamper our ability to cumulate research findings. More importantly, however, the more fundamental weakness embedded in all of these prior definitions is that they embed both antecedents and consequences of reputation within the reputation construct itself*" (Fombrun 2012:100).

It is clear that there is still no full agreement on the definition of corporate reputation. According to the approach of Fombrun (2012), it is more important to understand the reputational landscape and the differences between antecedents and consequences of such intangible asset.

In addition, analysing the key attributes of these definitions (see Table 1), the central roles of stakeholders emerge, particularly the roles of "specific stakeholder groups" (Fombrun 2012). According to Fombrun (2012), the refinement of the

Table 1 Prior definitions of corporate reputation

Authors (year:page)	Definitions of reputation (key attributes are in bold)
Fombrun (1996:72)	A **perceptual representation** of a company's past actions and future prospects that describes the firm's **overall appeal to all** of its key constituents when **compared with other leading rivals**.
Barnett et al. (2006:34)	**Observer's collective judgments** of a corporation based on **assessments** of the **financial, social, and environmental impacts** attributed to the corporate **over time**.
Walker (2010:370)	A relatively **stable**, issue specific **aggregate perceptual representation** of a company's past actions and future prospects **compared** against **some standard**.
Fombrun (2012:100)	**A Collective assessment** of a company's **attractiveness** to a **specific group of stakeholders** relative to a **reference group of companies** with which the company **competes for resources**.

Source: Our elaboration from Barnett et al. (2006), Walker (2010) and Fombrun (1996, 2012)

definition is useful in practice, solves main confusions in the debates between scholars and professionals and focuses on the core concepts of corporate reputation.

Several aspects (e.g., cultural and technical) differentiate stakeholder groups that have different ways of assessing a firm's reputation. Different reputations concern the same firm (Chun 2005), and there is no one reputation (Trotta et al. 2011).

As noted by Walker (2010:370), *"companies may have multiple reputations depending on which stakeholders and which issues are being looked at, but each reputation represents the aggregate perception of all stakeholders for that specific issue"*.

Different stakeholders use different "criteria" in their specific evaluation of reputation (Walker and Dyck 2014), and each criterion can be weighed differently depending on the stakeholder groups (Rindova et al. 2005).

Stakeholders' views (Freeman 1984) are useful in building and managing corporate reputations *in concreto*, particularly in recent years. According to Carreras et al. (2013:16):*"we are entering a new economic cycle that we can call economy of intangible assets and corporate reputation. In this new context, the roles of companies and the traditional balance of power are changing. This means that power is shifting over to stakeholders' hands (public opinion, customers, employees, regulators, shareholders, suppliers, etc.), and the new role of companies and institutions is to be at the service of the stakeholders"*. Focusing on what is observed and assessed by different groups of stakeholders allows us to explore the links among the concepts of corporate reputation, image and identity (see, among others, Fombrun and Van Riel 1997; Barnett et al. 2006; Da Camara 2011). Some scholars argue that the concepts of identity, image and reputation overlap, whereas others use these concepts indistinguishably (see, for a review, Chun 2005; Walker 2010; Foreman et al. 2012). Cian and Cervai (2014) offer an interesting analysis of reputation as *"an umbrella construct"* that includes "corporate image", "organizational identity", "organizational projected image", and all their main antecedents and related factors. In the reputation-building and management process, identity, image and reputation must always be aligned (Cornelissen 2014). Any dissonance between these concepts can lead to a crisis or a performance losses (Chun 2005; Cian and Cervai 2014).

2 Bank's Reputation: Determinants and Consequences

The crucial role of reputation is self-evident in the banking and financial industries. Reputation is a concept related both to the *"raison d'être"* of banks and the *special* nature of banking business in the context of contemporary financial intermediation theories (Diamond 1984, 1991; Boot et al. 1991, 1993; Bhattacharya and Thakor 1993; Chemmanur and Fulghieri 1994; Allen and Santomero 1998; Boot 2000).

Despite these considerations, reputation analysis in the banking sector (and in the financial sector) has long been ignored by scholars, practitioners and regulators. In response to fraud cases, scandals and the meltdown, this topic has become more fashionable, particularly its linkages with ethics (Leiva et al. 2014; Shanahan and Seele 2015), but it remains poorly investigated. The debate on reputation necessarily involves a reflection on the role and responsibility of scholars, professionals, policymakers and regulators. As stated by Helm (2011:13): *"reputation also is a reflection of the moral principles our economies and corporations adhere to and therefore also relevant form a deontological perspective"*. For these reasons, the topic is becoming more popular, particularly for banks and financial firms.

According to Walter (2014:301), *"(r)eputational matters for financial services companies are significantly more serious for this sector than other industries, because financial services comprise what are arguably 'special' businesses. This is for two reasons: first, because they deal with other people's money, and secondly, because problems that arise in financial intermediation trigger serious external costs, which during the crisis were subsequently 'collectivised' through government intervention"*.

Reputation is particularly important for banks and financial firms because the services they provide are intangible (Fombrun 1996; Wang et al. 2003), and the *"transactions are based on trust in the fulfilment of future promises* (Gaultier-Gaillard and Louisot 2006:425). Financial systems are also exposed to systemic events that could amplify reputational damages (De Bandt and Hartmann 2000). These considerations show that reputation is one of the most valuable (intangible) assets for any bank and most of all for global financial institutions (Stansfield 2006:470).

With respect to the link between reputation and trust in the banking industry, Romenti (2006:3) notes that "*a positive reputation represents an indication of the capital a company has in its credibility, reliability and trustworthiness (...) in relation to its stakeholders*", and it is useful in crisis management.

Trust is fundamental in the banking industry: *"while trust is fundamental to all trade and investment, it is particularly important in financial markets, where people part with their money in exchange for promises. Promises that are not worth the paper they have written on if there is no trust"* (Sapienza and Zingales 2012:124).

The specificities of the banking system and the financial industry affect regulators', professionals' and scholars' approaches to reputation.

In the case of the banking industry, which is characterized by information asymmetries, the need to preserve reputation should deter banks from opportunistic behaviour (Fang 2005), and the effectiveness of reputation serves as an enforcement mechanism (Buckley and Nixon 2009; von der Crone and Vetsch 2009). Therefore, "reputational concerns" (Corbett and Mitchell 2000) should be of utmost importance in decision-making processes.

For all of these reasons, we judged that it is an appropriate time to re-examine banks' reputation issues, starting from understanding the antecedents and consequences.

The primary determinants of corporate reputation are understood on a general level from the lens of Fombrun (2012:103), who identifies three main sources: *"the personal experiences that stakeholders have with an organization, the corporate initiatives and communications that managers make to strategically influence stakeholder perceptions, and the specialized coverage the organizations receives from influential intermediaries such as analysts, journalists, and others gatekeepers linked through social networks"*.

Several works discuss the most relevant criteria used for building and measuring reputations *in concreto*. In particular, Fombrun et al. (2000) provide an overview of the state of the art in reputation measurement and propose an instrument based on the following dimensions: emotional appeal, products and services, financial performance, vision and leadership, workplace environment, and social responsibility (see Chap. 2).

Rindova et al. (2005) identify two distinct (but interrelated) dimensions of organizational reputation, *perceived quality* and *prominence*, which have different antecedents. In their model, certifications provided by institutional intermediaries have a strong influence on a firm's prominence.

Limiting the analysis to the banking industry, general intermediaries (e.g., media) and expert intermediaries (e.g., rating agencies, analysts) play a keyrole in the process of information production and distribution (communication). Media data and media content are critical factors in reputation building and management (Fombrun and Shanley 1990; Deephouse 2000; Van Schaik and Garcia 2007; Tlou and Govender 2015; Van den Bogaerd and Aerts 2015), given the growing role of social media. In particular, global media and communication channels represent opportunities, challenges and threats for banks' reputations (Leiva et al. 2014).

The press' role is particularly important in the disclosure of misconduct and fraud. "*(P)ress articles based on reporter analysis seem to create significant changes in the market's assessment of a firm*" (Miller 2006:1024).

The special features of the banking sector emphasize the keyrole played by corporate disclosure practices and communication strategies (Gaultier-Gaillard and Pratlong 2011).

Banks' misconduct and enforcement of rules of conduct are also under the magnifying glass. Using a "law and finance" approach, academia investigates the links between the intensity of the enforcement powers of regulators and financial penalties for banks' misconduct (La Porta et al. 2006; Armour et al. 2010; Dyck et al. 2013). Linkages between reputation issues and enforcement of sanctions exist (Armour et al. 2010).

Some authors analyse the reputation effects of financial regulation enforcement. Karpoff and Lott (1993) find large reputational penalties related to press announcements of criminal fraud. Kang (2008) notes that reputational penalties are remarkable in the case of directors' interlocks.

By analysing the effects of sanctions decided by the French Financial Markets Authority on firms' reputation, Kirat and Rezaee (2015) identify three events that can have significative effects on stock prices: the opening of an investigation by the Authority, the issuance of a monetary sanction, and the publication of information about a sanction.

Therefore, the announcement of sanctions in the press and the opening of investigations represent triggering events that cause reputational losses. According to Djama (2013), financial markets are more reactive to the opening of an investigation for misconduct because of its "disciplinary effect".

With respect to banks, Ruiz et al. (2014) provide—*inter alia*—a literature review of the dimensions of banks' reputations. It noted that in the case of banks' reputations, scholars consider the quality of products and services to be of greatest importance. However, the results of their research do not confirm this assumption. Their empirical analysis shows that financial strength and leadership are the most important dimensions *in concreto*. In addition, their work confirms the relevance of the relationship between emotional dimensions (customer satisfaction and trust) and reputation (Ruiz et al. 2014:271).

Generally speaking, a positive financial and economic performance could amplify the company's ability to create value over time and give it prestige. In the case of the banking industry, this attribute refers to banks' abilities to guarantee customers' deposits (Ruiz et al. 2014:264).

In times of crisis, this dimension likely becomes more significant. Financial performance is considered to be both an antecedent and a consequence of reputation (de la Fuente Sabate and de Quevedo Puente 2003; Lange et al. 2011). For this reason, it is worth distinguishing between prior financial performance (as an antecedent) and financial performance (as a consequence) (Ali et al. 2015).

Complex linkages are also identified in the literature between social and environmental responsibility and reputation. As a result of the special nature of banks and the effects of financial crisis, this issue is currently under the magnifying glass (see Chap. 2).

Additionally, vision and leadership on the one hand and workplace environment on the other represent two important key dimensions of reputation. They help characterize the culture of the bank and its rules of conduct.

Focusing on cognitive dimensions, Ruiz et al. (2014) include the "integrity dimension", which is only partially attributable, in our opinion, to social actions and is understood as the *"degree of responsibility, transparency, ethics and honesty practiced by organizations"* (Ruiz et al. 2014:264). However, they find an inverse relationship between integrity and reputation and social actions (Ruiz et al. 2014).

These criteria are also included in a list of the 15 most determining factors for banking institutions created by Gaultier-Gaillard and Pratlong (2011).

Obviously, antecedents can turn into hazards and represent risk drivers (Gatzert et al. 2015). In this regard, banks are particularly sensitive to reputational risk (Walter 2013); the banking literature emphasizes risks related to reputation.

Research on consequences shows several positive effects (Gatzert 2015): A good reputation improves customer loyalty (Ruiz et al. 2014) and the satisfaction of key stakeholders (Helm 2007), and it contributes to reducing the cost of capital (Armitage and Marston 2008).

In summary, various studies have been conducted that aim to give insight into a series of issues concerning the dimensions, antecedents and consequences of banks' reputations. First, although lists of the potential determinants of reputation have been created, the theoretical relationship has not always been confirmed empirically. This deficit could be due to several reasons, including the geographical area analysed, the time window considered, the stakeholder groups involved and stakeholders' different perspectives on the antecedents of corporate reputation (Ali et al. 2015:1105).

Second, a (causal and bidirectional) relationship between determinants and consequences sometimes exists.

Finally, in the case of banks' reputations, more attention is devoted to reputational risk.

3 Reputational Risk: Regulatory Approach and Management Connections

The first definition of reputational risk was elaborated in 1995 by the FED (1995): "*reputational risk is the potential that negative publicity regarding an institution's business practices, whether true or not, will cause a decline in the customer base, costly litigation, or revenue reductions*". This definition is short but conceptually extensive. Indeed, on the one hand, the definition identifies the causes of reputational risk, which, according to the American Authority, are to be found essentially in adverse publicity and bad news, which can damage banks' images. On the other hand, however, the effects of the manifestation of reputational risk are defined; they can be both economic (e.g., the contraction of earnings, costs related to disputes) and non-economic (e.g., the reduction of the customer base, the loss of stakeholders' confidence).

In 1997, the Basel Committee stated that: "*reputational risk arises from operational failures, failure to comply with relevant laws and regulations, or other sources. Reputational risk is particularly damaging for banks since the nature of their business requires maintaining the confidence of depositors, creditors and the general marketplace*" (BCBS 1997:23). In this definition, the regulatory intervention appears to be more articulated than in the American definition. More in detail, we identify at least three aspects worthy of consideration that the European Authority aims to highlight: a) reputational risk arises primarily from operational and non-compliance failures with regulations; therefore, it is essentially a result of the manifestation of other non-financial risks (primarily operational and non-compliance risk); b) the sources of reputational risk are not all identified *a priori*. The Basel Committee, in fact, refers to "*other sources*", agreeing that although it is a second-order risk, the manifestation of reputational risk is not completely controllable. Finally, c) reputational risk may be particularly harmful because its manifestation can lead to a crisis of confidence in the performance of banking. After approximately 4 years, the Basel Committee stated: "*reputational risk poses a major threat to banks, since the nature of their business requires maintaining the confidence of depositors, creditors and the general marketplace. Reputational risk is defined as the potential that adverse publicity regarding a bank's business practices and associations, whether accurate or not, will cause a loss of confidence in the integrity of the institution. Banks are especially vulnerable to reputational risk because they can so easily become a vehicle for or a victim of illegal activities perpetrated by their customers*" (BCBS 2001:4). The greater extension of this proposal shows the attempt of regulation to provide a more refined definition of reputational risk. Indeed, on the one hand, it recalls the importance of the trust component; on the other hand, it also pays attention to the communicational factor. The spread of negative news concerning bank management is considered potentially damaging for banks' reputation, regardless of the validity or otherwise of this news (see also the FED 2008). As the news becomes more unfavourable, the probability of the manifestation of reputational risk and consequently the scope of the damage produced increase. Therefore, communication processes appear crucial for reputation, both positively and negatively. In summary, the intensity of reputational damages certainly depends on the nature of behaviour that violates rules and environmental expectations (Walter 2013). It is strongly influenced by the possibility of transmission to the outside, or through internal channels, of the information on the detrimental event. In the banking market, the "*official*" channels that disseminate information are manifold, including the following:

a) the investigations carried out by the Supervisory Authorities. Their annual reports generate a wealth of information on the quality of the business relationships of a bank. From these reports, it is possible to infer whether a bank (and/or its directors) has incurred administrative fines or penalties, whether it has undergone extraordinary inspections, whether it has violated rules regarding competition, and whether it is involved in judicial investigations;
b) the *Alternative Dispute Resolution (ADR)* between banks and customers. By reporting their activity, this system is an important vehicle of information about not only the quality of contractual relationships but also the commitment of

individual financial institutions to respecting and enhancing customer relationships (see Box 1).

Box 1 ADR and the Reputational Sanctions: A Focus

In some European countries, it is expected that financial intermediaries who do not respect the decisions made by respective *Alternative Dispute Resolution* be made public. The names of such banks are reported on the authority's website, in their annual reports or in the national press, along with a description of the practices found incorrect. This practice is adopted in Italy, where the *Arbitro Bancario Finanziario* has been active since 2009, and in Spain, where the *ADR* is part of the *Servicio de Reclamaciones*.

These two institutions cannot make binding decisions (as a judge can); however, by publicizing the non-fulfilment of the banks, they determine an obvious "*reputational sanction*". In this way, the regulator intends to stimulate the market discipline. On the contrary, in Germany and France, the *Alternative Dispute Resolution* does not provide any type of sanction against financial intermediaries who not respect their decisions. In England, a mixed system operates. On one hand, the decisions made by the *Financial Ombudsman Service* (FOS) have the force of executive title against banks, and in case of non-compliance, they may be accompanied by a fine imposed by the FSA; on the other hand, there are no plans in England to publicize financial intermediaries that are non-compliant. In the USA, platforms managed by private institutions that specialize in arbitration and conciliation services exist. The most important *ADR providers* are the *American Arbitration Association Inc.*, the *National Arbitration Forum* and *JAMS*. Currently, no ADR systems are incardinated in public regulatory authorities, and there is no "*reputational sanction system*".

Source: Our elaboration from Boccuzzi (2010) and non-judicial authority websites.

After a few years, the regulator developed other important definitions of reputation risk with the intent to capture as much as possible all major defining elements. Over time, the regulator tried to add new items to arrive at a definition that is always more complex and representative of the real "*modus operandi*" of such risk. Table 2 chronologically traces the most important key features provided by the main definitions of reputational risk developed by the Supervision.

The last definition dates back to 2009, when, the regulator stated that among other aspects, reputational risk "*exists throughout the organization*" (BCBS 2009a:19). The regulator highlighted two important connotations of this risk: the strong pervasiveness and transversality with respect to the company structure, which makes it not only difficult to manage—to the point of becoming "*the most intractable risk in terms of the overall hierarchy of risks faced by financial intermediaries*" (Walter 2013)—but also a "*unicum*" in the banking organization.

Table 2 The key features of the main regulatory definitions of reputational risk

Definitions of reputational risk/ authority documents (year:page[a])	Distinctive features in main regulatory definitions
FED—Federal Reserve System (1995)	• The spread of negative news can cause the manifestation of reputational risk. • Whether this news is true is irrelevant. • The effects of reputational risk may be economic and non-economic.
BCBS—Basel Committee on Banking Supervision (1997:23)	• Reputational risk follows from the manifestation of other types of risk (operational and compliance risks). • It is not possible to identify in advance all the possible sources of reputational risk. • Reputational risk is highly harmful for the banking business.
BCBS—Basel Committee on Banking Supervision (2001:4)	• Communicational factors are important: communication processes appear critical for corporate reputation in both positive and negative senses. • The manifestation of reputational risk can also exclude a direct responsibility of the financial intermediary because the latter can be a mere vehicle of fraudulent activity carried out by the customers.
BCBS—Basel Committee on Banking Supervision (2006:144)	• Reputational risk is dissociated from operational risk. • Although it represents a second-order risk, reputational risk is autonomous and independent at the definitional, operational and management levels.
CEBS (now *EBA, European Banking Authority*) (2006:40)	• There is a net connection between reputational risk and economic value destruction, and the manifestation of this risk may affect earnings and/or capital. • There are two clusters of stakeholders: a) *transactional stakeholders*(customers, shareholders, investors and the regulator, cited by the CEBS), which most likely feed direct interests toward the bank (because they are linked to the bank by a contractual relationship, and b) *tangential stakeholders*, such as the press, the media, NGOs, tradeunions, competitors and the general public (not mentioned by the CEBS), whose expectations, however, can be considered more marginal (because such stakeholders are linked to the bank by a non-contractual relationship; Manjarin 2012; Abrahams 2008).
BCBS—Basel Committee on Banking Supervision (2009a:19)	• Increased importance and emphasis are attributed to reputational risk. • The perceptive nature and the multidimensional character (multi-stakeholder view) of reputational risk are recognized. • Reputational risk has a strong cause-effect relationships with other types of risk (e.g., liquidity, market risk). • Economic implications related to reputation loss are recognized.

(continued)

Table 2 (continued)

Definitions of reputational risk/ authority documents (year:page[a])	Distinctive features in main regulatory definitions
	• Reputational risk can compromise the funding opportunities of banks also through the interbank market and securitization processes (therefore, bank-customers relations include relations between banks and other financial intermediaries, expanding the scope of this risk).

[a]The page number refers to the page containing the text where the reputational risk definition appears

Source: Our elaboration of the Supervisory Authority' documents cited in the table

As seen in Table 2, there are two key elements that are echoed in all proposed definitions. Reputational risk is, on the one hand, related to other specific risks of the banking business (primarily, operational and compliance risk); on the other hand, it constitutes a risk that is logically distinct from other types of risk. It follows that banks must make use of valid approaches that are capable of evaluating the links between reputational risk and other risks but simultaneously isolate this risk to achieve appropriate measurement and management techniques.

3.1 The Management of Reputational Risk: The Point of View of Regulation

In the first phase, the regulator focuses primarily on elaborating specific definitions of reputational risk. Then, when financial scandals have become more frequent, the attention shifts primarily to the management and measurement of this risk that all banks should implement.

The first major action in this direction was in 2004, when the Basel Committee on Banking Supervision published the document that transposed the Basel II Accords (BCBS 2006). Through this measure, on one hand, the regulator separates, on both operational and conceptual levels, this risk from operational risk by modifying a conviction expressed only a few years ago. On the other hand, the Basel Committee urges banks to develop special techniques of reputational risk management, although it acknowledges the difficulties of measuring this non-financial risk ("*although the Committee recognizes that 'other' risks, such as reputational and strategic risk, are not easily measurable, it expects industry to further develop techniques for managing all aspects of these risks*", BCBS 2006: *section* 742). More specifically, reputational risk is placed between so-called "*second-pillar*" risks, which are different from risks that require a mandatory minimum of capital (e.g., credit, market and operational risks, so-called "*first-pillar risks*"). Hence, in this first phase, the regulator does not impose the detention of regulatory capital against reputational risk. Rather, it urges financial intermediaries to internally evaluate the adequacy of its capital base until the capital held is sufficient to support all risks associated with the banking activity.

In this way, reputational risk fully enters the logical framework of the risk assessment process of the bank, assuming a specific role within the *enterprise risk-management process* (Regan 2008). Even in the absence of an apposite capital buffer, it is essential to pay attention not only to the mechanisms of interaction between reputation risk and other types of banking risk but also to measurement methods, which, although difficult to implement, must be developed (BCBS 2012: 47).

In 2009, the Basel Committee published a package of measures to strengthen the three pillars of the Basel II (see *Enhancements to the Basel II framework*). On this occasion, the Authority also aimed to establish specific management guidelines while confirming the location of the reputational risk under Pillar II. First, it stated: a) "*banks should have policies in place to identify sources of reputational risk*" (BCBS 2009a:19), particularly when "*when entering new markets, products or lines of activities*" (BCBS 2009a:20). Specifically, among the sources of reputational risk, all business lines of the bank are included, along with the liabilities, off-balance sheets, and special purpose vehicles with which the bank operates. The risk of such transactions must be properly assessed and integrated in the processes of the risk appetite of the bank and subsequently addressed in the self-assessment of the capital allocation (ICAAP, *Internal Capital Adequacy Assessment Process*) and the development of appropriate liquidity contingency plans. Second, the Basel Committee recommends that: b) the "*stress testing procedures carried out by banks—take account of reputational risk*" (BCBS 2009a:20) to better understand the pervasiveness of negative consequences associated with the manifestation of this risk. Finally, c) "*in order to avoid reputational damages and to maintain market confidence, a bank should develop methodologies to measure as precisely as possible the effect of reputational risk in terms of other risk types (e.g., credit, liquidity, market or operational risk) to which it may be exposed*" (BCBS 2009a:20). With this statement, the Committee intended to focus on the true and potential interaction between reputational risk and other types of banking risk. It is therefore clear that reputational risk should be analysed, managed and monitored not in *standalone mode* but through the examination of the mutual influence with other types of risk from which "*reputational spill-over effects*" can result (BCBS 2009b:16). In the same years, the regulator urged banks to analyse the performance of some indicators (such as complaints and disputes) that are representative of a possible deterioration of the banks' reputation, along with the occurrence of negative effects, particularly if they are economic in nature (e.g., losses, disbursements). At the same time, it is important that such an assessment is associated with the examination of certain operational and/or organizational factors (e.g., conflicts of interest, organizational complexity, structured products) to highlight any gaps or dysfunction. The regulator gives importance not only to the original events that can trigger the reputational risk but also to the organizational structures that, if not properly prepared, can certainly facilitate the manifestation of this risk (Bank of Italy 2008).

3.2 Reputational Risk in the System of Banking Risks

As stated, the relationships between reputational risk and other banking risks are of two types: a) causal and b) interactive. The causal relationships primarily affect the grouping of operational risks (operational risk, legal and non-compliance risk) and risks of a business nature (business and strategic risk; Patarnello 2010). In particular, this aspect emerges from regulations that, in multiple definitions of reputational risk, show that such risks primarily originate "*from operational failures and failure to comply with relevant laws and regulations*" (BCBS 1997:23a). Therefore, the relationships between reputational risk and compliance/operational risk appear direct and pervasive. Whenever a bank does not comply with the system of rules governing the banking business, it is likely to incur a reputational sanction that will likely increase with the significance of the violation against the collective well-being. Hence, it is necessary to take advantage of a *Compliance Function* to predispose appropriate organizational measures not only to prevent regulatory violations but also to neutralize any effect on banks' reputations. Very similar is the link between reputational risk and legal risk; the latter is due to the emergence of disputes with both customers and Regulatory Authorities. Finally, the connection is important between operational and reputational risk ratified not only by regulations but also by the doctrine that has investigated their implications by identifying significant empirical evidence.

Using event-study methodology, many authors have analysed the effect of operational losses on the market value of listed companies (De Fontnouvelle et al. 2006; Cummins et al. 2006; Gillet et al. 2010; Plunus et al. 2012; Sturm 2013). In most cases, it is reported that the market more strongly penalizes operating loss that has occurred by highlighting consequentially the existence of a mere reputational damage (Cummins et al. 2006; Plunus et al. 2012). The event types that cause the most reputational effects are due to human resources and processes. Indeed, the collapse in stock prices is greater and more immediate (Biell and Muller 2013) when the operating loss is due to internal fraud (De Fontnouvelle et al. 2006; Gillet et al. 2010; Schwizer et al. 2010; Biell and Muller 2013; Fiordelisi et al. 2014) or when it occurs in companies with a higher level of debt (Sturm 2013) or profitability (Fiordelisi et al. 2013).

On the contrary, interactive relationships involve essentially the managerial risks (including credit, liquidity and market risk). Among these the liquidity risk is very important. Indeed, not only the Basel Committee but also other important Regulatory Authorities have addressed the issue of the mutual repercussions of reputational crisis on a liquidity crisis (FED 2010). The manifestation of reputational risk can certainly have serious repercussions for a bank's ability to meet its payment obligations; furthermore, though temporary, illiquidity is likely to have reputational effects that can exacerbate the *status quo* and transform a liquidity crisis into a default condition. It is also worth paying attention to financial liabilities levels and to their related implications for reputational risk, which can negatively affect not only the funding opportunities of the bank but also the ability to place on the market instruments that are a part of regulatory capital, thereby jeopardizing the financial soundness of a bank (FED 2010; BCBS 2014).

Finally, a more recent connection established by regulators is between reputational risk and compensation systems and thus between reputational risk and *compensation risk management*. The first Authority that has institutionalized this association is the *Financial Stability Forum*, which in the *Principles for Sound Compensation Practices* (April 2, 2009) states that "*compensation must be adjusted for all types of risk(….). Risk adjustments should account for all types of risk, including difficult- measure risks such as liquidity risk, reputation risk and cost of capital*" (FSF 2009:2). This opinion is shared by the Basel Committee on Banking Supervision, which years later stated that "*risk measurement should be comprehensive and address known financial risks (such as market, credit and liquidity), as well as non-financial risks (such as legal, reputational and compliance risks) and other operational risks*" (BCBS 2011:21). In more detail, the link between *reputational* and *compensation risk* has two important implications: First, it urges financial intermediaries to include executive pay in the metrics for measuring corporate reputation, identifying and adopting relevant qualitative indicators of the efficiency and correspondence of these practices to the dictates of regulation (which after the international crisis has become increasingly stringent). On the other hand, linking the remuneration packages to reputational risk could also increase pay levels (Deephouse 1997; Winfrey and Logan 1998) if the bank were to enjoy an excellent reputation and thus reward managers for having reached this important milestone (Cordeiro et al. 2000; Milbourn 2003). However, because it is not easy to exactly quantify reputational risk, regulators urge banks to use special proxies, including "*risk indicators, capital requirements or scenario analysis*" (EBA 2015:61).

3.3 The Dynamics of Reputational Risk: Sources, Effects and Stakeholders Involved

It is crucial to investigate the dynamics of reputational risk by analysing the sources, the effects and the stakeholders involved in the manifestation of such risk.

According to regulators and the recent literature (Walter 2013; Cummins et al. 2006; Gillet et al. 2010), reputational risk arises from a "*primary*" business event that is essentially a type of financial or non-financial risk of greater importance for a bank. It is believed that reputational risk assumes the guise of a harmful additive event rather than alternative (Patarnello 2010). Therefore, it is a second-order risk because it follows the manifestation of another type of risk which assumes the qualification of "*original event*" (Fiordelisi et al. 2014). Consequently, damaging events that can compromise bank reputation are primarily "*endogenous*" because they are the direct result of the illegal conduct of managers or of omissions in the performance of the control functions and the monitoring of management. These events may be classified into four categories:

a) operational losses that could have the greatest reputational influence if they are caused by internal fraud (Fiordelisi et al. 2014);
b) the violation of the corporate provisions (codes of conduct and/or ethical), legislation or self-regulation rules (self-regulatory codes);
c) legal disputes that elicit administrative or criminal penalties (imposed, for example, by the national supervisory authorities);
d) errors in business decisions generally associated with a *short-termism* and/or a failure to react quickly to cyclical changes.

All these situations can be qualified as "*endogenous sources*" of reputational risk. They will cause a reputational loss that will increase with the strength of the amplification process resulting from the activation of "*reputational variables*", identified in the type of environment in which the bank operates, in the importance of the corporate brand and the effectiveness of communication processes (Gabbi 2004).

There are also cases in which the responsibility of the intermediary appears more marginal. This happens, for example, in the presence of an adverse evolution of the environment or in economic conditions that increase sovereign risk (Walter 2013). In other cases, however, the reputation of a bank may be affected by the reputational crisis of another financial intermediary, usually a competitor with whom the bank considers having trade relations. Some scholars have noted that in the financial sector, particularly when the economic condition is adverse, a contraction of the reputational capital of a bank (particularly if it has systemic importance) can certainly affect the reputation and equities prices of other financial intermediaries. "*This "industry effect" is especially strong in the banking sector, where even the more responsible banks have had to struggle with the public perception that they, too, have been partly responsible for the financial crisis and mistreating their consumers*" (Reputation Institute 2015:3).

These events, in which banks do not hold direct and subjective responsibility, may be considered "*exogenous sources*" of reputational risk. They reveal another characteristic of this type of risk, i.e., that it is not completely controllable by an individual bank. Therefore in order to manage the reputational risk, sectorial control methodologies and the systemic actions agreed upon by the different financial intermediaries must also be implemented (Walter 2013). The banks "*needs to work together to restore trust among stakeholders and return to its core tenets of responsibility and providing the highest-quality services to consumers worldwide*" (Reputation Institute 2015:3).

The second aspect to consider to understand the dynamics of reputational risk concerns the stakeholders involved in the negative event that damages the bank. In this case, CEBS (2006) discerns two categories of stakeholders:

a) *transactional stakeholders* (e.g., *customers, shareholders, employees, investors and regulators)*. Most likely, they feed direct interests in the operations of the bank because they are linked to it by a contractual relationship;
b) *tangential stakeholders* (such as *the media, non-governmental organizations, trade unions, rating agencies, competitors and the general public)*,whose

expectations may be considered different because they are linked to the bank by a not-contractual relationship (Manjarin 2012; Abrahams 2008).

This distinction is useful for the success of the political management of reputational risk. The specific identification of stakeholders involved allows for a better calibration of the interventions to focus them on the stakeholders most affected by the reputational event (Walker and Dyck 2014).

Finally, we also must analyse the consequences that a bank may suffer when reputational risk occurs. In this regard, a first important distinction concerns the nature of the effects that, on the basis of this criterion, may be strictly economic (*direct effects*) or non-economic (*indirect effects*; Dell'Atti et al. 2012). In the first case, the consequences of the manifestation of reputational risk directly generate a loss of economic nature affecting certain values of financial statements; in the second case, however, the reduction of banks' economic value is mediated by the activation of some qualitative variables that only at a later cause economic loss.

According to Dell'Atti et al. (2012) and Walter (2013) cases of non-economic reputational effects can include the following: *the loss of market share caused by customers' disaffection; the reduction of the effectiveness of the diversification of geographical and sectorial strategies (regarding both funding and loans); legislative and regulatory actions, such as inspections by the supervisory authorities and/or involvement in criminal proceedings; and difficulties in recruiting and retaining qualified staff.*

On the contrary, economic reputational effects are primarily related to: *the imposition of administrative sanctions, fines and legal fees; funding contraction; the increase in the cost of funding in terms of venture capital and debt capital; the deterioration of capital solvency and the consequent danger of running into a liquidity crisis; the increase in shares' volatility and/or the contraction of their market value; and direct and indirect costs directed to recovering the lost reputation.*

However, independently of this distinction, it should be noted that all reputational consequences are able to generate significant economic losses that negatively affect banks' shares value. Not only can several reputational negative effects occur simultaneously; it is not uncommon that the manifestation of one of can lead to others, thereby triggering a systemic reaction that makes it difficult or impossible to identify the original effect.

4 Understanding Reputational Crisis in the Banking Industry: Concepts for Improvements and a Proposed Model

Despite the relevance of the topic, few studies have focused on reputational crisis in the banking and financial industries.

Booth (2000:197) defines reputational crisis as "*the loss of the common estimation of the good name attributed to an organization*" whereas Zyglidopoulos and Phillips (1999:335) qualify reputational crisis as "*a situation in which important stakeholders negatively re-evaluate their opinions and beliefs about the firm*".

In the case of banking industry, the main key characteristics of reputational crisis are (Dell'Atti et al. 2012:251):

a) the triggering event that can be internal or external;
b) reputational effects/damages that can be various (financial and non-financial) and differ across banks;
c) the interpretation and reaction of internal and external bank stakeholders.

Note that stakeholders' reactions depend on several variables, including the nature of the event and the interpretation of information about this event available in a bank's ecosystem. We can distinguish between two different types of communications and disclosure provided by banks: information and communications that the bank controls, and information, data and news that are beyond the control of the bank. Dell'Atti et al. (2012) compared several case studies of banks' reputational crisis and noted that the market reacts and punishes banks with behaviour that is not aligned with stakeholders' expectations. In particular, fraud or, more generally, misconduct, which are within banks' responsibilities, are punished harder. It is interesting to note that the intensity of market reaction could also depend on specific institutional features and the way of handling the crisis (CIMA 2007:15). In addition, many reputational crisis are caused by failures in governance and the internal control systems of the bank (Dell'Atti et al. 2012).

The main findings of our review of the state of art that are significant with regard to banks' reputation and reputational crisis are: 1) Determinants are often different and connected in many different ways. 2) Effects may vary with the characteristics of the bank (e.g., type of activity, size, age, geographic markets), of the ecosystem and of the period. 3) Reputational losses also depend on the type of communication and disclosure realized by the bank. As argued above (with regard to banks' reputations), different groups of relevant stakeholders are very important. This is also true *a fortiori* in the case of reputational crisis, in which relevant stakeholders play a decisive role in the interpretations of events and banks' responses. Additionally, we note that in financial systems, authoritative and specialized actors (e.g., rating agencies, financial analysts, scholars, specialized journalists) can be perceived as gatekeepers, analysing information from various sources and relaying it to other stakeholders. In particular, regulatory and supervisors authorities indirectly confirm—in the eyes of the public opinion—the accuracy of the information.

Based on these considerations, we consider it useful to suggest—with respect to the categories of stakeholders-a more articulate categorization of relevant stakeholders, by distinguishing 1) regulators and supervisors and 2) media, analysts and scholars. These are two different groups of stakeholders ad hoc, with respect to the transactional stakeholders and tangential stakeholders.

Finally, our review highlights that in the banking industry, information is a key element of the relationships between banks and stakeholders, and reputation is based on information.

By this reasoning, we can conclude that each reputational crisis appears to be specific and unique. Therefore, in our opinion, the qualitative approach is the best way to conduct an exploratory analysis of reputational crisis, with the goal of better understanding the differences and similarities between individual case studies.

In the following, we propose a model that uses a set of reputational indicators. We believe that these indicators are important reputational signals that are useful for qualitative analysis. The model (proposed in the Appendix) consists of six sections (A, B, C, D, E, and F). Each section is dedicated to a major cornerstone of banks' reputations, as noted in our review.

The model is composed of 43 reputational indicators that can be distinguished as external or internal variables. Internal variables concern data, documents or actions made by banks, whereas external variables are those related to relevant information produced by several independent actors in a bank. Because bank has no over control these variables, they are considered external.

The proposed model is useful to serve as a guideline for monitoring bank's reputation and understanding reputational crisis.

Turning to the details of the model, Section A and Section B explore the quality of the relationships with relevant and specific groups of stakeholders (e.g., regulators, supervisory authorities, media, analysts). Section A detects whether and how banks are involved in administrative or judicial litigations, investigations or extraordinary inspections from supervisory authorities. Section B searches for anomalies in the announcements provided by authoritative stakeholders, such as rating agencies, analysts, and journalists, with special attention devoted to media coverage and visibility.

Section C refers to quantitative or financial-economic ratios available on financial markets, whereas Section D consists of economic and financial ratios derived from banks' financial statements or other official documents. Finally, Sections E and F are dedicated to data and documents related to ethics and values.

To help facilitate the understanding and use of more complex variables related to the proposed model, detailed explanations are provided for the Sections C, D, E, and F in the following sub-paragraphs.

A final clarification is necessary. The proposed reputational variables do not cover all the investigations. Future research is expected to continue exploring the qualitative aspects of banks' reputations and reputational crisis.

4.1 A Focus on Sections C and D

In Section D of our model, we aim to analyse the following indicators:

- customer deposits;

- interbank deposits;
- the conditions of economic and financial balance;
- the cost of funding and the cost of equity;
- the incidence of derivatives in financial statements;
- the conditions of liquidity and capital adequacy.

In particular, regarding customer and interbank deposits, we aim to analyse the relative changes in the reputational capital of the banks in relation to their real and potential customers' depositors. We can measure banks' reputations towards depositors by an economic criterion for estimating differential results. In this way, the value of the reputational capital towards depositors coincides with the benefits to be calculated in differential way compared to medium or normal situations of competitors (who cannot take advantage of this relational capital). The change in the reputational capital of banks towards their real and potential customer depositors can be estimated in percentage terms by the following formula:

$$\Delta\ \mathrm{CRC} = (\Delta\ \text{annual bank deposits}) - (\Delta\ \text{average deposits})$$

where:

- Δ CRC measures the variation in the reputational capital towards customers, and it can also be understood as an estimate of the change in the value of banks' reputation towards customer depositors[1];
- Δ annual bank deposits is the annual percentage change in the "Total Deposits" of the bank analysed;
- Δ average deposits is the average annual percentage change of "Total Deposits" of a panel of banks competitors.

This differential analysis can be conducted distinguishing: *a*) total customer deposits from *b*) interbank deposits (total deposits from banks). In the second case, the change in the reputational capital of banks in the interbank market can be estimated in percentage terms using the following formula.

$$\Delta\ \mathrm{CRB} = (\Delta\ \text{annual interbank deposits of the bank}) \\ - (\Delta\ \text{average volumes of interbank deposits})$$

where:

- Δ CRB measures the variation in the reputational capital in the interbank market, and it can also be understood as an estimate of the change in the value of the banks' reputation towards other banks;
- Δ annual interbank deposits is the annual percentage change in "total deposits from banks" of the bank analysed;

[1] Considering the relative value and not the absolute value, we delete the distortions caused by the different sizes of the banks analysed.

- Δ average interbank deposits is the average annual change in "total deposits from banks" of a panel of bank competitors.

The conditions of economic and financial balance can be analysed by the reclassification of the balance sheets and the income statements.

To approximate another measure of the reputation of the banks towards depositors and shareholders, we aim to estimate the percentage cost of customer deposits and the percentage cost of equity. Regarding the percentage cost of funding, we will determine the average rate paid by the bank for the passive collection from customers.[2] Regarding the determination of the cost of equity (Ke), we apply the formula of the CAPM:

$$Ke = Rf + \beta * (Rm - Rf)$$

where:

- Rf is the risk-free integrated country risk factor, identified in the average annual return (December 31 of each year) of the 10-year treasury bond issued by the state.
- β is the measure of the volatility of a stock relative to the market, which is the correlation factor between the yield logarithmic actual title of the bank and the overall yield of the reference market compared to the variance of the total returns of the market.
- (Rm − Rf) is the risk premium required by the market.

Regarding the amount and effect of speculative derivatives in the financial statements, we aim to analyse derivatives in the financial statements in relation to the assets and liabilities measured at fair value. We will analyse the conditions of liquidity and capital adequacy of the banks by different ratios.

Finally, in Section C of our model, we aim to conduct a technical analysis of the share price of the bank and then calculate a monetary value representing the reputation of the bank in the financial markets. To estimate a monetary value representing the reputation of banks in financial markets, it is possible to multiply the value of the net assets of the banks—equity—for the difference between the actual value of the ratio "price to book value (P/BV)" of banks on the market and a theoretical measure of this relationship, which we can also infer based on the profitability of banks:

$$CRMF = [(P/BV) - (Roae/Ke)]*Equity$$

where:

[2] The calculation method is based on the relationship between the annual interest expenses and the average of the last 2 years of the total liabilities.

- *CRMF* is the value of the reputational capital of banks in the financial markets;
- *P/BV* represents the value of the ratio "price to book value" really valued in the market;
- *Ke* is estimated by the CAPM approach;
- *Roae/Ke* provides an approximate estimate of the theoretical ratio "P/BV"; i.e., it incorporates the current profitability of the bank. It represents the capacity of creating economic value for shareholders;
- *Equity* is the net assets of the banks.

According to this estimation methodology, negative values of CRMF indicate that the market does not have value, and it incorporates in the share price the earning capacity of the bank. Positive values of CRMF indicate that the market, in addition to recognizing and enhancing its profitability, attributes to the bank also expectations of future economic value creation.

4.2 A Focus on Sections E and F

Section E of our model aims to analyse the social performance of a bank. To understand and rate the CSR performance of a bank, we select nine sub-indicators. First, we verify if the bank draws up a social report, determine whether it adopts the GRI model and identify its application level. This information constitutes a preliminary test to appreciate the effective CSR commitment of the bank. Then, we analyse other important social reporting tools that any bank could implement. They are the policy on *Anti-Money Laundering* (AML) and the policy related to the control and management of reputational risk. We believe that the employment of specific policies regarding such important issues (such as AML and reputational risk) represents an indicator of the importance that the bank gives to CSR concerns. Subsequently, we verify whether the bank is included in one or more ethical indices or in important reputational rankings, including those created by Fortune Magazine and Reputation Institute (see Chap. 2).

Finally, the last CSR sub-indicators aim to check whether the bank adopts and publishes (on the website) an ethical code, whether sanctions are provided in case of the violation of such ethical code and lastly whether the bank adopts procedures on gender diversity or financial inclusion.

To recognize the reputational performance of banks and to verify whether a reputational crisis could occur, it is important to focus on the *corporate governance system* (Section F). First, we analyse the board effectiveness by verifying whether the CEO is also chairman of the board (CEO-duality) and the presence of independent directors and determining whether the bank has established an ethical or CSR committee. Then, we focus on management compensation by verifying whether the bank provides information on its remuneration policy and determining the "*soundness*" of its pay system. To this end, five micro-criteria are selected. Finally, we also check whether the bank has established a remuneration committee, if it has established a compliance function and if has appointed a responsible governor of this function. In addition, women's presence (%) and their positions held in the corporate governance system are examined. We found all this information by consulting the Financial or Corporate Governance Reports of the bank.

Appendix: A Model for Understanding Reputational Crisis[a]

Reputational indicators	Description	Source
Section A—Information about the quality of stakeholder relationships		
A.1 Customer complaints	Check the number/increase of customer complaints	Website, financial report
A.2 Employee reduction	Check if the bank has reduced the number of its employees	Financial report, Bankscope
A.3 Stakeholder engagement systems	Check if the bank adopts stakeholder engagement systems	Social report
A.4 Extrajudicial litigations (disputes)	Check if the bank is involved in extrajudicial litigations	Website
A.5 Administrative sanctions from the National Supervisory Authority	Check if the bank managers have received sanctions by the National Central Bank	Website of National Central Bank (*Supervisory Bulletin*) and media
A.6 Administrative sanctions from the National Supervisory Regulator on the markets	Check if the bank managers have received sanctions by the Financial Market Supervisory Authority	Website of Financial Market Supervisory Authority (Supervisory Bulletin) and media
A.7 Inspections from the National Supervisory Authority	Check if the bank has received extraordinary inspections	Financial report
A.8 Involvement in judicial investigations	Check if the bank is involved in judicial investigations	Media/national and international press
A.9 Antitrust sanctions (check penalties)	Check if the bank has received sanctions for violations of competition rules	Antitrust Website
Section B—Information provided by authoritative and independent actors		
B.1 Downgrading by rating agencies	Analyse the performance of several individual and issuer rating of the major rating agencies, Moody's, Standard & Poor's and Fitch. Check if the bank has suffered a downgrading and its intensity	Bankscope
B.2 *Media coverage*: Negative press reports	Analyse the quality (positive/negative) of the press reporting	National/international press
B.3 Sentences given to corporate officers (bank managers)	Check if bank managers have been convicted	National/international Press

(continued)

Reputational indicators	Description	Source
B.4 Other negative judgments (from, e.g., Corporate Governance or ethical agencies)	Check if other rating agencies (on Governance, on CSR) have issued negative judgments	Websites of rating agencies, Press
Section C—Information about market measurement		
C.1 Contraction of the share price on the stock exchange (excluding cyclical and sectorial phenomena)	Technical analysis of share price of the bank compared to an sector index	Elaboration on financial-market data
C.2 Increase in the sales of the bank securities in periods of falling prices		Elaboration on financial-market data
C.3 Reduction of the value of the reputational capital of banks in the financial markets	CRMF = [(P/BV) − (Roae/Ke)]*Equity	Elaboration on financial-market data and Bankscope
Section D—Information about accounting measurements		
D.1 Deposit contraction (measured in relative terms compared to the mean change in the industry)	Δ CRC	Elaboration from Bankscope data
D.2 Contraction of the volumes of interbank deposits (measured in relative terms compared to the mean change in the industry, as a point D.1)	Δ CRB (bank reputational capital)	Elaboration from Bankscope data
D.3 Economic losses in the 5 years preceding the reputational crisis	Check if the bank has suffered economic losses	Financial report, Bankscope
D.4 Increase in the funding cost (K_d)	Interest expense on customer deposits/average customer deposits	Elaboration from Bankscope data
D.5 Increase in the equity cost (K_e)	CAPM approach	Elaboration from financial/market data
D.6 Amount/percentage of speculative derivatives		Financial report, Bankscope
D.7 Reduction of the degree of liquidity	Analyse the dynamics of more liquidity indicators	Elaboration from Bankscope data
D.8 Deterioration of asset quality	Analyse the dynamics of most indicators of asset quality	Elaboration from Bankscope data
D.9 Level and quality of capital	Analyse the capital composition of the bank and its development over the years (Tier 1 ratio vs. Total Capital ratio)	Elaboration from balance sheet data
D.10 Leverage ratio	Check the debt level of the bank	Bankscope

(continued)

Reputational indicators	Description	Source
Section E—Information about ethical performance		
E.1 Social report	Check if the bank draws up a social report	Website of bank
E.2 Compliance level to GRI	Check if the bank adopts the GRI model and determine the application level	Social report
E.3 Inclusion of the bank in ethical indices	Check if the bank is included in one or more ethical indices	Analysis of the composition of the most important ethical indices
E.4 Inclusion in reputational rankings	Check if the bank is included in reputational rankings	Analysis of reputational rankings
E.5 Specific policy for the control/management of reputational risk	Check if the bank draws up/adopts a policy on reputational risk	Website, social report
E.6 Policy on AML (Anti-Money Laundering)	Check if the bank draws up/adopts a policy on Anti-Money Laundering	Website, social report
E.7 Adoption of an ethical code and publication on the website	Check if the bank adopt and publish an ethical code	Social report
E.8 Sanctions for violations of the ethical code	Check if the bank imposes sanctions in case of violation of the ethical code	Website, social report
E.9 Policies/procedures regarding gender diversity/financial inclusion	Check if the bank adopts procedures of financial inclusion	Social report
Section F—Information about organizational and corporate governance system		
F.1 CEO duality	Check if the CEO is also chairman of the board	Corporate Governance report
F.2 Low/modest independence of the board (% of independent directors <50 %)	Check the board independence	Corporate Governance report
F.3 CSR or Ethical Committee	Check if the bank has established a CSR committee	Financial report, Corporate Governance report
F.4 Remuneration Policy	Check if the bank provides information on its remuneration policy	Corporate Governance report
F.5 Remuneration system: – *bonus even in the presence of economic losses,* – *no multi-year performance indicators,* – *high incidence of variable pay compared to the fixed regarding the CEO compensation,* – *no deferred compensation plan,* – *guaranteed bonuses and/or golden parachute*	Check the level of short-termism of executive remunerations	Corporate Governance report

(continued)

Reputational indicators	Description	Source
F.6 Remuneration committee	Check if the bank has established a remuneration committee	Corporate Governance report
F.7 Compliance function and/or its responsible party	Check if the bank has established a compliance function and has appointed a responsible governor of this function	Financial report, Corporate Governance report
F.8 Gender diversity	Check the women's presence (%) and their positions held	Financial report, Corporate Governance report

[a]This Appendix is the result of a collaboration between Stefano Dell'Atti, Annarita Trotta, Antonia Patrizia Iannuzzi and Vincenzo Pacelli

References

Abrahams D (2008) Brand risk: adding risk literacy to brand management. Gower Publishing Limited, Hampshire

Ali R, Lynch R, Melewar TC et al (2015) The moderating influences on the relationship of corporate reputation with its antecedents and consequences: a meta-analytic review. J Bus Res 68(5):1105–1117

Allen F, Santomero AM (1998) The theory of financial intermediation. J Bank Financ 21:1461–1485

Armitage S, Marston C (2008) Corporate disclosure, cost of capital and reputation: evidence from finance directors. Br Account Rev 40(4):314–336

Armour J, Mayer C, Polo A (2010) Regulatory sanction and reputational damage in financial markets. Oxford Legal Studies Research Paper No. 62/2010; ECGI – Finance Working Paper No. 300/2010. http://ssrn.com/abstract=1678028 or doi:10.2139/ssrn.1678028. Accessed 9 Mar 2015

Bank of Italy (2008) Guide to supervisory activities. Circular No. 269 of 7 May 2008

Barnett ML, Pollock TG (2012) Charting the landscape of corporate reputation research. In: Barnett ML, Pollock TG (eds) The Oxford handbook of corporate reputation. Oxford University Press, Oxford, pp 1–15

Barnett ML, Jermer JM, Lafferty BA (2006) Corporate reputation: the definitional landscape. Corp Reput Rev 9(1):26–38

BCBS—Basel Committee on Banking Supervision (1997) Core principles for effective banking supervision, September. http://www.bis.org/publ/bcbs30a.pdf

BCBS—Basel Committee on Banking Supervision (2001) Customer due diligence for banks, October. http://www.bis.org/publ/bcbs85.pdf

BCBS—Basel Committee on Banking Supervision (2006) International convergence of capital measurement and capital standards. A revised framework comprehensive version, June. http://www.bis.org/publ/bcbs128.pdf

BCBS—Basel Committee on Banking Supervision (2009a) Enhancements to the Basel II framework, July. http://www.bis.org/publ/bcbs157.pdf

BCBS—Basel Committee on Banking Supervision (2009b) Principles for sound stress testing practices and supervision, May. http://www.bis.org/publ/bcbs155.pdf

BCBS—Basel Committee on Banking Supervision (2011) Range of methodologies for risk and performance alignment of remuneration, May. http://www.bis.org/publ/bcbs194.pdf

BCBS—Basel Committee on Banking Supervision (2012) Core principles for effective banking supervision, September. http://www.bis.org/publ/bcbs230.pdf

BCBS—Basel Committee on Banking Supervision (2014) Guidelines Corporate governance principles for banks. Consultative document, October. http://www.bis.org/publ/bcbs294.pdf
Bennett R, Kottasz R (2000) Practitioner perceptions of corporate reputation: an empirical investigation. Corp Comm Int J 5(4):224–234
Bhattacharya S, Thakor AV (1993) Contemporary banking theory. J Finan Intermed 3:2–50
Biell L, Muller A (2013) Sudden crash or long torture: the timing of market reactions to operational loss events. J Bank Financ 37(7):2628–2638
Boccuzzi G (2010) I sistemi alternativi di risoluzione delle controversie nel settore bancario e finanziario: un'analisi comparata. Quaderni di ricerca giuridica n. 68, Banca d'Italia, settembre
Boot AWA (2000) Relationship banking: what do we know? J Financ Intermed 9(1):7–25
Boot AWA, Thakor AV, Udell GF (1991) Credible commitments, contract enforcement problems and banks: intermediation as credibility assurance. J Bank Financ 15(3):605–663
Boot AWA, Greenbaum SI, Thakor AV (1993) Reputation and discretion in financial contracting. Am Econ Rev 83:1165–1183
Booth SA (2000) How can organizations prepare for reputational crisis. J Conting Crisis Manag 8 (4):197–207
Buckley RP, Nixon J (2009) The role of reputation in banking. J Bank Finance Law Pract 20:37–50
Carreras E, Alloza A, Carreras A (2013) Corporate reputation. LID Publishing, London
CEBS (2006) Guidelines on the application of the supervisory review process under Pillar 2 (CP03 revised), 25 January
Chemmanur TJ, Fulghieri B (1994) Investment bank reputation, information production, and financial intermediation. J Financ 49(1):57–79
Chun R (2005) Corporate reputation: meaning and measurement. Int J Manag Rev 7(2):91–109
Cian L, Cervai S (2014) Under the reputation umbrella. An integrative multidisciplinary review for corporate image, projected image, construed image, organizational identity, and organizational culture. Corp Comm Int J 19(9):182–199
CIMA – The Chartered Institute of Management Accountants (2007) Corporate reputation: perspectives of measuring and managing a principal risk. London, UK. www.cimaglobal.com
Corbett J, Mitchell J (2000) Banking crises and bank rescues: the effect of reputation. J Money Credit Bank 32(3):474–512
Cordeiro J, Veliyath R, Eramus EJ (2000) Un empirical investigation of the determinants of outside director compensation. Corp Gov 8(3):268–279
Cornelissen J (2014) Corporate identity, branding and corporate reputation. In: Cornelissen J (ed) Corporate communication, a guide to theory and practice. Sage, London, pp 63–85
Cummins JD, Lewis CM, Wei R (2006) The market impact of operational risk events for U.S. banks and insurers. J Bank Financ 30(10):2605–2634
Da Camara NZ (2011) Identity, image and reputation. In: Helm S, Lierh-Gobbers K, Storck C (eds) Reputation management. Springer, Heidelberg, pp 47–58
De Bandt O, Hartmann F (2000) Systemic risk: a survey. ECB Working Paper No 35. https://www.ecb.europa.eu/pub/pdf/scpwps/ecbwp035.pdf. Accessed Nov 2000
De Fontnouvelle P, De-Jesus-Rueff V, Jordan J et al (2006) Capital and risk: new evidence on implications of large operational losses. J Money Credit Bank 38(7):1819–1846
De la Fuente Sabate JM, de Quevedo PE (2003) Empirical analysis of the relationship between corporate reputation and financial performance: a survey of the literature. Corp Rep Rev 6 (2):161–177
Deephouse DL (1997) The effect of financial and media reputations on performance. Corp Reput Rev 1(1–2):68–71
Deephouse DL (2000) Media reputation as a strategic resource: an integration of mass communication and resource-based theories. J Manag 26(6):1091–1112
Dell'Atti S, Iannuzzi A, Cavallaro G, Trotta A (2012) Understanding reputational crisis: evidence from the European banking sector. J Mod Account Audit 8(2):247–266

Diamond D (1984) Financial intermediation and delegated monitoring. Rev Econ Stud 51:393–414

Diamond DW (1991) Monitoring and reputation: the choice between bank loans and directly placed debt. J Polit Econ 99(4):689–721

Djama C (2013) Fraudes à l'information comptable et financière et contrôle de l'AMF : une étude des réactions du marché financier français. Rev Franc Gestion 2(231):133–157

Dyck A, Morse A, Zingales L (2013) How pervasive is corporate fraud? Rotman School of Management. Working Paper No. 2222608. http://ssrn.com/abstract=2222608 or doi:10.2139/ssrn.2222608. Accessed 22 Feb 2013

EBA—European Banking Authority (2015) Draft Guidelines on sound remuneration policies under Article 74(3) and 75(2) of Directive 2013/36/EU and disclosures under Article 450 of Regulation (EU) No 575/2013 61, March

Fang LH (2005) Investment bank reputation and the price and quality of underwriting services. J Financ 60(6):2729–2761

FED – Board of Governor of Federal Reserve System (1995) Rating the adequacy of risk management processes and internal controls at state member banks and bank holding companies. Supervisory Letter, SR Letter 95-51, 14 November. http://www.federalreserve.gov/boarddocs/srletters/1995/sr9551.htm

FED – Board of Governors of the Federal Reserve System (2008) Commercial bank examination manual, examination strategy and risk-focused examinations, October. http://www.federalreserve.gov/boarddocs/supmanual/cbem/200904/0904cbem.pdf

FED – Board of Governors of the Federal Reserve System (2010) Commercial bank examination manual, division of banking supervision and regulation, November, Section 4020.1. http://www.federalreserve.gov/boarddocs/supmanual/cbem/cbem.pdf

Fiordelisi F, Soana MG, Schwizer P (2013) The determinants of reputational risk in the banking sector. J Bank Financ 37(8):1359–1371

Fiordelisi F, Soana MG, Schwizer P (2014) Reputational losses and operational risk in banking. Eur J Financ 20(2):105–124

Fombrun CJ (1996) Reputation: realizing value from the corporate image. Harvard Business School Press, Boston, MA

Fombrun CJ (2012) The building blocks of corporate reputation: definitions, antecedents, consequences. In: Barnett ML, Pollock TG (eds) The Oxford handbook of corporate reputation. Oxford University Press, Oxford, pp 94–113

Fombrun CJ, Shanley M (1990) What's in a name? Reputation building and corporate strategy. Acad Manag J 33(2):233–258

Fombrun C, Van Riel C (1997) The reputational landscape. Corp Rep Rev 1(1–2):5–13

Fombrun CJ, Gardberg NA, Sever JM (2000) The Reputation Quotient[sm]: a multistakeholder measure of corporate reputation. J Brand Manag 7(4):241–255

Foreman PO, Whetten DA, Mackey A (2012) An identity-based view of reputation, image and legitimacy: clarifications and distinctions among related constructs. In: Barnett ML, Pollock TG (eds) The Oxford handbook of corporate reputation. Oxford University Press, Oxford, pp 179–200

Freeman RE (1984) Strategic management: a stakeholder approach. Cambridge University Press, Cambridge

FSF—Financial Stability Forum (2009) Principles for sound compensation practices, 2 April

Gabbi G (2004) Definizione, misurazione e gestione del rischio reputazionale degli intermediari bancari. Banca Impr Soc 1:51–78

Gatzert N (2015) The impact of corporate reputation and reputation damaging events on financial performance: empirical evidence from the literature. http://ssrn.com/abstract=2576627 or doi:10.2139/ssrn.2576627. Accessed 10 Mar 2015

Gatzert N, Schmit JT, Kolb A (2015) Assessing the risks of insuring reputation risk. J Risk Insur. doi:10.1111/jori.12065

Gaultier-Gaillard S, Louisot JP (2006) Risks to reputation: a global approach. Geneva Pap Risk Ins 31:425–445

Gaultier-Gaillard S, Pratlong F (2011) Le risque de réputation: le cas du secteurbancaire. Manag Avenir 8(48):272–288

Gillet R, Hübner G, Plunus S (2010) Operational risk and reputation in the financial industry. J Bank Financ 34(4):224–235

Gotsi M, Wilson AM (2001) Corporate reputation: seeking a definition. Corp Comm Int J 6 (1):24–30

Helm S (2007) The role of corporate reputation in determining investor satisfaction and loyalty. Corp Rep Rev 10(1):22–37

Helm S (2011) Corporate reputation: an introduction to a complex construct. In: Helm S, Lierh-Gobbers K, Storck C (eds) Reputation management. Springer, Heidelberg, pp 3–16

Helm S, Lierh-Gobbers K, Storck C (eds) (2011) Reputation management. Springer, Heidelberg

Kang E (2008) Director interlocks and spillover effects of reputational penalties from financial reporting fraud. Acad Manag J 51(3):537–555

Karpoff JM, Lott JR Jr (1993) The reputational penalty firms bear from committing criminal fraud. J Law Econ 36(2):757–802

Kirat T, Rezaee A (2015) Do financial markets react to regulatory sanctions? Evidence from France. Paper presented at the 2015 SASE Conference, Inequality in the 21st Century, London, 2–4 July 2015

La Porta R, Lopez-de-Silanes F, Shleifer A (2006) What works in securities laws? J Financ 61:1–32

Lange D, Lee PM, Dai Y (2011) Organizational reputation: a review. J Manag 37(1):153–184

Leiva R, Ferrero I, Calderòn R (2014) Corporate reputation and corporate ethics: looking good or doing well. Universidad de Navarra. Working Paper n. 05/14

Manjarin R (2012) Reputational risk management. GARP Switzerland Chapter Meeting Geneva. http://www.garp.org. Accessed 27 Nov 2012

Milbourn TT (2003) CEO reputation and stock-based compensation. J Financ Econ 68(2):233–262

Miller GS (2006) The press as a watchdog for accounting fraud. J Account R 44(5):1001–1033

Patarnello A (2010) Il rischio reputazionale: caratteristiche e collocazione nel sistema dei rischi della banca. In: Anolli M, Rajola F (eds) Il rischio di reputazione e di non conformità. Strumenti e metodi per la governance e la gestione operativa. Bancaria Editrice, Roma

Plunus S, Gillet R, Hübner G (2012) Reputational damage of operational loss on the bond market: evidence from the financial industry. Int Rev Finan Anal 24(4):66–73

Regan L (2008) A framework for integrating reputation risk into the enterprise risk management process. J Financ Transf 22:187–194

Reputation Institute (2015) How do consumers view the banking industry worldwide? March. https://www.reputationinstitute.com/Resources/Registered/PDF-Resources/global-banking-industry-reputation.aspx

Rindova VP, Williamson IO, Petkova AP et al (2005) Being good or being known: an empirical examination of the dimensions, antecedents, and consequences of organizational reputation. Acad Manag J 48(6):1033–1049

Romenti S (2006) Corporate reputation, crisis management and stakeholders partnerships. An Italian case study. Paper presented at Iran 3rd International Conference on Public Relations, Teheran, 16–17 November

Ruiz B, Esteba A, Gutierrez S (2014) Determinants of reputation of leading Spanish financial institutions among their customers in a context of economic crisis. Bus Res Q 17(4):259–278

Sapienza P, Zingales L (2012) A trust Crisis. Int Rev Financ 12(2):123–131

Schwizer P, Soana MG, Maucci G et al (2010) Rischio reputazionale e perdite operative. Un'analisi empirica sulle banche quotate. Bancaria 11:27–48

Shanahan F, Seele P (2015) Shorting Ethos: exploring the relationship between Aristotle's Ethos and Reputation Management. Corp Reput Rev 18(1):37–49

Stansfield G (2006) Some thoughts on reputation and challenges for global financial institutions. Geneva Pap R I-Iss P 31(3):470–479
Sturm P (2013) Operational and reputational risk in the European banking industry: the market reaction to operational risk events. J Econ Behav Organ 85(46):191–206
Tlou UB, Govender KK (2015) Identifying common reputation drivers for South African banks using media reports. J Econ 6(1):62–73
Trotta A, Iannuzzi A, Cavallaro G et al (2011) Banking reputation and CSR: a stakeholder value approach. In: Gummesson E, Mele C, Polese F (eds) Proceedings of The Naples Forum on Service – Service Dominant Logic, Network and System Theory and Service Science: Integrating Three Perspectives for a New Service Agenda, Giannini, Naples
Van den Bogaerd M, Aerts W (2015) Does media reputation affect properties of accounts payable? Eur Manag J 33(1):19–29
Van Schaik DJ, Garcia HF (2007) Reputation management: the key to successful public relations and corporate communication. Routledge, New York, NY
Von der Crone HC, Vetsch J (2009) Reputation and regulation. In: Klewes J, Wreschniok R (eds) Reputation capital, building and maintaining trust in the 21st century. Springer, Heidelberg, pp 179–195
Walker K (2010) A systematic review of the corporate reputation literature: definition, measurement, and theory. Corp Rep Rev 12(4):357–387
Walker K, Dyck B (2014) The primary importance of corporate social responsibility and ethicality in corporate reputation: an empirical study. Bus Soc Rev 119(1):147–174
Walter I (2013) The value of reputational capital and risk in banking and finance. Int J Bank Account Finance 5(1/2):205–219
Walter I (2014) Reputational risk in banking and finance: an issue of individual responsibility? J Risk Manag Finan Ins 7(3):299–305
Wang Y, Lo HP, Hui YV (2003) The antecedents of service quality and product quality and their influences on bank reputation: evidence from the banking industry in China. Manag Serv Qual 13(1):72–83
Winfrey FL, Logan JE (1998) Are reputation and power compensating differentials in CEO compensation? Corp Reput Rev 2(1):61–76
Zyglidopoulos S, Phillips N (1999) Responding to reputational crises: a stakeholder perspective. Corp Reput Rev 2(4):333–350

Annarita Trotta is a Professor of Banking and Finance at University Magna Græcia (UMG) of Catanzaro (Italy). She holds a PhD in Business Administration from the University Federico II of Naples (Italy), where she was an assistant Professor of Banking on the Faculty of Economics from 1995 to 2001. From 2001 to 2006, she was an Associate Professor at the University of Catanzaro. Since 2006, she has been a professor of Economics and Management of Financial Institutions and Markets at UMG, where she teaches Banking, Financial Markets, and Corporate Finance.

She is currently a member of the PhD Council of the School of Theory of Law and European Legal and Economic Systems at UMG and a member of the Evaluation Unit of the LUM Jean Monnet University (Italy).

She is also a member of the Committee of Advisors of Ordines (for Interdisciplinary Research on European Institutions) and a member of the editorial boards of the following journals: "China – USA Business Review", and "Economics World".

Over her 20-year academic career, Trotta has authored (or co-authored) more than 50 scientific publications and 4 books. Her primary areas of research are Social and Sustainable Finance; Impact Investing; Alternative Finance and Sustainability; Reputational risk and reputational crisis in the banking sector; Corporate Social Responsibility in the banking sector; Subprime crisis and Credit Rating Agencies; Local banking and information asymmetries; Credit risk; Small business, Venture Capital and Informal Venture Capital; Bank-small business relationships; and Finance and Medicine.

Antonia Patrizia Iannuzzi is a Researcher of "Banking and Finance" at University of Bari "Aldo Moro" (Italy) where she teaches the course "Economics of Financial Intermediaries" at the Ionic Department in Legal and Economic System of Mediterranean. Moreover she holds a PhD in "Banking and Finance" from the University of Roma "Sapienza (Italy) and she was a Research Fellow in Financial Markets and Institutions at University of Bari "Aldo Moro" (Italy, years 2005–2010) and University of Catanzaro "Magna Graecia" (Italy, years 2010–2014). Since 2008, she has co-taught "Banking and Finance" at the Department of Economics of University of Foggia, where she taught some courses (*Integrative Course of Economics of Financial Intermediaries, Economics of Insurance Companies, Professional course on Corporate Lending*). At present, she is a ordinary member of the "*Italian Association of Professors of Economics of Financial Intermediaries and Markets*" and consultative member of the scientific committee of CESAC ("*Interuniversity Research Center on the Guarantee Institutions*"), University of Foggia and University of Bari "Aldo Moro". Moreover, she has been a speaker at various national and international conferences and a reviewer of some international journals.

Since 2005, she has authored (or co-authored) 22 scientific publications. Her main research and teaching interests are related to corporate reputation and reputational risk in the banking sector, corporate governance, stakeholder engagement and management compensation, corporate social responsibility, ethical funds and bank–firm relationships.

Vincenzo Pacelli is a Tenured Assistant Professor of "Banking and Finance" at University of Foggia (since November 2008), where he is also Academic Senator (since October 2010). He holds a PhD in "Banking and Finance" from the University of Roma "Sapienza" (Italy). Currently, he teaches the courses "Financial Portfolio Management" and "Economics of Financial Intermediaries – Advanced Course" at the Department of Economics of University of Foggia. In addition, he taught the course "Banking and Finance" at the Department of Economics of University of Bari.

He is a member of the Council of PhD School in "Management and Finance" at University of Foggia, member of the organizing committee and chair of different International Conference, ordinary member of the "Italian Association of Professors of Economics of Financial Intermediaries and Markets" and member of the scientific committee of "CeSAC". He is also a member of the Editorial Board of the *Journal of Intelligent Learning Systems and Applications*, published by Scientific Research Publishing, Inc. USA, and he was an editor or reviewer for the following journals: *Applied Economics, Journal of Intelligent Learning Systems and Applications, Lecture Notes in Computer Sciences, Entropy, British Journal of Economics, Management & Trade.*

Since 2005, he has authored (or co-authored) more than 40 scientific publications. His major areas of research are as follows: Governance, Performance and Risks in Banks; Forecasting in Financial Markets; Intangibles in Banks; Credit Risk Management; Reputational Risk Management; Artificial Intelligence in Banking and Finance; Asset Allocation.

Reputation, Reputational Crisis and Corporate Social Responsibility of Banks: Measurement and Relationships

Stefano Dell'Atti and Antonia Patrizia Iannuzzi

Abstract The chapter focuses on the relationships between corporate reputation and corporate social responsibility. First, the main and most important measurement metrics of corporate reputation are analysed. Second, the focus shifts to CSR and an investigation of the measurement tools most frequently adopted by the scholars. Finally, an interesting analysis on the linkages between reputational crisis and the corporate social responsibility of banks is conducted. In this context, we highlight the role that CSR plays with regard to corporate reputation, the characteristics and the effectiveness conditions for CSR to operate as a reputational driver and, finally, when CSR can resolve the reputational crisis of a bank.

1 Corporate Reputation and CSR: The Measurement Metrics

To enhance and better manage corporate reputation, one must first understand how to measure this asset. Indeed, we cannot increase reputational capital if it is not first properly measured (Gardberg and Fombrun 2002). We apply similar considerations to corporate social responsibility (CSR). For this reason, the current chapter focuses first on the measurement metrics for both reputation and CSR. The aim is to realize a comprehensive overview of the main measurement tools for these assets. Thereby, we can also verify the main similarities and differences between corporate reputation and social responsibility. As will be evident in the second paragraph of this chapter, these two assets (reputation and CSR) are inextricably linked by

---

This chapter is the result of a collaboration between the authors. In particular, Stefano Dell'Atti contributed to paragraphs 2 and 2.1; Antonia Patrizia Iannuzzi contributed to paragraphs 1 (and connected sub-paragraphs), 2.2, and 2.3.

S. Dell'Atti (✉)
University of Foggia, Foggia, Italy
e-mail: stefano.dellatti@unifg.it

A.P. Iannuzzi
University of Bari "Aldo Moro", Bari, Italy
e-mail: antoniapatrizia.iannuzzi@uniba.it

S. Dell'Atti, A. Trotta (eds.), *Managing Reputation in The Banking Industry*,
DOI 10.1007/978-3-319-28256-5_2

important reciprocal relationships that a preliminary analysis of the measurement metrics certainly allows us to highlight.

1.1 The Metrics for Measuring Corporate Reputation

The issue of measuring corporate reputation has attracted the interest of many scholars who, over time and in various ways, have attempted to provide an answer to this important question (Walker 2010).

A first large classification of approaches to measuring corporate reputation leads to distinction between quantitative and qualitative metrics. The first measures aim to provide a numerical score; they are generally based on financial or market variables and assess reputation regardless of the opinion expressed by the stakeholders. Additionally, they do not provide a quantitative score as a final output, which is a synthetic indicator capable of expressing the total value of corporate reputation. However, the qualitative methodologies represent a barometer of corporate reputation and, thus, indirectly show the level of the bank's exposure to reputational risk. By contrast, quantitative metrics are based on the expectations of stakeholders and aim to synthesize, through an appropriate quantitative score, the opinions expressed at a given time. Therefore, while the quantitative metrics can be equated essentially to a financial value, the qualitative metrics are mostly measures of perceptive character.

1.2 The Quantitative Metrics for Measuring Corporate Reputation

We can distinguish different quantitative approaches for measuring corporate reputation, including the *Intellectual Capital Approach*, the *Accounting—Financial Approach,* the *Marketing Approach* (or approach based on the brand value), the *Market-based Approach* and, finally, the *Reputational Value at Risk (*or *Reputational VaR)* (Gabbi and Patarnello 2010; Soprano et al. 2009).

At present, the approach that is most often used in the banking sector is based on market data (*Market-based Approach*). Indeed, to measure the negative impact caused by the manifestation of reputational risk (that is a negative measure of corporate reputation), several authors use the event study approach, which has led to interesting conclusions. More specifically, this approach seems to confirm the hypothesis that when "reputational sensitive" events occur, i.e., events with high reputational impact caused mainly by operational losses, the bank suffers a financial loss greater than the book value due to the joint manifestation of the reputational risk (De Fontnouvelle et al. 2006; Gillet et al. 2010; Schwizer et al. 2010; Biell and Muller 2013; Fiordelisi et al. 2014; Palmrose et al. 2004; Sturm 2013). However, in addition to such pioneering studies, there are new research perspectives. Among the latter, the following are worth mentioning:

a) the practice of conducting a more accurate analysis of reputational events through accumulated knowledge of cases and situations likely to affect the value of reputation. In this way, a "*database of reputational events*" can be built to realize increasingly more accurate predictive investigations;
b) the improvement of the qualification of reputational events and the creation of an *ad hoc* model for measuring reputational risk to consolidate the approaches taken in the various hierarchical levels;
c) the need to improve methods of measuring not only the severity of reputational risk (*ex-post view*) but also the frequency, calculating the probability that within a specified time frame, the reputational event could occur (*ex-ante view*);
d) the need for industry associations or a national and/or international Supervisory Authority to define best practices for management and measurement, including at the sectoral level (Reputation Institute 2015).

1.3 The Qualitative Metrics for Measuring Corporate Reputation: Professional Models Versus Academic Models

We can also discern different qualitative approaches to assessing corporate reputation (Helm and Klode 2011). The literature suggests several classifications; the most important classifications are based on the type and/or number of stakeholders involved in the estimation process.

Indeed, some authors develop measures involving only one category of stakeholder, especially the customers of the company (Walsh and Beatty 2007). Other authors, however, take into account the views expressed by different parties that, for various reasons, gravitate around the company. Consequently, in the first case, the final score will be of *uni-stakeholder character*; in the second case, the estimates will be of the *multi-stakeholders type*.

Conversely, a second proposal distinguishes between objective and subjective instruments that assess corporate reputation (Carreras et al. 2013). The former are based on testing and evaluations conducted by individuals with high expertise (*highly informed experts*) and, thus, aim to produce an impartial value of reputation. The subjective measurement tools, however, are called such because they are based, essentially, on the perceptions and expectations of the other categories of stakeholders. Therefore, whereas the objective tools are designed to determine "*the degree to which a group of stakeholders actually thinks, feels and admires that company with or without reason, and right or wrong*" and, thus, can be assimilated to an excellent certification, the subjective measurement tools aim to synthesize "*the degree to which a group of stakeholders actually thinks, feels and admires that company with or without reason, and right or wrong*" (Carreras et al. 2013:354).

To put more simply, according to this view, the Fortune reputational rankings belong to the objective instrument category because they result from the opinions of Top managers and financial analysts, who are persons with high expertise. By contrast, the *RepTrak Pulse* of the Reputation Institute constitutes a subjective measurement tool because it results from the opinions expressed by the consumers of the company and expresses essentially the emotional involvement of these stakeholder groups (see *infra*).

In this context, however, because the intent is not only to achieve an overview of the main tools for assessing corporate reputation but also to identify similarities, differences and difficulties of such measurement models, we decided to simply distinguish between a) professional background models and b) academic models. The main difference between the two approaches regards only the subject that makes the elaboration because while the former are developed by consulting firms, magazines and others, sometimes in partnership with academic scholars, the latter are only performed by the doctrine. Concerning the output, however, the two approaches are equivalent in terms of providing specific reputational scores.

Regarding the models of the professional field, the development of the first rankings dates back to the 1980s. At first, the methodological approach is quite simple: after defining the areas under investigation (reputational dimensions), a selected stakeholder group, which expresses their judgements on a determined sample of companies, is interviewed. The most important of these first reputational rankings is the *American Most Admired Companies* (AMAC), which was developed in 1983 by the US Magazine Fortune. In the future, these ranking will be named the *World's Most Admired Companies* (WMAC) because Fortune has expanded the sample of companies under investigation. Over time, other similar initiatives were created to develop parallel indicators but relative to other geographical areas (Fombrun 2007; Carreras et al. 2013).

Subsequently, to overcome some important criticalities raised by these first measurement proposals, the professional field, in partnership with academia, has sought to improve the methodological approach by developing new reputational indicators. One such indicator is the *Reputation Quotient* (RQ), developed in 1999 by a team of professors (Fombrun et al. 2000a) in collaboration with the consulting firm *Harris Interactive* and now revised in a new version, which was developed only by the consulting firm. The principal value of this indicator is that it has expanded both the range of stakeholders involved in the analysis and the number of evaluation criteria. Indeed, unlike the Fortune score, which is based on only a few items (initially, there were seven items but now there are nine), the *Reputation Quotient* (RQ) not only is a multi-stakeholder score but it also focuses on 20 indicators that are grouped into six reputational dimensions that were selected through a bottom-up approach, i.e., by conducting a series of pilot studies (Fombrun et al. 2000a). Moreover, a further important aspect regards the introduction of the "emotional factor" in addition to the more rational dimensions: the *emotional appeal factor*. The basic items of this factor are as follows: *good feeling, admiration* and *respect, trust*—note that corporate reputation is not simply the result of objective assessments; it also derives from the emotional involvement of the company's main stakeholders (Davies et al. 2004).

Finally, compared to the first reputational rankings (still elaborated), with the introduction of the RQ, the methodology has been enriched by a rigorous conceptual background. Indeed, while the elaboration of *Fortune's WMAC* is not based on a detailed definition of corporate reputation or what is measured, since the construction of the RQ, the analysis has also incorporated such components (Fombrun et al. 2000a).

Rather similar to the RQ, but constituting an advanced version, the *RepTrak ™ Pulse* was developed by Reputation Institute in 2006. This ranking is a "*simplified emotion-based measure of corporate reputation*" (Ponzi et al. 2011:16) because its implementation focuses on an appropriate balance between emotional factors (*esteem, good feeling, trust*, and *admiration* that consumers feel towards a company) and more rational elements linked to six reputational dimensions. The theoretical framework is strong; developed on the basis of *signalling theory* and the *resource-based view* (RBV), the score aims to "*conceptualize corporate reputation as beliefs about companies and disentangle the drivers of reputation from the construct itself*" (Ponzi et al. 2011:16). However, what differentiates the ranking of the Reputation Institute is mainly the stakeholders interviewed. The stakeholder reference group does not relate to the managerial figures but to the general public or consumers, appropriately balanced with respect to age and gender.

Finally, the *MERCO index* (*Monitor Empresarial de Reputación Corporate*), whose main advantage is that it is based on a multi-steps and multi-stakeholders methodology, is worth noting. More specifically, such ranking not only involves several stakeholders groups, including both the Top managers and the consumers (and, therefore, the general public) in the analysis process, but also is developed in two different evaluative phases, with the aim of perfecting the final score. The aim of the implementation of a second step of analysis is to confirm or reject the result obtained from *previsional ranking* which is the output of the first phase (Carreras et al. 2013). Additionally, the final score of this ranking, unlike the previous rankings, is certified by the KPMG auditing firm on the basis of the *International Standard ISAE 3000*.

Restricting the analysis only to the banking and financial sector, all the rankings mentioned offer interesting information and allow the use of industry and geographic area filters. Among all ranking institutions, Fortune produces the most disaggregated information because, as regards the financial sector, it proposes the ranking of approximately seven different areas: 1) *Consume credit card and related services*, 2) *Financial data services*, 3) *Insurance: Life and Health*, 4) *Insurance: property and casualty*, 5) *Megabanks*, 6) *Securities and Asset Management*, and 7) *Superregional Banks*. In all areas, the ranking distinguishes between companies with higher reputation and the so-called "*contenders*", which have obtained a score lower than the industry average.

In addition, the Reputation Institute produces several sectoral reports annually, including the ranking of American banks with higher reputations in collaboration with the financial daily "*American Banker*" (*2014 US Most Reputable Banks*).

The latest reports indicate that the banking sector has not yet bridged the reputational gap that other industries have bridged because it is still suffering the effects of the international crisis, of which it is considered the main culprit. The reputational drivers on which banks should invest more are related to the products and services provided, the governance processes and the CSR strategies (Reputation Institute 2015).

1.4 The Qualitative Metrics for Measuring Corporate Reputation Proposed by the Doctrine

Qualitative academia models are elaborated only by the doctrine. The first attempts by scholars to measure the reputational asset date back to the 1970s. At that time, the attention focused mainly on the concept of the credibility of the enterprise (Newell and Goldsmith 2001). Only later, since the 1980s, specific studies on the measurement of corporate reputation have been conducted. The models proposed by the doctrine are quite heterogeneous (Helm and Klode 2011) with respect to the theoretical base (*institutional theory*, *resource-based view* and *signalling theory*, see Walker 2010), the derivation process of the model (*reflective model* versus *formative model,* see Helm 2005; Carreras et al. 2013:381) and, finally, the operating and managerial implications achievable (Walker 2010; Carreras et al. 2013). The following are among the best-known approaches:

a) the *Reputation Index* of Cravens et al. (2003), which is based on 4 reputational dimensions (*leadership, strategy, culture* and *innovation)* and 21 elementary items;
b) the *Corporate Personality Scale* of Davies et al. (2004), which is based on seven reputational qualitative dimensions related to characteristics of human personality (*Agreeableness*: honest, socially responsible; *Competence*: reliable, ambitious; *Enterprise*: innovative, daring; *Ruthlessness*: arrogant, controlling; *Chic:* stylish, exclusive; *Informality:* easy going; *Machismo*: tough);
c) the *SPIRIT model* of MacMillan et al. (2004), which is based on tree reputational dimensions: *experiences* (sub-dimensions: communication, material benefits, experience of outside influences), *feelings* (sub-dimensions: trust and positive emotions), *intentions* (including sub-dimensions of supportive behaviours, advocacy and retention of stakeholders);
d) the *CBR—customer based reputation* of Walsh and Beatty (2007), which is based on five reputational dimensions related to *customer orientation, good employer, reliable and financially strong company, product and service quality, social and environmental responsibility.*

Unlike professional models, these approaches are characterized by limited empirical utilization because they are mostly usable only as part of the scientific research that developed them.

1.5 The Metrics for Measuring CSR

As with corporate reputation, there are different corporate social responsibility (CSR) measurement approaches aimed to express a synthetic assessment of the ethical performance of the company. With regard to the banking sector, the solutions most frequently used in the literature can be differentiated in two macro groupings:

1. *Ethical ratings*: mostly elaborated by consulting firms or external agencies, such as *Eiris* (de la Cuesta-González et al. 2006), *SAM, Ethibel* and *Axia* (Soana 2011), KLD (Goss and Roberts 2011; El Ghoul et al. 2011), *Standard Ethics, Vigeo, IW Financial, Calvert, Jantzi Research Inc., RiskMetrics, Investissement Responsible, Accountability Rating,* and *Thomson Reuters* (Ioannou and Serafeim 2012; Ciciretti et al. 2015). Additionally, we can also discern academic ethical ratings, which are scores elaborated by the doctrine with regard both to banks (Scholtens 2009; Birindelli et al. 2015) and other organizations (Sotorrío and Sánchez 2008; Turker 2009).
2. *Ethical indexes*: groups of securities of listed companies characterized by high ethical performance. They are produced by the company specializing in the creation and management of stock market indexes that, for the case of CSR indexes, is generally assisted by an external ethical rating agency (see *supra*). In this case, the measurement of a bank's ethicality is made by simply verifying whether the bank can be found on the selected ethical index (Chih et al. 2010; McWilliams and Siegel 2000).

1.5.1 Ethical Ratings

Similar to the traditional rating, which synthetizes the creditworthiness of the company, the ethical rating reflects an assessment that, in this case, concerns only the social performance of the firm. More specifically, the ethical rating represents a barometer of the intensity by which the firm puts in place corporate social responsibility policies and strategies. At a methodological level, the ethical ratings are processed by content analysis approach (Abbott and Monsen 1979; Beattie and Thomson 2007): first, the evaluation criteria are selected (KPI, *Key Performance Indicators*) and, then, the company's compliance with these criteria is assessed. This verification takes place by administering a questionnaire to the company (Turker 2009), by viewing directly the corporate documents (Birindelli et al. 2015) or by examining information from Supervisory Authorities, media and other communication channels (Scholtens 2009; Sotorrío and Sánchez 2008). Frequently, these cognitive tools are used in an integrated manner. The evaluation standards, which generally are based on a combination of positive and negative criteria, can vary widely and be quite numerous depending on not only the approach taken by the ethical rating agency but also the type of score that will be processed. More specifically, we can distinguish between the following two types of ratings:

a) *multi-dimensional ethical ratings;*
b) *mono-dimensional ethical ratings.*

While the former ratings aim to evaluate simultaneously multiple CSR dimensions of a company, the latter simply check only dimension. Examples of the first type are the "*ESG ratings*" issued, for example, by KLD and ASSET4 and designed to assess, at the same time, the environmental, social and governance performance of the company. The *RepRisk index* (RRI), which was developed by *RepRisk* consulting firm is always multidimensional. Unlike the other scores, it does not indicate the most ethical companies; rather, it indicates those most exposed to the ESG risks. Indeed, a high value on the index reflects a firm's lower level of ethicality. Examples of one-dimensional ethical ratings, however, include the *Pollution Performance Ranking* and the *Carbon Performance Leadership Index* (CPLI) because they only evaluate the environmental performance of the firm and the *CSR Online Awards Europe 10*, which focuses on only the disclosure of social reporting tools.

Finally, the ethical rating can be represented by a numerical score or a synthetic assessment via letters. In most cases, these scores are shown; in other circumstances, however, the provider only publishes the ranking and omits the score assigned to each company.

At present, there is a wide range of ethical rating/score solutions offered by the professional world. This range has raised some confusion and many questions. Indeed, in some cases, a company is excluded from an ethical rating but is still judged as good by another consulting firm. Moreover, the approach taken by different ethical agencies may be quite different. Often, the criteria and weighting system used vary considerably. For this reason, the project known as the *Global Initiative for sustainability ratings*, which is still in the implementation phase, was developed with the objective of defining a standard model of ethical rating elaboration that can be shared and accepted at the international level.

1.5.2 Ethical Indexes

Equity ethical or socially responsible indexes represent an important tool of business ethics (*Social Responsible Investment*). Indeed, when we compare them with the traditional indexes, we can immediately check the performance that this sector can offer over the traditional one. In addition, as a measurement tool for CSR, ethical indexes allow us to identify immediately the most ethical companies (that are the constituents of these indexes) without providing a summary measure of their level of ethicality. In reality, membership on an ethical index may be treated as a type of quality certification regarding the company's social and environmental commitment and a type of recognition of the company's social activities.

Concerning the methodology, ethical indexes are constructed in the same way as ethical ratings, i.e., using a combination of positive and negative criteria designed to assess the social performance of the company. While the negative criteria aim to exclude all the companies operating in productive sectors in contrast to the corporate social responsibility principles (such as alcohol, tobacco, weapons, pornography and gambling), the positive criteria assess the commitment of the company in terms of environmental, social (respect for human and civil rights) and governance concerns. Often, the starting point is a traditional index. By applying a proper screening policy, we delete issuers that do not meet the requirements of social corporate responsibility previously defined. Moreover, ethical ratings are frequently used to more easily identify the undertakings to be included among the indexes.

However, in addition to ESG criteria, the ethical indexes must observe other composition criteria, especially in terms of maximum weight to be assigned to the securities with the highest capitalization. This method also ensures the comparability of any ethical index with a traditional index, *condicio sine qua non* so that the performance comparisons (between ethical and traditional finance) result fair and correct.

Finally, even in this case, it is possible to distinguish between the following two types of indexes:

a) *multi-dimensional ethical indexes*, which are used to assess the social performance of the company in several respects, including the environment, the relationships with stakeholders and the corporate governance system;
b) *one-dimensional ethical indexes*, which are used to highlight the social performance of the company in regard to a single dimension (environment, social or corporate governance) or industry sector.

For example, examples of the first type of ethical indexes are the *MSCI KLD 400 Social Index* and the *MSCI World ESG index*, while a mono-dimensional ethical index is the *FTSE CDP Carbon Strategy,* which aims to assess only the environmental performance of the enterprise. This index, indeed, includes companies that, for various reasons, incur costs and take initiatives to address the emergence of toxic emissions.

As previously mentioned, in the case of ethical indexes, we do not obtain an ordinal measure of the CSR level attributable to each firm (as in the case of ethical ratings whose output is constituted, mainly, by a numerical score); rather, it is possible to only discern the companies that best meet the sustainable finance principles. In the empirical literature, dummy variables are used to select the organizations included on ethical indexes and, therefore, characterized by the best social performance.

1.5.3 Other Measurement Approaches for CSR

Finally, other less important approaches to measuring CSR used by scholars concern the verification of the firm's adoption of relevant international standards (such as the *Equator* or the *Wolfsberg Principles*, see Scholtens and Dam 2007; Chih et al. 2010); the attainment of ethical certifications and compliance with guidelines on ethical conduct, such as those approved by the *United Nations Global Compact*, the *OECD*, the *Global Impact*, the *UNEP Finance Initiative*, the *Carbon Disclosure Project* and, finally, the *GRI* (*Global Reporting Initiative*). Furthermore, in these cases, scholars frequently use dichotomous dummy variables to discern banks that are compliant with selected ethical standards. Indeed, if the bank is compliant, it is given a value of one; otherwise, it is given a value of zero.

1.6 The Measurement of Corporate Reputation and CSR: Can We Hypothesize an Integrated Approach?

One aspect that certainly unites the corporate reputation and CSR concerns the large number of metrics proposed in the literature or by economic and professional fields. On the one hand, this shows the extreme accuracy of and the great interest that the scientific and professional community has in these issues. On the other hand, this aspect also involves a degree of uncertainty and confusion (Carreras et al. 2013). Indeed, the proliferation of measurement instruments, which are often quite different from each other, implies the need to make a choice in an attempt to use the tool most appropriate to one's knowledge needs. Moreover, this selection is not without implications. Frequently, the use of one approach to measuring corporate reputation and/or CSR over another approach affects the research results by supporting the investigation objectives to a greater or lesser degree. For this reason, given the absence of an ideal evaluation model, in the previous paragraphs, we provided an overview of the main measurement instruments for both corporate reputation and CSR with the aim of realizing some critical reflections on their adoption to develop metrics that are increasingly complete and effective.

However, through the joint analysis of the two measurement approaches (reputation and CSR), an interesting aspect emerged: in many cases, the dimensions analysed are indistinguishable from one another because they aim to analyse roughly the same aspects, including, in particular, *corporate governance*, the *quality of products and services*, and the *level of corporate innovation*. Moreover, in most cases, CSR is included among the reputational drivers due to a strong correlation with respect to reputational asset (Reputation Institute 2014). Similarly, some providers include reputation among the ethical dimensions to be analysed to develop a CSR indicator. Finally, it is not uncommon to find the use of reputation scores to synthesize the level of ethics of an organization in the literature (Turker 2009), although this method has not entirely shared (Liston-Heyes and Ceton 2009).

This overlap leads us to reflect on the possibility of developing an integrated approach to jointly measure the ethical and reputational performance of a bank. However, for this to happen, it is necessary to refine the two measurement approaches. Indeed, if there is a clear similarity in "*what*" reputation and CSR metrics measure, significant differences emerge on "*how*" the measurement is conducted. More specifically, the reputational scores are constructed by reworking the perceptions that one or more stakeholder groups have of a company. In contrast, the ratings or ethical indexes are based mostly on the analysis of corporate documents, failing to examine the sentiment surrounding the organization. In other words, with regard to governance processes, if the goal is to build a corporate reputation indicator, the assessment will focus on how stakeholders judge that system; however, if the focus moves to the CSR, the analysis will be more objective because it will be conducted by consulting the corporate documents, interviewing the managerial class, or administering a questionnaire to the company (Turker 2009). It is obvious that these two measurement systems will make use of different data and information but may be integrated. More specifically, it is possible that stakeholders make judgements based on aspects other than the objective characteristics of the company. This may depend on the type and quality of publically available information, how these are spread and filtered by the company, and aspects related to the personality of the stakeholders involved in the analysis, such as their degree of education, age, skills and preferences, etc.

For this reason, it is not improper to assume the development of an approach that combines and integrates the subjective assessments, which characterize the measurement of reputational asset, and the most objective measures, which distinguish the CSR analysis, into a single synthetic judgement. Such an attempt would also overcome some of the critical issues related to reputation scores, including the excessive reliance on subjective assessments and, therefore, on the target stakeholders selected for the estimation of the indicator.

Certainly, a combination that is properly balanced between subjective and objective assessments could generate an indicator that is not only more complete but also less random because it is subjected to a testing process and empirical evidence. To this end, we could assume a *multi-steps approach*: first, the subjective measures should be implemented to verify how the company's behaviour is perceived and judged by the public; then, we may proceed with the objective estimates to integrate, validate and refine those related to the performance reputation. The final output of this combination will be a numerical score that can be understood as a synthesis of the "*ethical reputation*" of the company.

2 Reputational Crisis and the Corporate Social Responsibility of Banks: What Are the Relationships?

A cross analysis of the reputational crisis and CSR is still not widely debated in the literature (Melo and Garrido-Morgado 2012; Esen 2013). However, such an analysis is very important for several reasons.

The link between reputation and CRS started long ago. For banks, this relationship represents two aspects of the same coin (Hillenbrand and Money 2007), although there is still debate on how to develop that connection and its management implications (Hillenbrand and Money 2007; de Quevedo-Puente et al. 2007; Esen 2013).

The logical link between the two issues is represented by the fiduciary bank relationship and the social function of banks. In the broadest sense, the corporate social responsibility of a bank is nothing more than an effective exercise of its objective function. Careful planning of business processes, together with the supervision of banking business, a detailed organizational structure and an efficient system of internal controls could enable the customer relations—which are governed and solidified in function of the trust relationship—to contribute positively to building the bank's good reputation on the market in the medium-long term. Conversely, a reputational risk can be symptomatic of a loss of customers' confidence; in turn, the latter may result from several factors. In summary, when the cornerstones on which the banking business rests are weakened, we can say that the social function of the bank is no longer apparent, which may cause the manifestation of reputational risk (Walter 2013).

Therefore, although they are not always analysed in the literature in an integrated manner, the issues of corporate reputation and corporate social responsibility in the banking sector are easily attributable to common goals (Hoepner and Wilson 2012).

In fact, there are banking entities oriented toward ethics and social responsibility and for which the link with the company's reputation becomes almost unavoidable and binding, revealing a very strong identity. In these cases, it is the same business (for example, ethical mutual funds, the business of green economy, social and sustainable investments, etc.), strongly oriented towards CSR issues, that requires a risk management planning process that can estimate the negative effects of a possible failure of the business, with negative consequences on reputation. Indeed, in these cases, the reputation of the financial intermediary is nothing but its sense of social responsibility.

However, for other banks, a strong orientation towards CSR issues serves as a "*protective barrier*" against adverse events not only of external origin, such as an economic crisis (Xifra and Ordeix 2009), but also of internal origin, such as a reputational crisis (see *infra*, Box 1 on *Société Générale* reputational crisis).

2.1 Reputation and CSR: A "Triple" Consequential Relationship

From the point of view of an enterprise, there are many reasons to adopt CSR practices (Fombrun et al. 2000b; Esen 2013). Indeed, the doctrine has long showed significant benefits, including the development of increasingly strong customer relations (Lin et al. 2009; Mulki and Jaramillo 2011). More specifically, customers show a greater predisposition to buy products (Smith and Alcorn 1991), a greater willingness to pay a higher price (Creyer and Ross 1997) and, finally, less sensitivity to supporting the costs associated with the change of the brand to sustain, mainly, the companies involved in ethical activities. Then, the relationships with economic performance are not less important: indeed, the main research studies (Simpson and Kohers 2002) report a positive connection, noting that the development of social responsibility practices will promote businesses' profitability, especially in the long term (Beurden and Gössling 2008; Scholtens 2009; Callado-Muñoz and Utrero-Gonzalez 2011). Often, the link between ethical and economic performance is not evaluated assuming a direct relationship; rather, it is mediated by another intangible asset, which is also strongly linked to CSR (Vitezić 2011; Esen 2013; Walker and Dyck 2014). More specifically, research states that the implementation of social responsibility strategies, by increasing the value of corporate reputation, also enhances the economic value creation. In other words, the profitability of the company would result from the development of the reputational capital, which, in turn, would constitute the main (positive) result of the implementation of social responsibility practices (Fombrun et al. 2000b; Esen 2013).

The consequential link between ethical and reputational performance appears, therefore, unequivocal (Walker and Dyck 2014). However, if we analyse the various metrics for measuring corporate reputation, we can easily see that corporate social responsibility is always mentioned because it represents one of the main reputational drivers (Esen 2013; Walker and Dyck 2014). However, it may happen that this relationship is manifested with different intensities depending on the industrial sector (Williams and Barrett 2000), the economic cycle (Jacob 2012) or the different socially responsible activities (Brammer and Pavelin 2006). More specifically, Brammer and Millington (2005) show that the growth of reputational capital, which is associated with the increase of expenses for philanthropic activities, varies significantly in the different industrial sectors. Indeed, these authors observe that philanthropy greatly affects the reputation of those companies linked to sectors with significant social externalities, such as the alcoholic beverages and tobacco sectors. This finding suggests that philanthropy (expression of the CSR practices) can help companies to expiate behaviour that is not socially responsible. Philanthropy acts as a "*protective barrier*" against the negative perceptions of stakeholders. Similarly, Jacob (2012) notes that the link between CSR and reputation is influenced by the economic environment in which the firm operates. Indeed, the author, observes that during the recent sub-prime mortgage crisis, the influence of the working conditions (workplace) on the reputational capital of a company became more marginal. This is due to the deterioration of working conditions, which was the main consequence of the crisis and made employees and their expectations less influential at a reputational level (Jacob 2012).

Overall, therefore, considering the relationship with corporate reputation, a triple role can be assigned to CSR. First, corporate social responsibility is a tool that increases the value of corporate reputation (Esen 2013). Such awareness began in the 1990s (Fombrun and Shanley 1990) but only later received greater consideration (Gardberg and Fombrun 2002; Brammer and Pavelin 2006; Esen 2013; Walker and Dyck 2014) with regard to emerging economies (Rettab et al. 2009) and at different stages of economic instability (Xifra and Ordeix 2009). The reason for this link is found under signalling theory, in which social performance represents an antecedent of corporate reputation (Turban and Greening 1997; Janney and Gove 2011; Maden et al. 2012). Indeed, by developing CSR practices, the company would send signals to meet the stakeholders' expectations and, thus, increase the value of its reputation.

Additionally, social responsibility is ascribed the function of protecting the value of corporate reputation (Fombrun et al. 2000b). Indeed, the risk of incurring reputational losses is one of the main reasons that lead companies engage in social responsibility practices (Fombrun et al. 2000b; Peloza 2006). Klein and Dawar (2004) believe that CSR represents, for the enterprise, a form of "*insurance policy*" against negative events. More specifically, these scholars argue that consumers' high perception of the CSR activities of the company minimizes the attributions of guilt for any faults in products sold (Minor and Morgan 2011). Therefore, even in the absence of a direct impact on corporate profitability, CSR produces value because it can help to mitigate the negative effects of a detrimental event, safeguarding the value of the reputational asset (Klein and Dawar 2004). If then, in addition to good ethical and reputational performance, major and effective disclosures are provided, the protection level against financial scandals will be maximized and the market's reaction will be less harmful (Janney and Gove 2011).

Finally, another function that we can attribute to corporate social responsibility regards the recovery phase of reputation loss. Indeed, when a reputational crisis occurs, CSR can certainly help to minimize the reputational damage by mitigating the negative impact of fraudulent behaviour. However, in this case, it is good to make a clarification because the ethical commitment of a company can be a double-edged sword. High involvement in social responsibility practices can expose companies to more severe judgement if they become responsible for fraudulent conduct (Janney and Gove 2011). Specifically, when a company has a high reputation for a given dimension of CSR, violations connected with this dimension are likely to be severely punished. In other words, if a company is known for having a good corporate governance system, a scandal that affects this system will be severely punished by the market. Conversely, if the governance system of the firm already suffers from a poor reputation, any flaws in this sector will certainly have less reputational impact (Janney and Gove 2011).

A further implication of the controversial relationship between reputation and CSR concerns the influence that these assets have on the behaviour of investors, especially on shareholder activism. Recent studies show that the development of corporate social responsibility practices leads to a better reputation but, at the same time, creates some negative externalities (King and McDonnell 2015). Companies with better reputations, which are more well-known and visible, are also likely to more easily become the target of operations boycotts by activists. Indeed, to give more emphasis and visibility to their protests, these stakeholders will choose businesses with better reputations because these firms are the most known to the public. In turn, these companies will tend to satisfy the activists' expectations to avoid triggering an adverse reaction by the market and losing economic value. Thus, a vicious circle is created in which, rather than constituting a form of insurance, CSR is likely to make companies more vulnerable (King and McDonnell 2015).

2.2 Reputation and CSR: A More Complex Relationship

In fact, the relationships between CSR and corporate reputation are not just consequential. Numerous studies reveal more complex connections characterized by interdependence, reciprocity and/or interactive effects (Trotta et al. 2011). More specifically, it is claimed that business reputation represents not only a consequence of a good CSR strategy but also an antecedent of this practice. It increasingly appears that reputation is a prerequisite for the success of a CSR strategy, that is a *conditio sine qua non* to be more socially responsible.

In particular, the doctrine highlights two basic conditions. The first is the possession of a good reputation, without which the company's implementation of CSR practices may not be effective (Schuler and Cording 2006). The second condition, however, concerns the compatibility of the ethical and reputational performance. In other words, to develop economic and reputational value, CSR strategies must not only be implemented by companies that already have a good reputation but also be consistent with the company's image. Otherwise, if the image projected by implementing CSR practices is not aligned with the firm's reputation, the firm is likely to produce dis-value caused by the incurrence of costs that are not offset by economic value creation (Schuler and Cording 2006; Du et al. 2010).

Servaes and Tamayo (2013) have the same opinion. They observe that the cost of promoting CSR activities can have a negative impact when such strategies are not consistent with the full value of corporate reputation. In other words, "*CSR efforts have to be aligned with the firm's prior reputation to create value*" (Servaes and Tamayo 2013: 1058). Therefore, companies with a bad reputation run the risk of not achieving any benefit from implementing CSR strategies because "*such activities may appear disingenuous and may well have the opposite effect*" (Servaes and Tamayo 2013: 1059). To change this trend, it is necessary to intervene in customer engagement policies to understand why such stakeholders have negative perceptions and, thus, elicit a positive change. Finally, Du et al. (2010) corroborates these considerations by supporting the notion that the preliminary possession of a good reputation amplifies the positive effects associated with the communication of CSR policies.

In summary, it is evident that CSR is not always a good strategy and produces value by improving the company's image. This may depend on the reasons underlying the implementation of such strategies and how they are perceived by the stakeholders. When the company does not enjoy good credibility, CSR policy implementation can feed the suspicion of hidden or selfish motives rather than enhancing the company's reputation; therefore, it can be counterproductive. This risk can be mitigated when neutral external sources give the company a good ethical rating or when the relationship between CSR/advertising is high or when the company promotes its ethical commitment continuously and pertinently (Yoon et al. 2006) through relevant public relations activities (Esen 2013).

Ultimately, we can state that trust in a company is a key driver of social responsibility, the indispensable condition for CSR practices to be valued positively and have the desired effects. In the absence of trust (and, therefore, of reputation) in the company, any CSR strategy could be futile (Osterhus 1997) or even counter-productive (Strahilevitz 2003).

2.3 CSR as a Reputational Driver: Characteristics and Effectiveness Conditions

As previously mentioned, among the reputational drivers, there are both qualitative and quantitative factors (Esen 2013). Among these, CSR is centrally located because it is considered the most important reputational driver (Esen 2013). Additionally, especially for certain stakeholders, CSR would have a reputational impact far greater than the economic performance (Walker and Dyck 2014). This qualification derives from some characteristics that distinguish CSR policies and attribute the reputational potentialities analysed in the preceding paragraphs to them. More specifically, it can be stated that the CSR is:

a) *A multivalent driver* with regard to the different stakeholder categories. As previously mentioned, the process of measuring corporate reputation is greatly influenced by the category of stakeholders involved in the estimation process and, therefore, the expectations of each of them. Compared to other reputational drivers, CSR maintains its importance and effectiveness for all stakeholders groups considered for estimating corporate reputation. In other words, regardless of the corporate reputation measure developed, CSR will always have a central position because this driver keeps its positive potentiality regardless of the type of stakeholder (Fombrun et al. 2000b; Esen 2013).
b) *A cross driver* regarding the business organization. Good CSR practices can (and must) be developed by all the firm's staff, from the senior management to the front office employees. This aspect gives CSR a greater potentiality of impact and higher levels of penetration and diffusion both inside and outside the business organization.
c) *An easily communicable driver* because CSR is measured and announced with an *ad hoc* reporting tool, which is the Social Report.
d) *An easily measurable driver*. As we have shown (Sect. 1.5), the doctrine and the commercial practice have long since developed numerous ethical ratings that can certainly be used as reference by the company to elaborate in-house independent indicators of ethics or to monitor the importance of its social performance over time.
e) *A multi-directional driver* whose management and activation does not require special skills or expertise. Any company can develop CSR practices within

multiple business dimensions (corporate governance, workplace, stakeholders' engagement, the market relationships, etc.) without incurring conflicts or overlapping.

However, for CSR to increase the reputational asset value, certain conditions are necessary. More specifically, the CSR strategy must:

- *be congruent with respect to the business and/or production process put in place by the company*. In other words, if the firm belongs to the mining industry, where working conditions are generally more demanding, it should pay special attention to the claims of the employees such that stakeholders render their work in a healthy environment that respects their rights. Therefore, it is not sufficient to develop CSR practices; rather, it is crucial that these practices have an aim and are more consistent than the negative externalities produced by the corporate business;
- *involve all stakeholder categories, informing them of the ethical commitment of the company properly and continuously*. In doing so, it is extremely important to achieve a balance between an overly lengthy communication that is likely to create only scepticism (Morsing and Schultz 2006) and the transmission of minimal information. Indeed, the CSR processes are very important and should be made with foresight and resources by taking care of the content and the timing of realization;
- *be implemented by a company that already has a good reputation*. If the company does not have a good reputation, has a bad reputation, or has an ongoing financial scandal, the development of CSR practices can produce scepticism and be seen only as an expedient to mask some corporate misdeed (Yoon et al. 2006);
- *be credible in the eyes of all stakeholders, which must be given the opportunity to test the feasibility and practicality of the strategies*. Otherwise, the company runs the risk of being considered misleading, with deleterious effects on the building and growth of its corporate reputation;
- *be able to satisfy all stakeholders without damaging any of them*. In other words, to be very effective and have a positive impact on the reputational asset, a CSR policy should develop a "*win-win*" logic so that the company's efforts to improve its social performance benefit all stakeholders and are equally shared and supported by them;
- *be able to listen and involve all stakeholders at the same time*. By listening, the company will be able to know and understand the real expectations of its stakeholders. By developing engagement practices, it may also receive active and positive support to make CSR strategies increasingly effective and influential.

Finally, we can state that CSR positively impacts corporate reputation (see the Santander case study by Xifra and Ordeix 2009). Likewise, CSR has a positive influence in the case of a reputational crisis because it contains and minimizes the negative effects of the detrimental event (Dell'Atti et al. 2012). An example derives from the reputational crisis of the French bank *Société Générale*. The resolution of the crisis is ascribable to the interaction of several factors. Certainly, the capital strength of the French bank must be included, together with the management capacity of its Top managers, who understood the seriousness of the crisis immediately and put in place an action plan to wisely resolve and foresee the serious damage to the image of one of the most important European banks (Dell'Atti et al. 2012). However, a positive and purposeful role in the resolution of the reputational crisis was also played by CSR. As evidenced by Box 1, the CSR commitment of the French bank had a central role in minimizing the negative effects of the bank's reputational crisis.

Box 1 The Reputational Crisis of Société Générale and the Role of CSR

The reputational crisis of *Société Générale* resulted from a sensational financial scandal caused by an employee of that bank (a trader). Using various fraudulent operations (usurpation of codes to access computer controllers, falsification of documents, etc.), *Jérôme Kerviel* (the name of the trader) made, over time, a series of highly speculative and arbitrage operations on derivatives that subsequently proved incorrect and caused *Société Générale* to lose approximately 4.9 billion euros. This situation was announced to the press on January 24, 2008. However, despite the major economic loss suffered, the French bank was able to solve its problems in a short time by minimizing reputational impacts related to not only the collapse of the shares price but also the downgrading of the main economic and reputational rankings (Dell'Atti et al. 2012).

According to an analysis of financial statements, *Société Générale* appears to have long been engaged in building a good image in the market to become "*a major reference in Corporate Social Responsibility (CSR) and one of the leading European financial establishments in this field*" (Société Générale 2009: 139). This commitment has led the French bank not only to be included in the main stock (CAC 40, STOXX Europe 50, EURO STOXX 50, Euronext 100, MSCI PAN EURO) and ethical indexes (including, FTSE4Good and ASPI Eurozone) but also to be selected by the major French ethical funds as a target firm (Société Générale 2009, 2010, 2011). Additionally, it is noteworthy the decision to integrate CSR policies at all hierarchy organizational levels to avoid these strategies were disconnected from the other parts of the business. Indeed, the 2009 Annual Report stated that: "*the CSR management framework forms an integral part of the Group's structure, and comprises a number of different tools and structures at various levels of the Group's hierarchy (the corporate governance system, the compliance framework, the Risk Committees, the New Product Committees, Internal Regulations, Code of Conduct, Audit Charter, etc.)*" (Société Générale 2009: 139).

(continued)

Box 1 (continued)

Of similar importance for reputational goals is the independent compliance function, implemented by the French bank since 2006. Over the years and on an ongoing basis, this structure has been expanded to take into account the presence of new sources of risk and the changes in the environment and regulatory framework. The last renovation of this function dates back to September of 2010, likely in response to the reputational crisis of 2008. On that occasion, the French bank decided to replace the previous structure with a new department (*Compliance Department*) by extending the functions and assigning a larger staff (Société Générale 2009). Among the responsibilities assigned is the management of reputational risk, for which the French bank has not chosen to set up an *ad hoc* monitoring unit. However, an internal directive is aimed at all employees to define the policy for the management, minimization and prevention of reputational risk. For *Société Générale*, the management of this risk is a key objective to which all employees must contribute (see, more specifically, Société Générale 2011: 168). Finally, a further contribution to the resolution of the reputational crisis is the absence of previous adverse and harmful events that could have damaged the bank's image. At the time of the crisis, the reputation of the French bank seemed very solid and not at all compromised. As argued by the doctrine (see *supra*), the preliminary possession of a good corporate reputation not only serves as a "*protection barrier*" against adverse events but also allows the CSR strategies to best perform their reputational driver function to reconstruct the deteriorated image. This also explains why the internal consequences (on profitability and equity) of the reputational crisis have been marginal. Indeed, neither the funding of the bank nor its total capitalization suffered a relevant decrease. Both the traditional customers and some more important financial distributors showed a loyal attitude, thereby safeguarding the amount of bank funding. Additionally, the support received from some important investment banks was very important and decreed the success of the capital increase. Finally, customer complaints were contained, and the penalties imposed by authorities have involved only some bank managers and not the highest corporate officers.

Source: Our elaboration from Société Générale Registration Document (2009) and website.

References

Abbott WF, Monsen RJ (1979) On the measurement of corporate social responsibility: self-reported disclosures as a method of measuring corporate social involvement. Acad Manag J 22(3):501–515

Beattie V, Thomson SJ (2007) Lifting the lid on the use of content analysis to investigate intellectual capital disclosures. Account Forum 31(2):129–163

Beurden PV, Gössling T (2008) The worth of value – a literature review on the relation between corporate social and financial performance. J Bus Ethics 82(2):407–424

Biell L, Muller A (2013) Sudden crash or long torture: the timing of market reactions to operational loss events. J Bank Financ 37(7):2628–2638

Birindelli G, Ferretti P, Intonti M et al (2015) On the drivers of corporate social responsibility in banks: evidence from an ethical rating model. J Manag Governance 19(2):303–340

Brammer S, Millington A (2005) Corporate reputation and philanthropy: an empirical analysis. J Bus Ethics 61(1):29–44

Brammer SJ, Pavelin S (2006) Corporate reputation and social performance: the importance of fit. J Manag Stud 43(3):435–455

Callado-Muñoz F, Utrero-Gonzalez N (2011) Does it pay to be socially responsible? Evidence from Spain's retail banking sector. Eur Financ Manag 17(4):755–787

Carreras E, Alloza A, Carreras A (2013) Corporate reputation. LID Publishing Ltd, London

Chih HL, Chih HH, Chen TY (2010) On the determinants of corporate social responsibility: international evidence on the financial industry. J Bus Ethics 93(1):115–135

Ciciretti R, Fabretti A, Nicolosi M (2015) Social responsibility and responsible investments in Italy: an overview. In: Hebb T, Hawley JP, Hoepner AGF, Neher AL, Wood D (eds) The Routledge handbook of responsible investment. Routledge, London

Cravens K, Goad Oliver E, Ramamoorti S (2003) The reputation index: measuring and managing corporate reputation. Eur Manag J 21(2):201–212

Creyer EH, Ross WT (1997) The influence of firm behavior of purchase motive: do consumers really care about business ethics? J Consum Mark 14(6):421–432

Davies G, Chun R, da Silva RV et al (2004) A corporate character scale to assess employee and customer views of organization reputation. Corp Reput Rev 7(2):125–146

De Fontnouvelle P, De Jesus-Rueff V, Jordan J et al (2006) Capital and risk: new evidence on implications of large operational losses. J Money Credit Bank 38(7):1819–1846

de la Cuesta-González M, Muñoz-Torres MM, Fernández-Izquierdo MA (2006) Analysis of social performance in the Spanish financial industry through public data. J Bus Ethics 69(3):289–304

de Quevedo Puente E, de la Fuente Sabatè JM, Delgrado-Garcia JB (2007) Corporate social performance and corporate reputation: two interwoven perspectives. Corp Reput Rev 10 (1):60–72

Dell'Atti S, Iannuzzi A, Cavallaro G et al (2012) Understanding reputational crisis: evidence from the European banking sector. J Mod Account Audit 8(2):247–266

Du S, Bhattacharya CB, Sen S (2010) Maximizing business returns to corporate social responsibility (CSR): the role of CSR communication. Int J Manag Rev 12(1):8–19

El Ghoul S, Guedhami O, Kwok CCY, Mishra DR (2011) Does corporate social responsibility affect the cost of capital? J Bank Financ 35(9):2388–2406

Esen E (2013) The influence of corporate social responsibility (CSR) activities on building corporate reputation. In: Gonzalez-perez MA, Leonard L (eds) International business, sustainability and corporate social responsibility, Advances in sustainability and environmental justice. Emerald Group Publishing, Bingley, pp 133–150

Fiordelisi F, Soana MG, Schwizer P (2014) Reputational losses and operational risk in banking. Eur J Financ 20(2):105–124

Fombrun CJ (2007) List of list: a compilation of international corporate reputation ratings. Corp Reput Rev 10(2):144–153

Fombrun CJ, Shanley M (1990) What's in a name? Reputation building and corporate strategy. Acad Manag J 33(1):233–258

Fombrun CJ, Gardberg NA, Sever JM (2000a) The Reputation Quotient^{TM}: a multi-stakeholder measure of corporate reputation. J Brand Manag 7(4):241–255

Fombrun CJ, Gardberg NA, Barnett M (2000b) Opportunity platforms and safety nets: corporate citizenship and reputational risk. Bus Soc Rev 105(1):85–106

Gabbi G, Patarnello A (2010) Il valore della reputazione bancaria tra risk management e scelte strategiche. Banca Impr Soc 29(2):335–358
Gardberg NA, Fombrun CJ (2002) The Global Reputation Quotient Project: first steps towards a cross-nationally valid measure of corporate reputation. Corp Reput Rev 4(4):303–307
Gillet R, Hübner G, Plunus S (2010) Operational risk and reputation in the financial industry. J Bank Financ 34(4):224–235
Goss A, Roberts GS (2011) The impact of corporate social responsibility on the cost of bank loans. J Bank Financ 35(7):1794–1810
Helm S (2005) Designing a formative measure for corporate reputation. Corp Reput Rev 8 (2):95–109
Helm S, Klode C (2011) Challenges in measuring corporate reputation. In: Helm S, Liehr-Gobbers K, Storck C (eds) Reputation management. Springer, Berlin, pp 99–110
Hillenbrand C, Money K (2007) Corporate responsibility and corporate reputation: two separate concepts or two sides of the same coin. Corp Reput Rev 10(4):261–277
Hoepner AGF, Wilson J (2012) Social, Environmental, Ethical and Trust (SEET) issues in banking: an overview. In: Barth JR, Lin C, Wihlborg C (eds) Research handbook on international banking and governance. Edward Elgar, Cheltenham
Ioannou I, Serafeim G (2012) What drives corporate social performance? The role of nation-level institutions. J Int Bus Stud 43:834–864. doi:10.1057/jibs.2012.26
Jacob CK (2012) The impact of financial crisis on corporate social responsibility and its implications for reputation risk management. J Manag Sustainability 2(2). doi:10.5539/jms.v2n2p259
Janney JJ, Gove S (2011) Reputation and corporate social responsibility aberrations, trends and hypocrisy: reaction to firm choices in the stock option backdating scandal. J Manag Stud 48 (7):1562–1585
King BG, McDonnell MH (2015) Good firms, good targets: the relationship between corporate social responsibility, reputation, and activist targeting. In: Kiyoteru Tsutsui K, Lim A (eds) Corporate social responsibility in a globalizing world. Cambridge University Press, Cambridge, pp 430–454
Klein J, Dawar H (2004) Corporate social responsibility and consumers' attributions and brand evaluations in a product-harm crisis. Int J Res Mark 21(3):203–217
Lin CH, Yang HL, Liou DY (2009) The impact of corporate social responsibility on financial performance: evidence from business in Taiwan. Technol Soc 31(1):56–63
Liston-Heyes C, Ceton G (2009) An investigation of real versus perceived CSP in S&P-500 firms. J Bus Ethics 89(2):283–296
MacMillan K, Money K, Downing S et al (2004) Giving your organization SPIRIT: an overview and call to action for directors on issues of corporate governance, corporate reputation and corporate responsibility. J Gen Manag 30(2):15–42
Maden C, Arikan E, Telci EE et al (2012) Linking corporate social responsibility to corporate reputation: a study on understanding behavioral consequences. Procedia Soc Behav Sci 58:655–664
McWilliams A, Siegel D (2000) Corporate social responsibility and financial performance: correlation or misspecification? Strategic Manag J 21(5):603–609
Melo T, Garrido-Morgado A (2012) Corporate reputation: a combination of social responsibility and industry. Corp Soc Resp Environ Manag 19(1):11–31
Minor D, Morgan J (2011) CSR as reputation insurance: primum non nocere. Calif Manage Rev 53 (3):40–59
Morsing M, Schultz M (2006) Corporate social responsibility communication: stakeholder information, response and involvement strategies. Bus Ethics: Eur Rev 15(4):323–338
Mulki JP, Jaramillo F (2011) Ethical reputation and value received: customer perceptions. Int J Bank Mark 29(5):358–372
Newell SJ, Goldsmith RE (2001) The development of a scale to measure perceived corporate credibility. J Bus Res 5(3):235–247
Osterhus TL (1997) Pro-social consumer influence strategies: when and how do they work? J Mark 61(4):16–29

Palmrose ZV, Richardson VJ, Scholz S (2004) Determinants of market reactions to restatement announcements. J Account Econ 37:59–89
Peloza J (2006) Using corporate social responsibility as insurance for financial performance. Calif Manage Rev 48(2):52–72
Ponzi LJ, Fombrun CJ, Gardberg NA (2011) RepTrak™ pulse: conceptualizing and validating a short-form measure of corporate reputation. Corp Reput Rev 14(1):15–35
Reputation Institute (2014) Global CSR RepTrak ® 100 study and results. December. http://www.reputationinstitute.com/Resources/Registered/PDF-Resources/2014-CSR-RepTrak-100-Study.aspx
Reputation Institute (2015) How do consumers view the banking industry worldwide? March. http://www.reputationinstitute.com/Resources/Registered/PDF-Resources/global-banking-industry-reputation.aspx
Rettab B, Brik AB, Mellahi K (2009) A study of management perceptions of the impact of corporate social responsibility on organizational performance in emerging economies: the case of Dubai. J Bus Ethics 89(3):371–390
Scholtens B (2009) Corporate social responsibility in the international banking industry. J Bus Ethics 86(2):159–175
Scholtens B, Dam L (2007) Banking on equator. Are banks that adopted the equator principles different from non-adopters? World Dev 35(8):1307–1328
Schuler DA, Cording M (2006) A corporate social performance corporate financial performance behavioral model for consumers. Acad Manage Rev 31(3):540–558
Schwizer P, Soana MG, Maucci G et al (2010) Rischio reputazionale e perdite operative. Un'analisi empirica sulle banche quotate. Bancaria 11:27–48
Servaes H, Tamayo A (2013) The impact of corporate social responsibility on firm value. Manag Sci 59(5):1045–1061
Simpson WG, Kohers T (2002) The link between corporate social and financial performance: evidence from the banking industry. J Bus Ethics 35(2):97–109
Smith SM, Alcorn DS (1991) Cause marketing: a new direction in the marketing of corporate social responsibility. J Consum Mark 8(3):19–35
Soana MG (2011) The relationship between corporate social performance and corporate financial performance on the banking sector. J Bus Ethics 104(1):133–148
Société Générale (2009) Registration Document
Société Générale (2010) Registration Document
Société Générale (2011) Registration Document
Soprano A, Crielaard B, Piacenza F, Ruspantini D (2009) Measuring operational and reputational risk: a practitioner's approach. Wiley, Hoboken, NJ
Sotorrío LL, Sánchez JLF (2008) Corporate social responsibility of the most highly reputed European and North American firms. J Bus Ethics 82(2):379–390
Strahilevitz MA (2003) The effects of prior impressions of a firm's ethics on the success of a cause-related marketing campaign: do the good look better while the bad look worse? J Nonprofit Pub Sector 11(1):77–92
Sturm P (2013) Operational and reputational risk in the European banking industry: the market reaction to operational risk events. J Econ Behav Organ 85(46):191–206
Trotta A, Iannuzzi A, Cavallaro G et al (2011) Banking reputation and CSR: a stakeholder value approach. In: Gummesson E, Mele C, Polese F (eds) Proceedings of The Naples Forum on Service – Service Dominant Logic, Network and System Theory and Service Science: Integrating Three Perspectives for a New Service Agenda, Giannini, Naples
Turban DB, Greening DW (1997) Corporate social performance and organizational attractiveness to perspective employees. Acad Manag J 40(3):658–673
Turker D (2009) Measuring corporate social responsibility: a scale development study. J Bus Ethics 85:411–427
Vitezić N (2011) Corporate reputation and social responsibility: an analysis of large companies in Croatia. Int Bus Econ Res J 10(8):85
Walker K (2010) A systematic review of the corporate reputation literature: definition, measurement, and theory. Corp Reput Rev 12(4):357–387

Walker K, Dyck B (2014) The primary importance of corporate social responsibility and ethicality in corporate reputation: an empirical study. Bus Soc Rev 119(1):147–174

Walsh G, Beatty SE (2007) Customer-based corporate reputation of a service firm: scale development and validation. J Acad Mark Sci 35(1):127–143

Walter I (2013) The value of reputational capital and risk in banking and finance. Int J Bank Account Financ 5(1/2):205–219

Williams RJ, Barrett JD (2000) Corporate philanthrophy, criminal activity, and firm reputation: is there a link? J Bus Ethics 26(4):341–350

Xifra J, Ordeix E (2009) Managing reputational risk in an economic downturn: the case of Banco Santander. Public Relat Rev 35(4):353–360

Yoon Y, Gurhan-Canli Z, Schwarz N (2006) The effect of corporate social responsibility (CSR) activities on companies with bad reputations. J Consum Psychol 16(4):377–390

Stefano Dell'Atti is a Professor of Banking and Finance at University of Foggia (Italy). He holds a PhD in Business Administration and Governance from the University Parthenope of Naples (Italy). He was an Assistant Professor in Banking and Finance at Faculty of Economics University of Foggia (from 1997 to 2000). From 2000 to 2003, he was an Associate Professor at University of Foggia. He is currently a Full Professor in Banking and Finance at University of Foggia (since 2003), where he teaches Banking and Finance and Strategy and Organization of Financial Intermediaries.

He is a member of the Council of PhD in Management and Finance at University of Foggia and Director of the Research Center Interuniversity on the Guarantee Institutions (CeSAC) of University of Foggia and University of Bari "Aldo Moro".

He is also a Member of the Editorial Board of Journal "Rivista Bancaria" and "Banche e Banchieri", and he was an editor and reviewer for a number of journals.

Over his 20-year academic career, he has authored (or co-authored) more than 50 scientific publications and 5 books. His major areas of research are as follows: Value and Intangibles in Banks; Reputational Risk; Small Banks, Guarantee Institutions; Efficiency of Financial Intermediaries, Regulation and Disclosure.

Antonia Patrizia Iannuzzi is a Researcher of "Banking and Finance" at University of Bari "Aldo Moro" (Italy) where she teaches the course "Economics of Financial Intermediaries" at the Ionic Department on Legal and Economic System of Mediterranean. Moreover she holds a PhD in "Banking and Finance" from the University of Roma "Sapienza" (Italy) and she was a Research Fellow in Financial Markets and Institutions at University of Bari "Aldo Moro" (Italy, years 2005–2010) and University of Catanzaro "Magna Graecia" (Italy, years 2010–2014). Since 2008, she has co-taught "Banking and Finance" at the Department of Economics of University of Foggia, where she taught some courses (*Integrative Course of Economics of Financial Intermediaries, Economics of Insurance Companies, Professional course on Corporate Lending*). At present, she is a ordinary member of the "*Italian Association of Professors of Economics of Financial Intermediaries and Markets*" and consultative member of the scientific committee of CESAC ("*Interuniversity Research Center on the Guarantee Institutions*"), University of Foggia and University of Bari "Aldo Moro". Moreover, she has been a speaker at various national and international conferences and a reviewer of some international journals.

Since 2005, she has authored (or co-authored) 22 scientific publications. Her main research and teaching interests are related to corporate reputation and reputational risk in the banking sector, corporate governance, stakeholder engagement and management compensation, corporate social responsibility, ethical funds and bank–firm relationships.

Part II
Learning from Case Studies

The Libor Case: A Focus on Barclays

Rosella Carè

Abstract The purpose of this chapter is to describe the reputational impact of the Libor case on Barclays by outlining the ensuing process of rebuilding trust and implementing cultural changes. This chapter is organized as follows. First, we briefly describe the major elements of the Libor scandal, including the investigations, fines and regulatory actions. Then, we propose a focus on Barclays, the company that arguably experienced the most significant impact of the media scandal in 2012. In our case study, we describe the course of events that led Barclays into a reputational crisis, identify and describe the core elements of the restructuring concept. In closing, we consider the lessons learned from this series of events.

1 Introduction: The Libor Rate-Fixing Scandal

The London Interbank Offered Rate (Libor) is the primary global benchmark for short term interest rates. Because it is used as the benchmark for trillions of loans, mortgages and financial products around the world, the Libor is considered one of the most crucial interest rates in finance and reflects the average rate at which banks can borrow unsecured funds from other banks. According to BIS statistics, more than 50 % of all syndicated loans signed in 2011 were linked to either the Libor or the Euro Interbank Offered Rate (Euribor) and a significant fraction of the world's bonds—amounting to at least $10 trillion—refer to one of these two rates (BIS 2013:3). Interbank markets are integral to the functioning of many other financial markets (Cui et al. 2012:2) and are especially closely linked to interest rate derivatives (forwards, futures and swaps) (IMF 2008:74). In addition, interbank rates play key roles in capital markets more generally.

The Libor scandal involves charges that banks rigged interest rates for two purposes: 1) to gain more profits and 2) to appear financially stable, especially

R. Carè (✉)
University Magna Graecia, Catanzaro, Italy
e-mail: care@unicz.it

S. Dell'Atti, A. Trotta (eds.), *Managing Reputation in The Banking Industry*,
DOI 10.1007/978-3-319-28256-5_3

during the financial crisis (O'Brien and Gilligan 2013). Agarwal and Jain (2015:111) state that during 2012, "an international investigation into the manipulation of interbank offered lending rates revealed a widespread plot undertaken by multiple banks—most notably, Barclays, UBS, Rabobank and the Royal Bank of Scotland—to leverage these interest rates for profit".

Concerns about perceived "uncorrected" Libor submissions initially surfaced in the media in 2008 (Abrantes-Metz 2012; Abrantes-Metz et al. 2012; Monticini and Thornton 2013; Fouquau and Spieser 2015). As explained by the Financial Services Authority[1] (FSA) (2012:28), "by April 2008, there was a more general perception that contributing banks' LIBOR submissions were not reflecting adequately conditions in the London interbank market. For example, this was reflected in a Wall Street Journal article published on 16 April 2008".

Several authors (Abrantes-Metz 2012; Abrantes-Metz et al. 2012; House of Commons Treasury Committee 2012; McConnell 2013; Monticini and Thornton 2013; Fouquau and Spieser 2015) note that a tipping point in the Libor scandal occurred upon the publication of an article in the Wall Street Journal in May 2008. In this article, the Journal assessed the borrowing rates reported by banks by comparing Libor rates with the cost of default-insurance. Until the financial crisis, the cost of insuring against bank defaults moved largely in tandem with Libor. However, during the financial crisis, the two measures began to diverge (House of Commons Treasury Committee 2012; King and Lewis 2014). After the Wall Street Journal analysis, King and Lewis (2014) noted that "most of the banks on the Libor panel have been investigated and several have settled allegations of malfeasance with U.S. and U.K. authorities, collectively paying billions of dollars in fines. In addition, several individual bankers face criminal charges, with at least two having already pled guilty, and numerous civil suits have been filed" (pp: 10).

O'Brien and Gilligan (2013) remarked that the FSA's enforcement notice indicates that there were two discrete phases of misreporting: the first phase occurred before mid-2007 and involved patterns or practices designed to distort Libor in a manner that benefited banks' current derivative positions, and the second phase involved the systematic reporting of the cost of debt in a manner designed to dampen public media coverage and/or regulatory scrutiny of banks.

Since 2009, the FSA, along with other regulators and public authorities in several countries—including the United States, Japan and the European Union—has been investigating a number of institutions for alleged misconduct relating to Libor and other benchmarks, including Euribor and Tibor (Hou and Skeie 2014). On July 2012, the Chancellor of the Exchequer commissioned Martin Wheatley, the managing director of the FSA and Chief Executive-designate of the Financial Conduct Authority (FCA), to undertake a review of the framework for the setting of Libor. The report contains a number of recommendations for the government, the British Bankers' Association (BBA) and the banks, as well as regulatory authorities

[1] In April 2013, the FSA was replaced by two new regulatory bodies, the Prudential Regulation Authority (PRA) and the Financial Conduct Authority (FCA).

both in the UK and internationally. Through a process of analysis and consultation, the Wheatley Review developed three fundamental policy recommendations: i) to reform the current framework for setting and governing LIBOR; ii) to determine the adequacy and scope of sanctions to address LIBOR abuse; and iii) to determine whether similar considerations apply to other price-setting mechanisms in financial markets and, if so, to provide provisional policy recommendations in these areas. The government accepted the recommendations of Martin Wheatley's independent review in full and significant reforms came into effect in 2013.

Following the Wheatley Review of LIBOR, responsibility for Libor administration was transferred from the BBA to a new administrator, the ICE Benchmark Administration (IBA), which is an independent subsidiary of the Intercontinental Exchange and is responsible for the end-to-end administration of benchmarks. The IBA was established for the sole purpose of administering benchmarks and is now a wholly-owned subsidiary of the Intercontinental Exchange group (ICE).

In 2012, the international investigation into the manipulation of interbank rates revealed "a widespread plot undertaken by multiple banks—most notably Barclays, UBS, Rabobank and the Royal Bank of Scotland—to leverage these interest rates for profit" (Agarwal and Jain 2015:111). In June 2012, Barclays was fined £59.5 million by the FSA, £200 million by the Commodity Futures Trading Commission (CFTC) and £160 million by the United States Department of Justice for engaging in rate manipulation. In December 2012, UBS agreed to pay $1.2 billion to the US Department of Justice (US DOJ) and CFTC, £160 million to the UK Financial Services Authority and CHF60m to the Swiss Financial Market Supervisory Authority for its role in Libor manipulation. In September 2013, ICAP (or - IEL-ICAP Europe Ltd) was fined $65 million by the CFTC and £14 million by the FCA (FCA 2013). Table 1 provides a summary of the UK Regulatory actions related to LIBOR activity.

Table 1 UK Regulatory fines related to LIBOR activity

Institution	£ million	Date	Activity	
Barclays	59.5	27 Feb 2012	Libor	Euribor
UBS	160.0	19 Dec 2012	Libor	Euribor
RBS	87.5	06 Feb 2013	Libor	
ICAP Europe	14.0	25 Sept 2013	Libor	
Rabobank	105.0	29 Oct 2013	Libor	
Martin Brokers (UK) Limited	0.6	15 May 2014	Libor	
Lloyds Banking Group	105.0	28 July 2014	Libor	Repo[a]
Deutsche Bank AG	227.0	23 Apr 2015	Libor	Euribor

Source: Our elaboration of FSA fines per year (data are available at http://www.fca.org.uk/firms/being-regulated/enforcement/fines)

[a]The FCA news release published on July 28, 2014 states that: "The Financial Conduct Authority (FCA) has fined Lloyds Bank plc (Lloyds) and Bank of Scotland plc (BoS), both part of Lloyds Banking Group (LBG), £105 million for serious misconduct relating to the Special Liquidity Scheme (SLS), the Repo Rate benchmark and the London Interbank Offered Rate (LIBOR)". Available at http://www.fca.org.uk/news/lloyds-banking-group-fined-105m-Libor-benchmark-failings

Following the Libor scandal, the European Commission adopted a proposal for regulating benchmarks with the goal of restoring public trust in financial benchmarks in the wake of the recent scandals. In addition, in December 2013, the European Commission announced fines on six financial institutions for their participation in cartels relating to Libor submissions for Japanese Yen during the period 2007/2010. These penalties were just the first round of fines imposed by the Commission; in October 2014, two international banks were fined, and in February 2015, the Commission fined the broker ICAP 14.9 million euros for its participation in several cartels relating to the Yen interest rate derivatives sector.

Currently, regulators in several countries—including Canada, America, Japan, the European Union, Switzerland and Britain—are investigating allegations that Libor and similar rates were manipulated by a large number of banks.

2 A Focus on Barclays[2]

Barclays Plc[3] is an international bank and financial services company based in London. Through the parent company and its numerous subsidiaries, Barclays provides services including corporate banking, investment banking, credit cards and retail banking.

Barclays Bank has a long corporate history and has undergone many changes. Established in 1690 as a goldsmith bank, Barclays' roots are in retail banking in London. At the end of the nineteenth century, Barclays grew significantly as a result of its amalgamation with 20 regional banks. Barclays was listed on the London Stock Exchange in 1902.

Today, Barclays is classified by the Financial Stability Board as 1 of 28 banks around the world that are so large that they are systemically important on a global scale. Barclays has operations in over 50 countries and territories and has approximately 48 million customers.

In June 2012, Barclays was fined by the UK Financial Services Authority (FSA) for its role in the LIBOR scandal.

In determining the appropriate penalty for Barclays, the FSA considered mitigating factors, including in particular the company's co-operation with the FSA

---

[2] The analysis, descriptions and findings are based on the assessment of documents that are publicly available on the Banks' web sites. The author has generally checked the veracity of the information obtained. Other individuals who consider the same information could reach different conclusions. This case study has scientific purpose and it is not intended to guide or influence the conduct or decisions, including any investment or other financial decisions, of any person. Accordingly, this chapter must not be relied upon for that purpose.

[3] The term 'Barclays' refers both to "Barclays Plc Group" and to "Barclays Bank Plc". For this chapter, we used documents published on the Barclays web site (http://www.barclays.com/) related to both Barclays Plc Group and to Barclays Bank Plc to obtain a complete picture of the company's historical evolution.

during its investigation. However, one US regulator, the CFTC, levied a fine of $200 million (£128.5 million) on Barclays, which was the largest fine ever issued by the CFTC. The Commission also found that Barclays issued false LIBOR reports at the direction of members of senior management to protect the company's reputation during the global financial crisis (CFTC 2012).

Numerous authorities opened investigations into Barclays' participation in the manipulation of benchmark currency exchange rates, including the FCA, the CFTC, the U.S. Securities and Exchange Commission (SEC), the US Department Of Justice Fraud Section (DOJ-FS) and Antitrust Division (DOJ-AD), the European Commission, the Serious Fraud Office (SFO), the Monetary Authority of Singapore, the Japan Financial Services Agency, the Prosecutors' Office in Trani (Italy) and various US State Attorneys General (Barclays Bank Plc Annual Report 2014:307). Barclays received negative media attention for several reasons related to liquidity issues (FSA 2012:24). During its investigation, the FSA found that Barclays' misconduct included: i) inappropriate submissions following requests by derivatives traders; ii) inappropriate submissions to avoid negative commentary in the media; iii) systems and controls failings; and iv) compliance failings. As explained by the House of Commons Treasury Committee (2012), Barclays has taken the initial brunt of the criticism because it settled first and thus was the first bank to have been found guilty of misconduct.

Furthermore, mass media outlets such as newspapers play an important role in influencing firms' reputations and in disseminating information to a broad audience. Between January 2008 and May 2015, 4705 articles concerning Libor manipulation were published in newspapers and their online counterparts.[4] The highest concentration of articles occurred in 2012, with 2052 articles published by traditional and new media outlets. This corresponds to the widespread media reaction to authorities' investigations and fines. However, 107 articles were published in 2011, which clearly demonstrates media interest in the topic of Libor manipulation before 2012. The search also included 2008, 2009 and 2010, but no results were found in those years (Fig. 1).

The documents come mainly from the UK (2736), U.S. (1453), Europe (639), Germany (287) and Switzerland (281). Finally, the entities mentioned most often are summarized in Fig. 2.

Figure 2 shows that Barclays is the entity cited most often in media articles. This distinction is further confirmed in Fig. 3.

[4] Automated keyword-based searches of online news archives in the media database Factiva reveal more than 4705 articles related to the words "Libor" and "manipulation". The search was conducted in May 2015. The selected time period was "01/01/2008–08/05/2015". Factiva provides a premier collection of the world's top media outlets, web media, and trade and consumer publications, giving immediate access to thousands of sources in 28 languages from nearly 200 countries. The database contains 35 years of articles, analyst reports and tweets. The top news sources in Factiva include the Wall Street Journal, Dow Jones Newswires, the New York Times, the Sydney Morning Herald, South China Morning Post and Le Monde. See http://new.dowjones.com/factiva-sources/

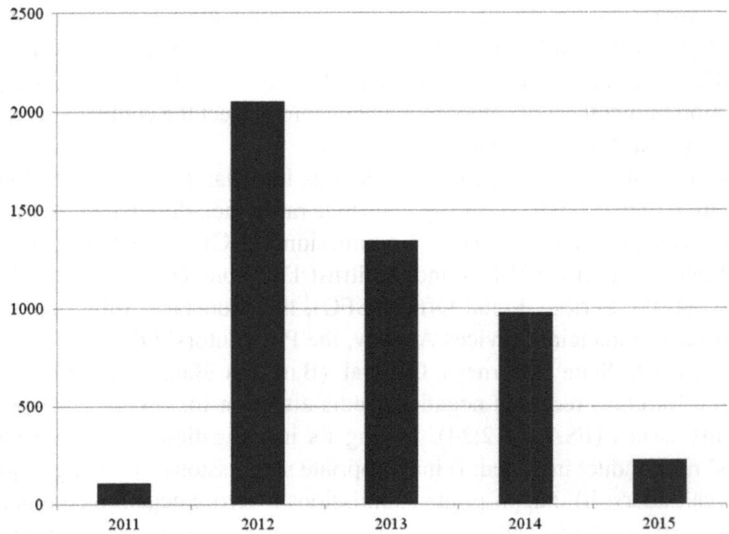

Source: Our elaboration of Factiva data

Fig. 1 Document distribution by date

The top three executives in terms of media mentions are related to Barclays Plc. Robert Diamond (Chief Executive), Marcus Agius (Chairman) and Jerry del Missier (Chief operating officer) resigned following the FSA investigation into interbank interest rates. Barclays saw its reputation decline significantly during 2012 (Rep Track 2013). Table 2 shows that between 2011 and 2012, Barclays' reputational score declined by more than 10 points.

The reputational damage to Barclays is confirmed by its 2014 Annual Report, which states that "there are a number of areas where the Group sustained financial and reputational damage during previous periods; and these consequences continued in 2014 and are likely to continue in 2015 and possibly beyond (pp: 122)".

Barclays Plc was involved in the scandal during 2012. However, the company responded immediately. For example, the scandal led to the resignation of Chief Executive Bob Diamond and Chairman Marcus Agius. Barclays' admission of misconduct, its cooperation and its remediation efforts make Barclays an interesting and intense case study for understanding the role of reputation in banking and the actions necessary to restore that reputation. The Barclays case study can also facilitate analysis of the following issues: i) the reputational consequences of violating the trust of market participants and regulatory authorities; ii) the impact

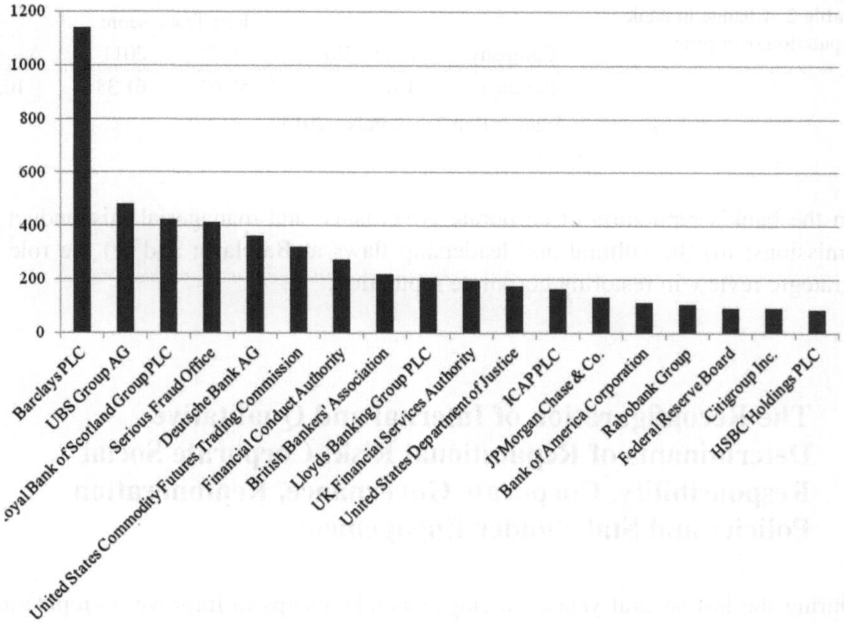

Source: Our elaboration of Factiva data

Fig. 2 Entities mentioned most often

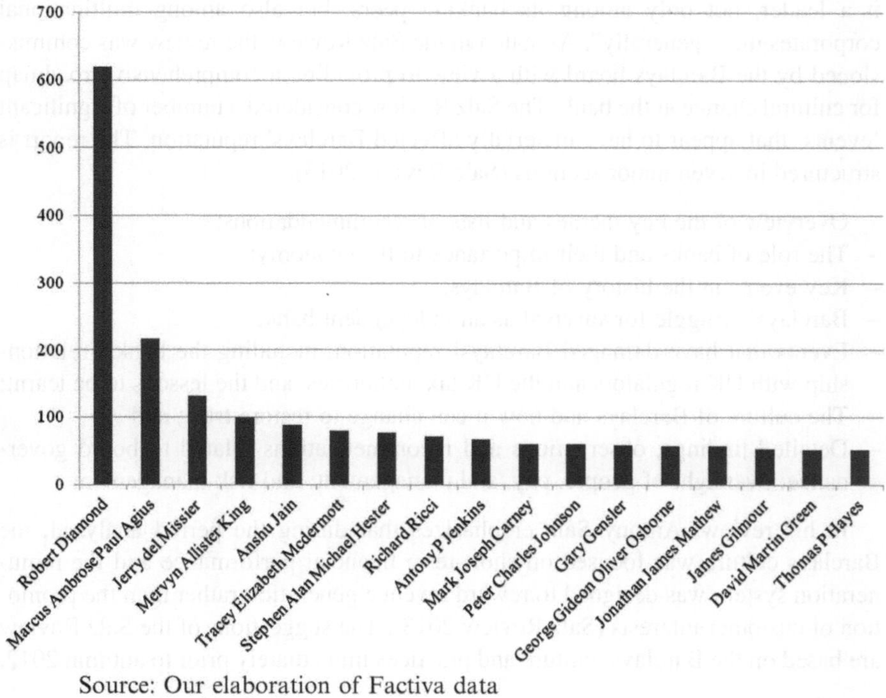

Source: Our elaboration of Factiva data

Fig. 3 Executives mentioned most often

Table 2 Change in bank reputation over time

Company	Rank (2012)	Rep Track score		
		2012	2011	Δ
Barclays	181	50.62	61.38	−10.77

Source: Rep Track Pulse, 2013

on the bank's reputation of corporate governance and managerial misconduct or omissions; iii) the cultural and leadership flaws at Barclays; and iv) the role of strategic review in restoring corporate reputation.

3 The Reconfiguration of Internal and Qualitative Determinants of Reputational Risk: Corporate Social Responsibility, Corporate Governance, Remuneration Policies and Stakeholder Engagement

During the last several years, Barclays has taken steps to improve its reputation, corporate governance and engagement in corporate social responsibility.

In July 2012, the Barclays board announced an independent external review (hereafter, the "Salz Review") of its business practices, which was intended to "determine how Barclays can rebuild trust and develop business practices that make it a leader, not only among its banking peers, but also among multinational corporates more generally". As stated in the Salz Review, the review was commissioned by the Barclays board with a view to providing a comprehensive roadmap for cultural change at the bank. The Salz Review considered a number of significant 'events' that appear to have materially affected Barclays' reputation. The report is structured in seven major sections (Salz Review 2013):

- Overview of the key themes and lists of recommendations;
- The role of banks and their importance to the economy;
- Key events in the history of Barclays;
- Barclays' struggle for survival as an independent bank;
- Events that have damaged Barclays' reputation, including the bank's relationship with UK regulators and the UK tax authorities, and the lessons to be learnt;
- The culture of Barclays and how it can change to restore trust; and
- Detailed findings, observations and recommendations related to board governance; oversight of people, pay, and management; and risk management.

In his review, Antony Salz emphasizes that during the period analysed, the Barclays culture was focused on short-term financial performance and the remuneration system was designed to reward revenue generation rather than the promotion of customer interests (Salz Review 2013). The suggestions of the Salz Review are based on the Barclays' culture and practices immediately prior to autumn 2012.

Suggestions can be grouped into 8 macro categories and articulated in 34 recommendations, which are summarized below (Salz Review 2013).

i) **Regulatory Relations**: Regulatory and business standards.
ii) **The board**: board experience; Non-Executive Directors; board information; the succession of Group Chief Executives; board coordination; board Committee for conduct, reputational and operational risk; board effectiveness; Strengthening Human Resources; and the board's role in compensation oversight.
iii) **Culture and Values**: Setting high standards; Bringing the Values to life; Monitoring progress; Code of conduct; Employee engagement; Recruiting and induction; Developing Barclays' future leaders; Issue escalation; and the independence and influence of the Control functions.
iv) **Balanced Scorecard**: Customers.
v) **Controls**: Risk culture and control framework; Conduct, reputational and operational risk; and Internal Audit.
vi) **Talent and Rewards**: Cohesive executive team; Improving the performance management process; Pay principles; Retail incentives; Discretionary pay; Long-term awards; Control functions' incentives; and Control functions' review of compensation.
vii) **Reputation Management**: Shareholder interaction and Learning from mistakes.
viii) **Transform Project Management Office**: Implementation.

After the Libor turmoil in 2012, Barclays undertook a comprehensive strategic review. In January 2013, Antony Jenkins announced the launch of new group-wide values, and on 12 February 2013, he announced changes to the scope of Barclays' business. Many of the suggestions of the Salz Review were implemented by the Barclays' board, either before (such as, for example, the changes made in January and February 2013) or after its publication.

The Transform Program announced by Barclays has three overall goals (Barclays Strategic Review 2013b):

- **Turnaround**: this purpose relates to the immediate need to stabilize the business and to maintain momentum after the events of 2012;
- **Return Acceptable Numbers**: this purpose relates to the need to deliver a return on equity (RoE) that is higher than the cost of equity (CoE) on a sustainable basis; and
- **Sustain FORward Momentum**: this purpose relates to the need to adapt the Barclays strategy going forward to ensure that does not return to a short-term bias.

Currently, Barclays has four key board-level committees that review and monitor risk across the Group: the board, the board Enterprise Wide Risk Committee, the board Financial Risk Committee and the board Conduct, Operational and Reputational Risk Committee (Barclays Bank Plc Annual Report 2014). In 2011, Barclays governance was structured as follows: the board (Group Chairman, two executive Directors, nine non-executive Directors), board Corporate Governance and Nominations Committee (Group Chairman and four independent non-executive Directors), board Audit Committee (Five independent non-executive Directors), board Risk Committee (Five independent non-executive Directors), board Remuneration Committee (three independent non-executive Directors and the Group Chairman)and board Citizenship Committee (Group Chairman and two independent non-executive directors) (Barclays Bank Plc Annual Report 2011). The new governance structure is the result of the company's transformation during the last several years.

The board Conduct, Operational and Reputational Risk Committee considers and evaluates the Group's operational risk profile and risk appetite and identifies and manages conduct and reputational risk. This committee replaced the board Citizenship Committee in January 2013 for the primary purpose of devoting more board time to the governance of non-financial risk (Response to the Salz Review 2013). Figure 4 provides a summary of the main activities of this committee.

In 2012, Barclays introduced the board Remuneration Committee to review its remuneration policy in line with the Transform Programme announced by Antony Jenkins. As announced in the 2012 Annual Report, the ratio of Group compensation to adjusted net operating income declined from 42 % in 2011 to 38 % in 2012. Furthermore, during 2014, variable pay decisions were made against a background of significant regulatory developments and market pressures. Figure 5 provides a summary of the Group incentive pool.

In 2013, the Group introduced the Enterprise Risk Management Framework (ERMF) to strengthen the company's governance relating to conduct and reputation

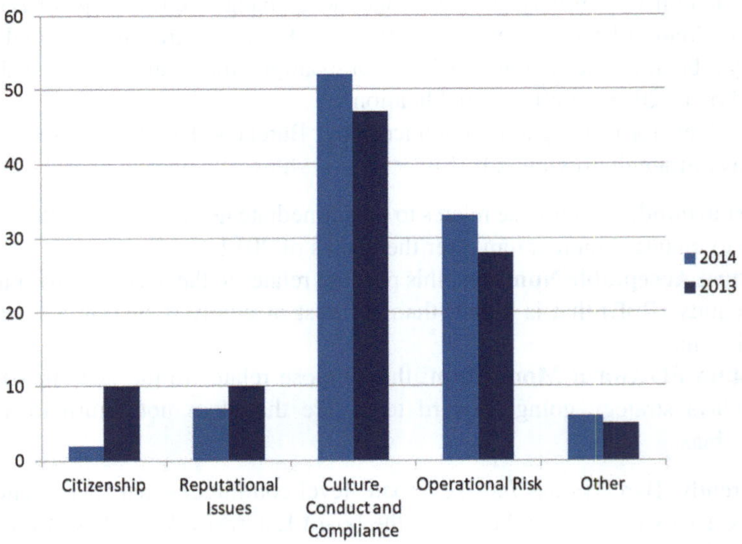

Source: Barclays Plc Annual Report (2014:54)

Fig. 4 Board conduct, operational and reputational risk committee allocation of time (%)

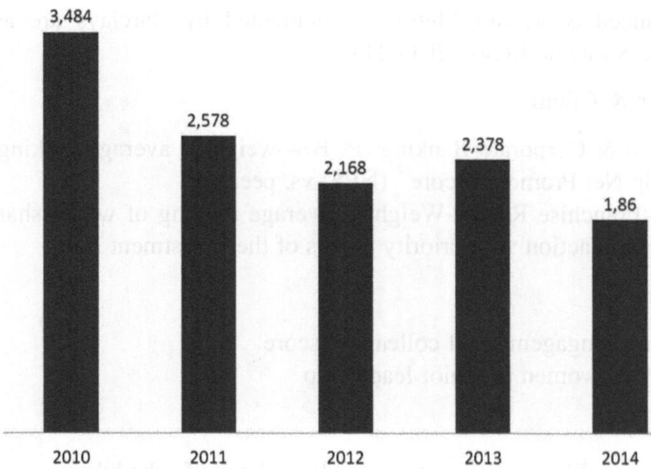

Source: Barclays Plc Annual Report (2014:28)

Fig. 5 Group incentive pool (£ million)

matters. Conduct and reputation risk were re-categorized as principal risks in 2013. The board Enterprise Wide Risk Committee was also created in 2013. This committee makes recommendations to the board regarding the Group's overall risk appetite and evaluates and reports details related to the Group's overall risk profile and risk monitoring (Barclays Bank Plc Annual Report 2014).

The reduction in the incentive pool is aligned with the reduction in statutory profit before tax (see Table 5). As stated in the Barclays Plc Annual Report (2014:27), "part of the reduction in the incentive pool year on year is due to the introduction of Role Based Pay (RBP) in 2014". The compensation to adjusted net income ratio decreased from 42.4 % in 2010 to 37.7 % in 2014.

The Transform Programme is considered by Barclays to be the vehicle for achieving necessary and fundamental cultural, financial and performance changes.

During 2012, Barclays developed a citizenship reporting process that was informed by and aligned with the financial reporting process, and in 2014, Barclays moved to further integrate citizenship reporting into the general financial reporting process by providing key citizenship performance disclosures within the Strategic Report included in the Annual Report. Barclays is currently moving towards further integration through the implementation of the 5C framework (Customer & Client, Colleague, Citizenship, Conduct and Company).

The 5C framework is related to the Balanced Scorecard approach. More specifically, the Balanced Scorecard establishes eight key measures around the 5Cs with the primary goal of reporting and monitoring Barclays' annual progress. In addition, both the 5C Framework and, consequently, the Balanced Scorecard Metrics can be immediately related to five stakeholder groups: customers and clients, staff/employees, regulators, communities and investors.

The Balanced Scorecard Metrics implemented by Barclays are as follows (Barclays Plc Strategic Report 2014:11):

1) **Customer & Client**
   - Personal & Corporate Banking (PCB)—weighted average ranking of Relationship Net Promoter Score® (NPS) vs. peer sets
   - Client Franchise Rank—Weighted average ranking of wallet share or customer satisfaction with priority clients of the Investment Bank
2) **Colleague**
   - Sustained engagement of colleagues score
   - Percent of women in senior leadership
3) **Citizenship**
   - Citizenship Plan—initiatives on track or ahead of schedule
4) **Conduct**
   - Conduct Reputation (YouGov survey)
5) **Company**
   - Adjusted Return on Equity
   - Fully Loaded CRD IV CET1 ratio

Barclays has received data indicating that certain improvements have been achieved over the last several years. For example, Barclays' scores in the periodic survey of global opinion makers conducted by YouGov have improved by 5 % (Barclays Plc Annual Report 2014:111). This measure is currently used to monitor progress in conduct management. As stated in the Annual Report (2014:212), "the conduct measure is developed through a conduct and reputation survey undertaken by YouGov across a range of respondents, including business and political stakeholders, the media, NGOs, charities and other opinion formers, and across key geographies (UK, Europe, Africa, the US and Asia)".

The Barclays Citizenship plan, which was launched in June 2012 and updated in July 2013, is an evolving set of global commitments organized around three areas (Barclays Plc Annual Report 2014:14): 1) Barclays' business practices; 2) contributions to growth; and 3) support of communities. Barclays' disclosures are prepared in accordance with the Global Reporting Initiative ('GRI') Indicator protocols and the Financial Sector Supplement. During the years 2012 and 2013, Barclays' disclosures were compliant with G3 (application level B), and in 2014, the company's disclosures were aligned with the Core option of the Global Reporting Initiative G4 Guidelines. Furthermore, Barclays has participated in a number of performance indices, benchmarks and environmental, social and governance (ESG) research ratings during the last several years.

During 2013, Barclays launched a new code of conduct that replaced a number of existing codes with one unifying document. This code outlines the values and

Table 3 Reputation term count

"Reputation"	
2014	175
2013	172
2012	111
2011	19
2010	16

Source: Our analysis of Barclays Plc Annual Report (2011, 2012, 2013a, 2014a)

behaviours fundamental to Barclays' long-term success. In addition, Barclay's Anti-Money Laundering (AML) policy establishes the following: global minimum standards, including the appointment of a Group Money Laundering Reporting Officer (GMLRO) and local Money Laundering Reporting Officers (MLROs);a risk-based approach for assessing and managing risks related to money laundering and terrorist financing; risk-based customer due diligence, identification, verification and "know your customer" procedures, including enhanced due diligence for customers that present higher risk; risk-based systems and procedures to monitor customer accounts and activity; procedures for reporting unusual activity internally and for reporting suspicious activity externally to the relevant law enforcement authorities; the maintenance of appropriate records; regular training for all relevant employees to enable them to understand and fulfil their legal obligations and to recognize risks that the bank's products and services are being used to assist money laundering or terrorist financing; appropriate communications and monitoring conformance arrangements to ensure that Barclays' policy requirements are understood and followed in practice; and the provision of appropriate managerial information and reporting to senior management to assess compliance with the AML and Counter-Terrorist Financing policies (Barclays Statement on Anti-Money Laundering 2014).

A search for the term "reputation" in Barclays' annual report confirms the company's renewed attention to reputation. Table 3 shows that the frequency of this term in Barclays' annual reports increased by more than 90 % over 4 years.

4 Quantitative Indicators, Credit Ratings and Share Price Analysis

In 2014, the Group's activities were resegmented into Core and Non-Core business units as part of the Group strategy update announced in May of that year (Barclays Bank Plc Annual Report 2014). The Core business comprises the following five business areas: Personal and Corporate Banking, Barclaycard, Africa Banking, Investment Bank, and Head Office. However, 2013 was a year of significant change for Barclays, and the company was affected by the business restructuring and de-risking process. Although the Group's adjusted profit before tax increased by

Table 4 Group statutory and adjusted profit

	£ million				
	2014	2013	2012	2011	2010
Statutory profit before tax	2256	2868	797	5770	5999
Statutory profit after tax	845	1297	181	3868	4499
Adjusted profit before tax	5502	4908	7599	5482	5641
Adjusted profit after tax	3798	2945	5440	4183	4271

Source: Barclays Plc Annual Report (2011, 2012, 2013a, 2014a)

Table 5 Key performance indicators

	2014	2013	2012
Adjusted dividend per share	6.5p	6.5p	6.5p
Adjusted dividend payout ratio	38 %	42 %	18 %
Dividends paid to shareholders	1057	859	733
Basic earnings per share	17.3p	15.3p	35.5p
Return on equity (adjusted)	5.1 %	4.1 %	n.a

Source: Barclays Plc Annual Report (2011, 2012, 2013a, 2014a)

Table 6 Barclays Bank Plc Financial Profile (million GBP)

	£ million				
	2014	2013	2012	2011	2010
Total assets	1,358,693.0	1,344,201.0	1,488,761.0	1,563,402.0	1,490,038.0
Deposits & ST funding	662,071.0	738,216.0	747,538.0	738,573.0	752,539.0
Equity	66,049.0	63,220.0	59,923.0	65,170.0	62,641.0
Net income	854.0	1308.0	33.0	4046.0	4563.0

Source: Our elaboration of Bankscope data

11 % in 2014, it had fallen by more than 35 % between 2012 and 2013. During 2013, the adjusted profit before tax decreased by 32 %, due to the cost of implementing the transformation program, and statutory profit before tax increased from £797 million to £2868 million (Table 4).

Group compensation costs decreased by 8 % between 2013 and 2014; dividends paid to shareholders increased by 23 % during the same period. Since 2010, there has been a significant shift in the allocation of earnings between employees and shareholders (Barclays Bank Plc Annual Report 2014). Although adjusted profit before tax increased by 12 % between 2013 and 2014, adjusted profit before tax in 2014 represents a 28 % decrease compared with 2012. Table 5 provides a summary of key performance indicators (KPIs).

The adjusted return on equity data shown in Table 5 demonstrates the organization's ability to generate long-term sustainable returns for shareholders. Table 6 provides an overview of the Barclays Bank Plc Financial Profile.

Table 7 Barclays' ratios

	2014	2013	2012	2011	2010
Capital					
Tier 1 ratio	13.00	15.70	13.20	12.90	13.50
Total capital ratio	16.50	19.90	17.00	16.35	16.91
Equity/total assets	4.85	4.70	4.03	4.17	4.20
Equity/cust & short term funding	9.98	8.56	8.02	8.82	8.32
Capital funds/liabilities	6.90	6.79	6.01	6.11	6.52
Capital funds/total assets	6.46	6.36	5.67	5.76	6.12
Capital funds/Dep & ST funding	13.25	11.58	11.28	12.19	12.11
Liquidity					
Interbank ratio	94.82	89.54	74.03	66.96	79.90
Net loans/total assets	31.48	32.30	28.47	27.63	28.72
Net loans/customer & ST funding	64.61	58.82	56.71	58.48	56.87
Liquid assets/Dep & ST funding	55.39	60.15	66.44	67.29	73.30

Source: Our elaboration of Bankscope data

Table 8 Barclays interbank ratio

Interbank ratio			
2011	2012	2013	2014
66.96	74.03	89.54	94.82

Source: Our elaboration of Bankscope data

During 2012, Barclays' Net Income fell by 74 % to 33.0 million (2011: 4046.0). However, the results also show that its business performance has been resilient (Table 7).

During the years 2012 and 2013, the Interbank Ratio increased by up to 17 %. Bonfim and Kim (2014:9) emphasize that "the interbank ratio allows one to assess another dimension of bank's funding liquidity risk, namely, whether banks are net borrowers or net lenders in interbank markets. Because we define this indicator as the ratio between loans to other banks and loans from other banks, a ratio above 100 % means that a bank is a net lender in interbank markets, which signals a more comfortable liquidity position than otherwise". Table 8 provides an overview of Barclays' Interbank Ratio during the period 2011/2014.

Barclays' ratio increased constantly during this period. Another demonstration of Barclays' performance resilience is that its credit rating was stable during these years (Table 9). In 2013, Barclays was downgraded one notch by Standard & Poor's because the rating agency perceived increased risk for certain large European investment banks due to tighter regulations and uncertain market conditions. Therefore, Barclays Bank Plc was downgraded from A+/A−1 to A/A−1 and Barclays Plc was downgraded from A/A−1 to A−/A−2 (Barclays Plc 2013a). In 2012, Moody's downgraded Barclays Bank Plc from Aa3/P−1 to A2/P−1 due to

Table 9 Ratings of Barclays Bank Plc

		Fitch judgement	Outlook
2014	Short-term debt	F1	Stable
	Long-term debt	A	
2013	Short-term debt	F1	Stable
	Long-term debt	A	
2012	Short-term debt	F1	Stable
	Long-term debt	A	
2011	Short-term debt	F1	Stable
	Long-term debt	A	

		S&P judgement	Outlook
2014	Short-term debt	A−1	Negative
	Long-term debt	A	
2013	Short-term debt	A−1	Stable
	Long-term debt	A	
2012	Short-term debt	A−1	Negative
	Long-term debt	A	
2011	Short-term debt	A−1	Stable
	Long-term debt	A	

		Moody's judgement	Outlook
2014	Short-term debt	P−1	Negative
	Long-term debt	A2	
2013	Short-term debt	P−1	Negative
	Long-term debt	A2	
2012	Short-term debt	P−2	Negative
	Long-term debt	A3	
2011	Short-term debt	P−1	–
	Long-term debt	A1	

Source: Barclays Bank Plc Annual Report (2011, 2012, 2013a, 2014)

the rating agency's repositioning of banks and securities firms with global capital market operations (Barclays Plc Annual Report 2013).

Figure 6 underscores the significant increase in sales volumes of the title between 5 days before and 5 days after (the event window) the diffusion of the FCA Final Notice (27 June). The analysis of sales volume within this event window allows us to depict the critical moments for the bank's reputation in the markets. The first critical moment relates to the increase in sales volume on June 27. On 28 June 2012, Barclays decreased 28.13p to 152.97p—a decline of more than 15 %—after the publication of the FSA Final Notice that announced a fine of £290 million for LIBOR manipulation. The second moment coincides with the resignation of the CEO and changes to the board (03 July).

Figure 7 analyses a 6-month window during 2012 to provide an overview of the most important events that affected Barclays' share price.

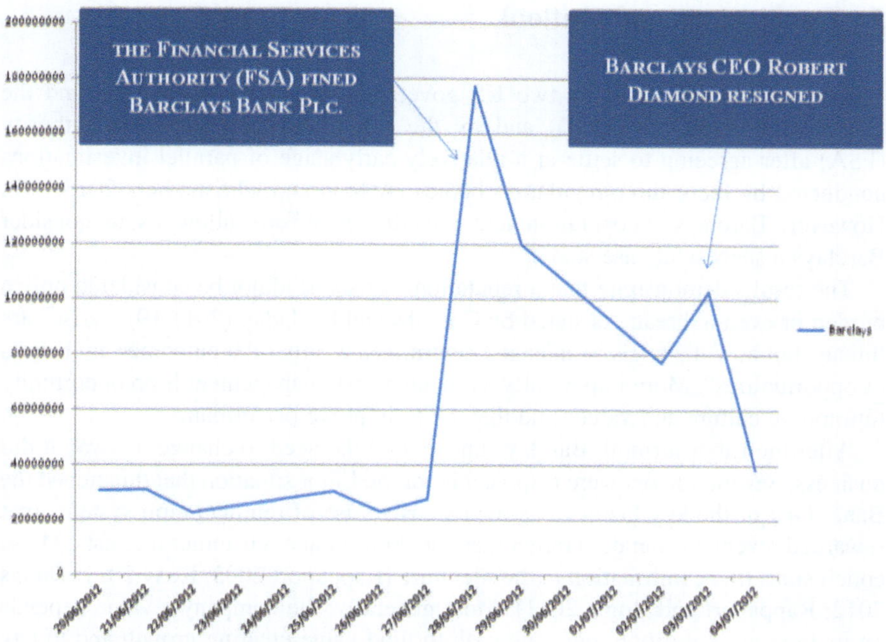

Source: Our analysis of Barclays' quote history

Fig. 6 Sales volume of the title

Source: Our analysis of Barclays' stock price time series

Fig. 7 Barclays' share price

5 Conclusions and Outlook

Barclays Bank was fined by two US government agencies (the CFTC and the Department of Justice (DOJ)) and by the UK's Financial Services Authority (FSA) after agreeing to settle at a relatively early stage of parallel investigations conducted by these three regulatory bodies (Ashton and Christophers 2015:197). However, Barclays' cooperation and remediation efforts allow us to consider Barclays a successful case study.

The results demonstrate that a reputational crisis need not be considered only a burden or even a threat. As stated by Coombs and Holladay (2011:19), "crises are threats, but how the crisis is managed determines whether the outcomes are threats or opportunities". More importantly, competent risk management is an opportunity to improve culture and values and thereby to improve performance.

After the Libor turmoil, Barclays understood the need to change the way it did business. Several factors were responsible for the Libor situation that threatened the Bank. One of the key factors was the extensive use of remuneration systems that rewarded revenue generation rather than the promotion of customer interests. These conclusions find confirmation in the literature (Rappaport 2005; Keay 2011; Dallas 2012; Rappaport and Bogle 2011). More generally, the company's value depends on its long-term ability to generate cash to fund value-creating growth and to pay shareholder dividends (Rappaport 2005:65). In this regard, Dallas (2012:267) emphasizes that: "short-termism, which is also referred to as earnings management (or, alternatively, managerial myopia), consists of the excessive focus of corporate managers, asset managers, investors and analysts on short-term results, whether quarterly earnings or short-term portfolio returns, and a repudiation of concern for long-term value creation and the fundamental value of firms".

Furthermore, although the unfavorable Libor event undermined Barclays' reputation among the public, it did not undermine its reputation in the markets. Barclays' financial results show that the company's performance has been resilient and has not been impacted by the scandal.

Based on the experiences observed in this case study, a number of success factors can be identified. The eight cornerstones of Barclays' successful reputational restructuring process can be summarized as follow:

1) **Awareness**. Barclays' awareness of the need for a cultural change is reflected in numerous actions, including, for example, the independent and external Salz Review. This review was commissioned with the intent to develop a comprehensive roadmap for cultural change at the bank.
2) **Timeliness**. The Barclays board implemented new Group-wide values and conducted a strategic review before the Salz Review was published. The timeliness aspect seems to be related to the need to immediately restore the bank's reputation.
3) **People**. After the Libor turmoil, the company's first response was the resignation of people directly involved in the investigation.

4) **Citizenship**. In 2013, Barclays developed a citizenship reporting process that was informed by and aligned with its financial reporting process. Through its Citizenship report, Barclays acknowledges stakeholder interest in more detailed technical information. The Barclays Citizenship Plan, launched in June 2012 and updated in July 2013, is an evolving set of global commitments that the Bank aims to fulfill in the coming years.
5) **Sustainability**. A restructuring/reorganization program is feasible only if the value of the restructuring can be adequately verified. The new reporting approach provides a series of key performance indicators to be monitored in the future.
6) **Structural changes.** Having expected a continued expansion of its business activities, Barclay's corporate organization was dominated by an excess concentration of resources in non-core activities, especially risky ventures. During 2014, the Group's activities have been reorganized into Core and Non-Core business units.
7) **Risk approach**. The Group has defined new levels of risk. The new risk appetite is approved by the board, which closely monitors and manages risk through, for example, the implementation of mandates and scale limits.
8) **Balanced scorecard**. The Balanced Scorecard defines eight specific commitments across the 5Cs (Customer & Client, Colleague, Citizenship, Conduct and Company) and helps to develop and monitor Barclays' progress on an annual basis.

References

Abrantes-Metz RM (2012) Why and how should the libor be reformed? Available at SSRN: http://ssrn.com/abstract=2094542. Accessed 04 Sept 2015

Abrantes-Metz RM, Kraten M, Metz AD et al (2012) Libor manipulation? J Bank Financ 36 (1):136–150

Agarwal A, Jain M (2015) Recent development in Libor. Abhinav-National Monthly Refereed J Res Comm Manag 4(3):107–114

Ashton P, Christophers B (2015) On arbitration, arbitrage and arbitrariness in financial markets and their governance: unpacking LIBOR and the LIBOR scandal. Econ Soc 44(2):188–217

Bank for International Settlements (2013) Towards better reference rate practices: a central bank perspective. Basel

Barclays Plc (2011) Annual Report. London

Barclays Plc (2012) Annual Report. London

Barclays Plc (2013a) Annual Report. London

Barclays Plc (2013b) Barclays' response to the Salz Review. London

Barclays Plc (2013c) Strategic Report. London

Barclays Plc (2014a) Annual Report. London

Barclays Plc (2014b) Statement on anti-money laundering. London

Barclays Plc (2014c) Strategic Report. London

Barclays Bank Plc (2011) Annual Report. London

Barclays Bank Plc (2012) Annual Report. London

Barclays Bank Plc (2013a) Annual Report. London

Barclays Bank Plc (2013b) Strategic Review. London

Barclays Bank Plc (2014) Annual Report. London

Bonfim D, Kim M (2014) Liquidity risk in banking: is there herding? Available at SSRN: http://ssrn.com/abstract=2163547. Accessed 04 Sept 2015

Commodity Futures Trading Commission (2012) Order instituting proceedings pursuant to Sections 6(C) and 6(D) of The Commodity Exchange Act, as amended, making findings and imposing remedial sanctions. Washington, DC

Coombs WT, Holladay SJ (eds) (2011) The handbook of crisis communication. Wiley-Blackwell, Oxford

Cui J, In FH, Maharaj EA (2012) What drives the Libor-OIS spread? Evidence from five major currency Libor-OIS spreads. Available at SSRN: http://ssrn.com/abstract=2173944. Accessed 04 Sept 2015

Dallas L (2012) Short-termism, the financial crisis, and corporate governance. Available at SSRN: http://ssrn.com/abstract=2006556. Accessed 04 Sept 2015

Financial Conduct Authority (2013) Final Notice 2013: ICAP Europe Ltd. Ref Number 188984. London

Financial Services Authority (2012) Report: Final Notice – FSA. Ref Number 122702. London

Fouquau J, Spieser PK (2015) Statistical evidence about LIBOR manipula tion: a "Sherlock Holmes" investigation. J Bank Financ 50:632–643

Hou D, Skeie DR (2014) LIBOR: origins, economics, crisis, scandal, and reform. Available at SSRN: http://ssrn.com/abstract=2423387. Accessed 04 Sept 2015

House of Commons Treasury Committee (2012) Fixing LIBOR: some preliminary findings. HC 481–I. London

International Monetary Fund (2008) Global Financial Stability Report. International Monetary Fund, Washington, DC

Keay A (2011) Risk, shareholder pressure and short-termism in financial in stitutions: does enlightened shareholder value offer a panacea? LFMR 5(6):435–448

King TB, Lewis KF (2014) What drives bank funding spreads? Available at SSRN: http://ssrn.com/abstract=2539711. Accessed 04 Sept 2015

McConnell PJ (2013) Systemic operational risk: the LIBOR manipulation scandal. J Oper Risk 8 (3):59–99

Monticini A, Thornton DL (2013) The effect of underreporting on LIBOR rates. J Macroecon 37:345–348

O'Brien J, Gilligan G (eds) (2013) Integrity, risk and accountability in capital markets: regulating culture. Bloomsbury Publishing, London

Rappaport A (2005) The economics of short-term performance obsession. Financ Anal J 61 (3):65–79

Rappaport A, Bogle JC (2011) Saving capitalism from short-termism: how to build long-term value and take back our financial future. McGraw Hill Professional, New York, NY

Reputation Institute (2013) UK RepTrakTM Pulse 2013. Forbes

Salz A (2013) The Salz review: an independent review of Barclays' business practices. London

Rosella Carè received a PhD in Health Care Management and Economics from the University Magna Graecia of Catanzaro and a PhD in "Sciences de Gestion" from the Conservatoire National des Arts et Métiers of Paris in March 2014 with a dissertation that focused on the sustainability of public expenditure. During 2012 and 2013, she was a visiting PhD student at the ESCP Europe of Paris. Currently, she teaches "Problem Solving and Decision Making", "Financial Markets and Instruments", and "Economics of Financial Markets" at the University Magna Graecia of Catanzaro. Her research interests are: Social and Sustainable Finance; Impact Investing; Alternative Finance and Sustainability; Reputational risk and reputational crisis in the banking sector.

The Case Study of Goldman Sachs

Vincenzo Pacelli

Abstract This chapter analyzes the case study of Goldman Sachs, highlighting the possible internal and environmental determinants of reputational risk. In particular, the chapter focuses on corporate social responsibility, corporate governance, remuneration policies, stakeholder engagement, quantitative indicators of the bank's financial statements, dynamics of the share price and deepens the impact of administrative or judicial inquiries and the dissemination of negative news through the media on the credit ratings and reputation of Goldman Sachs.

1 Introduction

Goldman Sachs Group, Inc., was founded in 1869 by Marcus Goldman, a German-born Jewish immigrant to the United States. Marcus Goldman included his son-in-law Samuel Sachs in the business in 1896, the year in which the company was quoted on the New York Stock Exchange.

Goldman Sachs passed unscathed, although with some difficulty, through the crisis of 1929. In the 1950s, under the leadership of Gus Levy, the Bank developed advanced investment techniques that allowed the trading of large volumes of securities outside the normal market sessions; this ability led Goldman Sachs to decide in 1956 to open the first Investment Banking division.

From 1999 to 2001 until 2007, Goldman Sachs, similar to other American investment banks, benefited from the liberal policies and credit support of the US government. In addition to generating extraordinary economic growth in the US until the beginning of 2007, these policies also made the financial services industry the premier industry in the US, representing approximately 40 % of the profits from the total of all US companies. In the US, the mortgage sector represented a fundamental component of the financial industry, as it was not only the main source of liquidity for most American families but also a necessary raw material used by

V. Pacelli (✉)
University of Foggia, Foggia, Italy
e-mail: vincenzo.pacelli@unifg.it

S. Dell'Atti, A. Trotta (eds.), *Managing Reputation in The Banking Industry*,
DOI 10.1007/978-3-319-28256-5_4

banks to manufacture and sell structured products based on the securitization of these loans. Until the beginning of 2007, this system had produced a great deal of wealth for US investment banks and flourishing emoluments for management. By way of example, Blankfein, the Chief Executive Officer (CEO) of Goldman Sachs, in 2007 personally earned $68 million, as did many other directors of investment banks on Wall Street. These flourishing emoluments of management represented an unpopularity factor when the subprime crisis burst. Encouraged by the extraordinary profits generated and authorized by a supervisory regime much less stringent than that for commercial banks, US investment banks fuelled their business with borrowed funds. The leverage ratio of US investment banks in 2007 was 32 to 1: a potentially explosive level when the apparently perfect mechanism of the early years of the century had misfired. And so it was. The situation began to change radically in 2007, when the increase in interest rates caused by the insolvency of many families and companies unable to cope with the cost of debt quickly became unsustainable; this state that was clearly reflected on the balance sheets of banks. This was the beginning of the *sub-prime* mortgage crisis, which struck even Goldman Sachs as it did the entire US financial system. On September 22, 2008, Goldman Sachs and Morgan Stanley, the last two surviving major US investment banks, on the brink of a liquidity crisis and in the absence of other strategic options were transformed into bank holding companies with the authorization of the Federal Reserve. This gave them access to the Fed's discount window and allowed them to enjoy the support that the government ensured commercial banks, but also required that they submit to much more stringent regulation and supervision. Within 7 months, the five largest US investment banks, the so-called *big five*, which were the pride of the US economic model, were gone. Two of them (Bear Stearns and Merrill Lynch) were acquired by two large commercial banks (respectively, JP Morgan Chase and Bank of America), another failed (Lehman Brothers) and the last two survivors (Goldman Sachs and Morgan Stanley), now close to the abyss, were deformed into between-bank holding companies (or into large commercial banks). This change represented the failure of the US investment bank model, a failure caused by errors of government economic policy, excessively risky and reckless investment policies, management greed, excessively liberal regulation and inadequate internal and external control systems (Pacelli 2014).

On October 3, 2008, the US Congress passed the *Emergency Economic Stabilization Act*, a plan devised by a team led by US Treasury Secretary Paulson, among other things, the former CEO of Goldman Sachs, to restore liquidity to the banking system and encourage the resumption of providing credit to the economy. The Paulson plan designated $700 billion for the purchase of illiquid assets on the financial statements of banks under the so-called *Troubled Assets Relief Program* (TARP). The plan was to re-establish a climate of confidence and stability to the system and to provide liquidity to banks, which would consequently return to providing credit to the economy. It was later estimated that the total cost of the government bailout passed $1 trillion. According to the government, the plan was necessary and indeed arrived with delay; according to others, the plan was wrong because it shifted onto American taxpayers the cost of management and political errors, fuelling a dangerous phenomenon of moral hazard. Basically, with the Paulson Plan, US taxpayers have paid the bill for unscrupulous, highly risky but equally profitable investment activity that was consciously engaged in over the years by business owners and managers who were paid to negotiate risks to craft these products, saving almost all from failure and ensuring these bankers salaries and severance packages worth millions. Obviously this scenario has certainly not favoured a climate of sympathy towards investment bankers. After this tsunami, US investment bankers started to run high risks that were often reckless but highly munificent. After the TARP and the crisis of 2008, in the first half of 2009, Goldman Sachs announced a profit of $5.2 billion and in June returned the $10 billion received from the government as part of TARP. The other banks receiving the Plan returned the funds received between 2009 and 2011. The activities of Goldman Sachs were resumed normally as well, and its risk exposure was absolutely not resized: in the second quarter of 2009, the VaR (Value at Risk) of the bank reached its historical peak of $245 million (Pacelli 2014).

After the tsunami of 2007–2009, which had affected the reputation of Goldman as well as the other US investment banks, other unpopular events further undermined the Goldman's reputation as regards public opinion rather than the markets. We refer to the Goldman's complicity in concealing the Greek public deficit and in the AIG crisis, the flourishing emoluments for management during a period of general crisis, and its obscure relationship with the US government.

In particular, on April 16, 2010, the Securities and Exchange Commission (SEC) filed a civil complaint against Goldman Sachs with the U.S. District Court (Southern District of New York). The complaint alleged that Goldman engaged in fraud in connection with a 2007 synthetic collateralized debt obligation (CDO) transaction, ABACUS 2007-AC1 SPV (ABACUS). The immediate capital market reaction was very negative, as Goldman Sachs' share price closed down more than 13 % that day, reflecting a reduction in market valuation of approximately $10 billion. This price reaction anticipated the very hostile reception that the firm received in subsequent Congressional hearings and, apparently, in the court of public opinion. It was also well in excess of the $550 million settlement that Goldman agreed upon with the SEC on 15 July 2010 (McCoy et al. 2010, p. 2).

These unpopular events probably undermined the Goldman's reputation in terms of public opinion but, as we will see, not in terms of the markets, as Goldman Sachs has successfully faced several financial scandals. Furthermore, Goldman Sachs gave the impression that it exited the financial crisis even stronger than it predicted, betting and making a great profit before its rivals, in part because the financial tsunami of 2007–2009 reduced the number of its competitor.

2 The Analysis of the Internal, Qualitative Determinants of Reputational Risk: Corporate Social Responsibility, Corporate Governance, Remuneration Policies and Stakeholder Engagement

In this section, we propose to conduct a brief analysis of the possible internal determinants of reputational risk for Goldman Sachs, focusing attention on corporate social responsibility, corporate governance, remuneration policies and stakeholder engagement.

Based on the company's documents, it is clear that today, especially after the financial crisis of 2007–2009, reputation management is a precise strategic priority for Goldman Sachs. Therefore, today the Bank has a more systematic, integrated and comprehensive system for monitoring and managing reputational risk.

In this regard, improvements have been made in four main strategic directions:

- the monitoring of individual transactions and approval of operational standards for different classes of transactions, with particular attention to those that present a high risk to reputation;
- better communication and greater transparency with customers and shareholders;
- greater attention to preventing conflicts of interest; and
- product innovation.

By analysing the official documentation of Goldman Sachs regarding Corporate Social Responsibility (CSR), it emerges that the Bank prepared a document entitled "Environmental, Social and Governance Report" in accordance with the guidelines of the Global Reporting Initiative (GRI) and the application of the level GRI G3. Goldman's attention towards the issue of Corporate Social Responsibility is also demonstrated by their presence, since the early 2000s, in the ethical "Dow Jones Sustainability Index", in the geographical divisions World and North America,[1] and by the publication on their own website of the Code of Conduct and Ethics, which shows that the Bank prohibits severe retaliation against anyone who in good faith reports possible violations of the this Code, threatening to initiate appropriate disciplinary action (Goldman Sachs 2015a).

In terms of anti-money laundering (AML), Goldman Sachs is committed to combating money laundering, terrorist financing, securities fraud and other financial offenses (collectively comprising "Money Laundering"), in compliance with all laws and regulations governing these activities. The AML program of Goldman Sachs is characterized by the following features:

- designation of a global AML compliance officer;

[1] Born in 1999 from the collaboration between Dow Jones Index, Stoxx Limited and Robeco—SAM, this index is the first index to evaluate the financial performance of the companies in the world with sustainable principles.

Table 1 Some reputational rankings and the positioning of Goldman Sachs

	2014	2013	2012
100 Best Global Brands[a]	47°	44°	48°
50 World's Most Admired Companies[b]	33°	34°	39°
60 Most Visible Companies[c]	n.a.	59°	59°

Source: Best Global Brands; World's Most Admired Companies; Most Visible Companies

[a] The Best Global Brands, created by Interbrands in 2000, assesses the contribution of the brand to the outcome of the entire business. The brand value, in fact, represents a unique indicator that merges the market, brand, competitors and financial data.

[b] The World's Most Admired Companies index is designed by the American magazine Fortune, with the contribution of the global consulting firm Hay Group. In this ranking, each company is evaluated with a score from 0 to 10, and the overall score is determined through a simple average of the individual scores.

[c] The Harris Poll RQ 2013 Summary Report, The Reputations of the Most Visible Companies—Executive Summary, February 2013. The research firm Harris Interactive every year estimates the so-called Reputation Quotient, a score (maximum of 100) that considers the value attributed to each of 20 features that, according to the research firm, revolve around the concept of reputation, each appropriately weighted and enclosed in six dimensions (Social Responsibility, Emotional Appeal, Products & Services, Workplace Environment, Financial Performance, Vision & Leadership).

- careful risk assessment;
- strict internal policies and procedures, including identifying the customer, managing sanctions, listing screening programs, monitoring suspicious activities and reporting, receiving and responding in a timely manner to re-requested information;
- staff training;
- independent tests (Goldman Sachs 2012).

In terms of its inclusion in reputational rankings, Goldman Sachs is present in numerous rankings on corporate reputation, as shown in the table 1.

Moreover, in 2013, Goldman Sachs was one of the few companies to have increased, compared to 2012, its RepTrak.[2]

With regard to the Bank's corporate governance, it, first of all, fundamentally emphasizes the presence of "CEO—duality" in recent years, as the Chairman of the Board of Directors simultaneously holds the position of Chief Executive Officer.

From the following table, we can note the evolution over the last few years of the degree of independence of the Board, which is always at or above 75 % (Table 2).

We also note the low presence of women on the Board over the last 5 years, as shown in the following table (Table 3).

Goldman Sachs has never initiated a specific company approval policy for new products within its organization and has never established an Ethics or CSR Committee.

[2] RepTrak (registered trademark of the Reputation Institute) is a model of emotional and rational measurement of reputation that evaluates the following factors: Products & Services, Innovation, Workplace, Governance, Citizenship, Leadership and Performance.

Table 2 Independence of Board

	2014	2013	2012	2011	2010	2009
Board members	13	12	13	12	11	12
Independent members	10	9	10	9	9	9
Independence	76.92 %	75.00 %	76.92 %	75 %	81.81 %	75 %

Source: Author calculations based on corporate data

Table 3 Presence of woman on the Board

	2014	2013	2012	2011	2010	2009
Board members	13	12	13	12	11	12
Female members	2	2	2	3	1	1
Female	15.38 %	16.67 %	15.38 %	25 %	9.09 %	8.33 %

Source: Author calculations based on corporate data

The key elements of Goldman Sachs' philosophy as regards its remuneration policy are to establish a direct relationship between the long-term evaluation of performance combined with an appropriate structure for remuneration practice. The remuneration policies of Goldman Sachs aim to

- evaluate performance over a multi-year horizon;
- discourage excessive or concentrated assumptions of risks;
- allow the attraction of young talent;
- align the total compensation for the company with performance over time (Goldman Sachs 2015b).

The remuneration policies of Goldman Sachs also aim to consider their managers as shareholders in the long term. In fact, the Bank believes that it is important for each administrator hold a stake in the company to align the interests of the administrator with those of shareholders. To achieve this aim, the Bank's policy requires that each administrator must maintain the ownership of at least 75 % of the shares of the Bank received until his tenure on the Board of Directors (Goldman Sachs 2014). There are expressly no treatments to administrators in the event of termination of office (a so-called "golden parachute").

The incidence of the variable representing the fixed part of top management's global remuneration was on average very high, ranging between 83.03 % and 96.77 % over recent years (Table 4). Although usual for an American investment bank, this level was probably considered by the markets to be an additional risk factor, as it encourages management to take high risks. In this sense, there is also an absence of procedures for the deferment of the variable component of total remuneration, and this shows a high propensity of executive pay toward short-termism and, consequently, again toward taking more risk by top management.

Table 4 Incidence of the variable for the fixed portion of salary in the total remuneration of "Top Management"

Cluster	2014	2013	2012	2011	2010
Top management	83.03 %	90.27 %	90.03 %	84.13 %	96.77 %

Source: Author calculations based on corporate data

Regarding the establishment of a Remuneration Committee, Goldman Sachs has established a Compensation Committee, consisting of not fewer than three independent members of the Board and with the following functions:

- determine and approve the remuneration of the CEO and other top managers;
- approve compensation and incentive plans;
- assist the Board in overseeing the development, implementation and effectiveness of business policies and strategies relating to the management function of human capital;
- prepare a report on executive compensation as required by the rules and regulations of the Securities and Exchange Commission (Goldman Sachs 2013b).

The stakeholder engagement policies of Goldman Sachs tend to identify themselves, in particular, with financial inclusion projects (Goldman Sachs 2013a), and they are characterized by management training programs for young women and by social startups, the financing of non-profit organizations and microcredit projects. Diversity is also appreciated within Goldman as an important resource, as it improves the corporate culture, helps to better serve customers and maximizes the economic return for shareholders.

3 The Influence of the Administrative and Judicial Inquiries and *Media* on Rating and Reputation

In this section we will analyse the impact of administrative or judicial inquiries and the dissemination of negative news through the media on the credit ratings and reputation of Goldman Sachs.

In recent years, Goldman Sachs has stabilized its rating (Table 5) after suffering a slight downgrading by the major international agencies (Moody's, Standard & Poors and Fitch) between 2008 and 2011 as the average of international investment banks. The following table shows all changes in Goldman's ratings by the major international agencies (Moody's, Standard & Poors and Fitch) between 2008 and 2014.

These ratings were issued despite numerous investigations and sanctions that led Goldman Sachs to manage several factors potentially threatening a reputational crisis after the international crisis of 2007–2009.

Table 5 Ratings of Goldman Sachs

		Fitch judgement	Outlook
December 2011	Short-term debt	F1	Stable
	Long-term debt	A	
December 2010	Short-term debt	F1+	Negative
	Long-term debt	A+	
December 2009	Short-term debt	F1+	Stable
	Long-term debt	A+	
December 2008	Short-term debt	F1+	Stable
	Long-term debt	AA−	

		Moody's judgement	Outlook
December 2013	Short-term debt	P−2	Stable
	Long-term debt	Baa1	
December 2012	Short-term debt	P−2	Negative
	Long-term debt	A3	
December 2008	Short-term debt	P−1	Negative
	Long-term debt	A1	

		S&P judgement	Outlook
December 2011	Short-term debt	A−2	Negative
	Long-term debt	A−	
December 2008	Short-term debt	A−1	Negative
	Long-term debt	A	

The first major investigation of the Securities and Exchange Commission (SEC) began on February 7, 2010 and aimed to understand whether Goldman Sachs had played a decisive role in the financial crisis of AIG. The implications of the investigation were particularly embarrassing for Goldman, as the SEC's survey revealed that Goldman Sachs would have pushed AIG into bankruptcy by issuing credit default swaps on subprime mortgages to indirectly affect the US mortgage market, which it had bet against since 2006.

On April 16, 2010, the Securities and Exchange Commission (SEC) filed another civil complaint against Goldman Sachs with the U.S. District Court (Southern District of New York). The complaint alleged that Goldman engaged in fraud in connection with a 2007 synthetic collateralized debt obligation (CDO) transaction, ABACUS 2007-AC1 SPV (ABACUS). The immediate capital market reaction was very negative, as Goldman Sachs' share price closed down more than 13 % that day, reflecting a reduction in market valuation of approximately $10 billion. This price reaction anticipated the very hostile reception received by the firm in subsequent Congressional hearings, and, apparently, in the court of public opinion. It was also well in excess of the $550 million settlement that Goldman agreed upon with the SEC on 15 July 2010 (McCoy et al. 2010, p. 2).

The reaction of Goldman Sachs was resolute. In a statement on its website, Goldman defined the accusations made by the SEC as "completely unjustified and unsubstantiated, both in practice and in the legal components", promising to vigorously defend the company and its reputation. However, after a few weeks, and especially after lengthy interrogations in Senate, Goldman Sachs changed its strategy, deciding not to venture against the SEC and Congress in a war that would have caused prolonged public exposure in the media. They risked further damaging their reputation and exacerbating hostile public opinion towards the Bank. On July 15, 2010, a plea bargain was reached to conclude the civil lawsuit for fraud of $550 million, the highest amount ever paid out by an American bank to close an agreement out of court. In the following months, other minor inquiries were conducting regarding Goldman Sachs by the SEC and the English Financial Services Authority (FSA).

Despite these governmental inquiries, Fortune classified Goldman Sachs as the international bank with the best reputation in its ranking World's Most Admired Companies in 2010 (with a score equal to 7.66 in a range from 0 to 10). This is only one example of how Goldman Sachs has been able to manage and to minimize the potentially negative effects of these inquiries on its reputation.

Focusing on the media coverage, we have analysed the diffusion of news on Goldman Sachs using the database of the Wall Street Journal, Class CNBC and the "Il Sole 24 Ore" from January 1, 2009, to August 31, 2013.

In particular, from the "Il Sole 24 Ore"[3] database from January 1, 2009, to August 31, 2013, we have analysed all articles that had Goldman Sachs as their subject, excluding the repeated news, and that did not have a neutral connotation (neither positive nor negative). Therefore we analysed 51 articles in an absolutely discretionary manner, finding that 62.8 % of the articles had a negative connotation. This percentage is not surprising because it was particularly negative period for public opinion toward the bank and because of the media's tendency to give prominence to negative news.

Below, we report five news stories selected by the media, analysing their impact on the share price of the bank as compared with the S&P 500 index 3 days before and 5 days after the diffusion of the news.

To analyse the dynamics of the stock price, net of cyclical and sectoral phenomena, we conducted a technical analysis comparing the trend of the share price of Goldman Sachs with the S&P 500 Index. As we can see, the "Galleon scandal" of October 2009 and the "ABACUS" inquiry of the Securities and Exchange Commission (SEC) of April 2010 are the news stories that produced the most reputational damage to Goldman Sachs (Table 6).

[3] See: http://www.ricerca24.ilsole24ore.com

Table 6 Analysis of news

Date news	Source	Summary
6 July 2009	Wall Street Journal	A former employee of Goldman Sachs was arrested by the FBI on charges of stealing the secret codes of the bank's trading system. The discovery raises serious questions about the security of Goldman Sachs' computer systems.

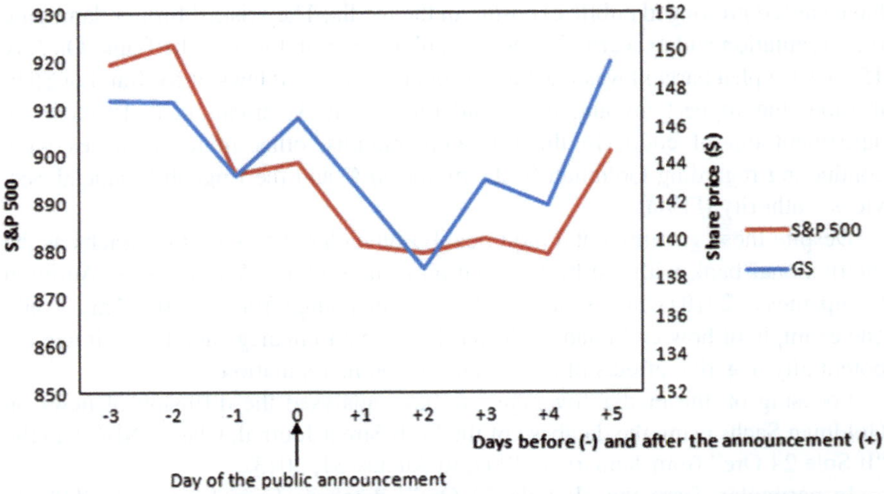

30 October 2009	Wall Street Journal	The Galleon scandal. It appears that some Goldman Sachs employees may be involved in the network of informants that provided relevant news to the manager of the hedge fund, in exchange for money.

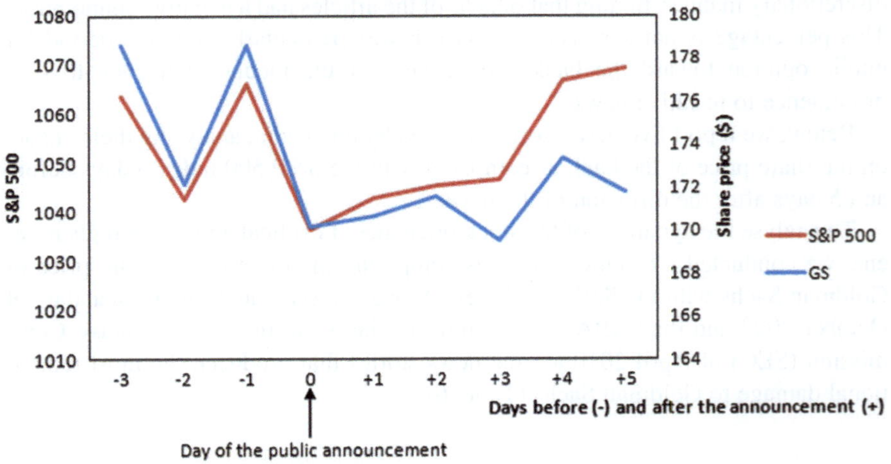

(continued)

Table 6 (continued)

Date news	Source	Summary
21 January 2010	Wall Street Journal	Goldman Sachs reduced the remuneration (including bonuses and benefits) by 20 % on annual basis. The bank also announced that they would give $500 million to charity. A move to "clean up its public image" after its policy on compensation and bonuses was sharply criticized by public opinion, the media and even by the USA President Obama.

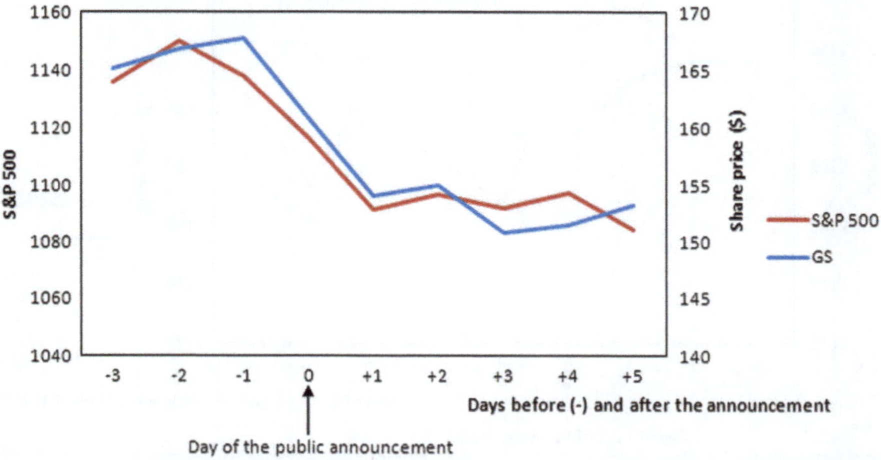

Date news	Source	Summary
16 April 2010	Wall Street Journal	The Securities and Exchange Commission (SEC) filed another civil complaint against Goldman Sachs with the U.S. District Court (Southern District of New York). The complaint alleged that Goldman engaged in fraud in connection with a 2007 synthetic collateralized debt obligation (CDO) transaction, ABACUS 2007-AC1 SPV (ABACUS).

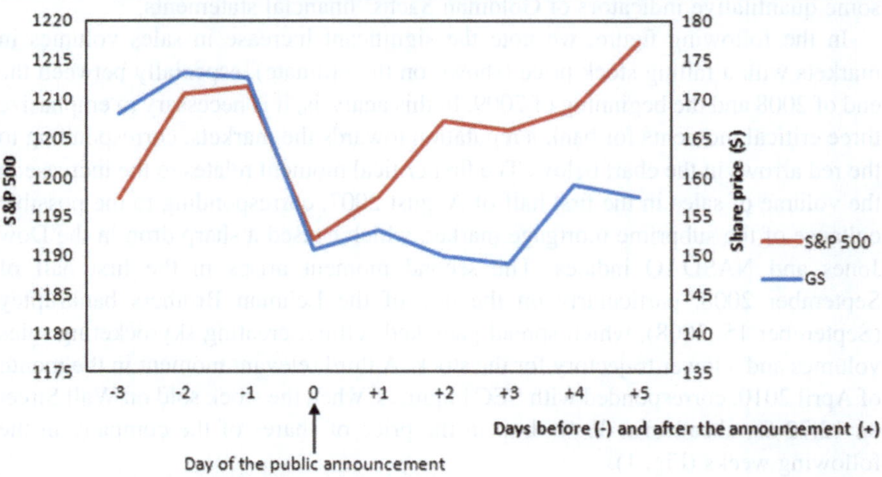

(continued)

Table 6 (continued)

Date news	Source	Summary
25 April 2010	Il Sole 24 Ore	Some internal emails of Goldman, announced by the investigations subcommittee of the Senate, reveal that the bank had not only made profits from its activities against speculative real estate, but then around 2007, when the crisis was about to explode, had a derisory attitude towards those who had not predicted the crisis.

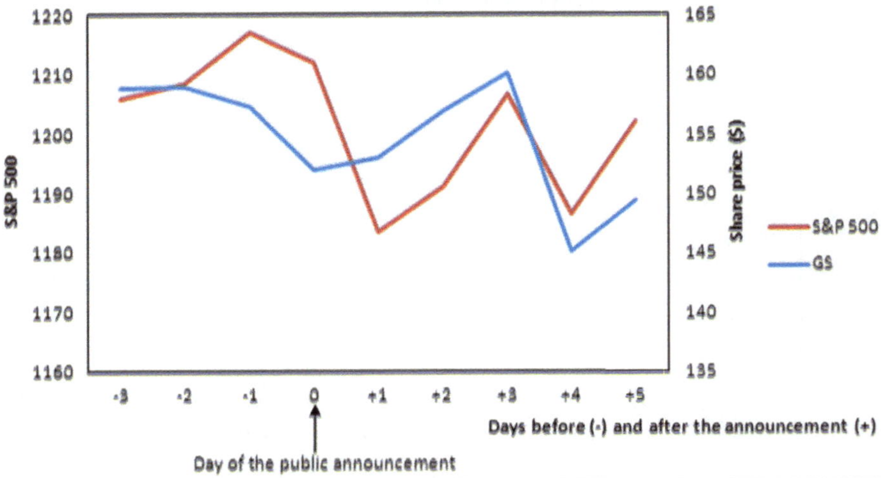

4 The Analysis of Share Price and Quantitative Indicators

In this section, we propose finally to analyse the dynamics of the share price and some quantitative indicators of Goldman Sachs' financial statements.

In the following figure, we note the significant increase in sales volumes in markets with a falling stock price (shown on the ordinate), especially between the end of 2008 and the beginning of 2009. In this analysis, it is necessary to emphasize three critical moments for bank's reputation towards the markets, corresponding to the red arrows in the chart below. The first critical moment relates to the increase in the volume of sales in the first half of August 2007, corresponding to the possible collapse of the subprime mortgage market, which caused a sharp drop in the Dow Jones and NASDAQ indices. The second moment arises in the first half of September 2008, particularly on the day of the Lehman Brothers bankruptcy (September 15, 2008), which spread panicked selling, creating skyrocketing sales volumes and a lower trajectory for the stock. A third relevant moment in the month of April 2010, corresponded with SEC inquiries, when the stock sold on Wall Street on 12.72 %, ahead of a 30 % drop in the price of shares of the company in the following weeks (Fig. 1).

To estimate a monetary value representing the reputation of banks in the financial markets, it is possible to multiply the value of the net assets of the banks—Equity—with the difference between the actual value of the "Price to

Source: Author calculations on Bloomberg data

Fig. 1 Analysis of the share price and volume of sales

Book Value (P/BV)" ratio of banks on the market and a theoretical measure of this relationship, as well as can be inferred by the profitability of banks:

$$\text{CRMF} = [(\text{P/BV}) - (\text{Roae/Ke})]^*\text{Equity}$$

where

- *CRMF* is the value of the reputational capital of banks in the financial markets;
- *P/BV* represents the value of the ratio "Price to Book Value" as actually valued in the market;
- *Ke* is estimated using the CAPM approach;
- *Roae/Ke* provides an approximate estimate of the theoretical "P/BV" ratio that incorporates the current profitability of the bank. In other words, it represents the capacity to create economic value for shareholders.
- *Equity* is the net assets of the bank.

According to this estimation methodology, negative values of CRMF indicate that the market does not value or incorporate into the share price even the earning capacity of the bank. Positive values of CRMF indicate, however, that the market, in addition to recognizing and enhancing the banks' profitability, also attributes to the bank expectations of future economic value creation.

Table 7 Performance of reputational capital on financial markets

	2014	2013	2012	2011	2010	2009
CRMF (value in millions $)	−72,327.07	−28,117.06	−58,518.30	−1578.46	−61,960.23	−75,795.53

Source: Author calculations based on corporate data

In all of the last 6 years, the estimated value of CRMF for Goldman Sachs was consistently negative, indicating that the market did not valorise or adequately incorporate the current earnings capacity of the bank in the share price. This is probably the only real symptom of the crisis on the bank's reputation in the markets (Table 7).

Following are the reclassified balance sheets and income statements of the Bank, by which we can appreciate the economic and financial balance conditions of the Bank (Tables 8 and 9).

In the two tables above (Tables 10 and 11), we analyse the relative changes in the reputational capital of Goldman Sachs in relation to their real and potential depositors. Following the methodology established in the first chapter, we can measure the bank's reputation as regards depositors using an economic criterion for estimating differential results. In this way, the value of the reputational capital as regards depositors coincides with the benefits to be calculated compared to the medium or normal situation of competitors (who cannot take advantage of this relational capital). In particular, the change in the reputational capital of banks as regards their real and potential depositors (Table 10) can be estimated in percentage terms using the following formula:

$$\Delta \text{ CRC} = (\Delta \text{ Annual Bank's Deposits}) - (\Delta \text{ Average Deposits})$$

where

- Δ CRC measures the variation in the reputational capital as regards customers, and it can also be understood as an estimate of the change in the value of the bank's reputation as regards depositors[4];
- Δ Annual Bank's Deposits coincides with the annual percentage change in the "Total Deposits" of Goldman Sachs;
- Δ Average Deposits coincides with the average annual percentage change in the "Total Deposits" of all USA commercial banks.

This differential analysis can be conducted distinguishing *a*) total customer deposits (Table 10) from *b*) interbank deposits (total deposits from banks) (Table 11). In the second case, the change in the reputational capital of banks in

[4] Considering the relative and not the absolute value, we will delete the distortions caused by the different size of banks analyzed.

Table 8 Reclassified balance sheets

Value in millions $	2014	2013	2012	2011	2010	2009	2008
Assets							
Current assets							
Cash and equivalents	109,316	110,804	122,340	120,272	93,519	74,954	122,404
Trade receivables	123,417	112,775	91,354	74,465	78,140	410,302	428,889
Other current assets	600,908	665,419	685,238	705,336	711,614	334,218	302,816
Total current assets	833,641	888,998	898,932	900,073	883,273	819,474	854,109
Fixed assets							
Other assets	22,599	22,509	39,623	23,152	28,059	29,468	30,438
Total non-current assets	22,599	22,509	39,623	23,152	28,059	29,468	30,438
Total assets	856,240	911,507	938,555	923,225	911,332	848,942	884,547
Liabilities and equity							
Trade and other payables	561,332	627,383	651,230	630,263	611,735	555,627	599,300
Short-term borrowings	44,540	44,692	44,304	49,038	47,842	37,516	52,658
Total current liabilities	605,872	627,075	695,534	679,301	659,577	593,143	651,958
Long term liabilities							
Long-term debt	167,571	160,965	167,305	173,545	174,399	185,085	168,220
Total non-current liabilities	167,571	160,965	167,305	173,545	174,399	185,085	168,220
Total liabilities	773,443	833,040	862,839	852,846	833,976	778,228	820,178
Stockholder's equity							
Total shareholder's equity	82,797	78,467	75,716	70,379	77,356	70,714	64,369
Total liabilities and shareholder's equity	856,240	911,507	938,555	923,225	911,332	848,942	884.547

Source: Author calculations based on corporate data

the interbank market can be estimated in percentage terms using the following formula.

$$\Delta \text{ CRB} = (\Delta \text{ Annual interbank deposits of the bank}) - (\Delta \text{ average volumes of interbank deposits})$$

where

- Δ CRB measures the variation in the reputational capital in the interbank market, and it can also be understood as an estimate of the change in the value of the bank's reputation as regards other banks;

Table 9 Reclassified income statements

Value in millions $	2014	2013	2012	2011	2010	2009	2008
Total revenues	30,481	30,814	30,283	23,619	33,658	37,766	53,579
Interest expense	4047	3392	3880	5192	5503	7407	31,357
Net revenues	34,528	34,206	34,163	28,811	39,161	45,173	22,222
Non-interest expense							
Compensation and benefits	12,691	12,613	12,944	12,223	15,376	16,193	10,934
Non-personnel expenses	9480	9856	10,012	10,419	10,428	9151	8952
Total non-interest expense	22,171	22,469	22,956	22,642	25,804	25,344	19,886
Income before taxes and dividends on trust preferred securities	12,357	11,737	11,207	6169	12,892	19,829	2336
Provisions for income taxes	3880	3697	3732	1727	4538	6444	14
Net income	8477	8040	7475	4442	8354	13,385	2322
Net income applicable to common stock	8077	7726	7292	2510	7713	12,192	2041

Source: Author calculations based on corporate data

Table 10 ΔCRC—Customer Reputational Capital

Values in thousands $	2014	Δ 2014–2013	2013	Δ 2013–2012	2012	Δ 2012–2011	2011
Total deposits USA Commercial Banks	10,945,515.40	5.35 %	10,389,364.82	3.75 %	10,014,122.73	8.18 %	9,256,787.19
Total deposits Goldman Sachs	830,080.00	17.23 %	708,070.00	0.97 %	701,240.00	52.08 %	461,090.00
ΔCRC	11.88 %		−2.78 %		43.90 %		

Source: Author calculations based on corporate data

Table 11 ΔCRB—Interbank Reputational Capital

Values in thousands $	2014	Δ 2014–2013	2013	Δ 2013–2012	2012	Δ 2012–2011	2011
Total deposits from Banks USA Commercial Banks	164,818.69	3.80 %	158,779.94	−11.35 %	179,114.07	7.59 %	166,474.67
Total deposits from Banks Goldman Sachs	591,350.00	−4.50 %	619,210.00	17.94 %	525,000.00	38.01 %	380,390.00
ΔCRB	−8.30 %		29.29 %		30.42 %		

Source: Author calculations based on corporate data

Table 12 Percentage cost of debt by customers

2014	2013	2012	2011	2010	2009	2008
0.69 %	0.79 %	0.87 %	0.95 %	0.84 %	0.81 %	3.31 %

Source: Author calculations based on corporate data

- Δ Annual Interbank Deposits coincides with the annual percentage change in the "Total Deposits from banks" of Goldman Sachs;
- Δ Average Interbank Deposits coincides with the average annual change in the "Total Deposits from banks" of all USA commercial banks.

With the analysis of Table 10, we can state that in the years 2012 and 2014, Goldman Sachs registered an increase in customer deposits significantly higher than the average for USA commercial banks, while it registered a result slightly worse than average in 2013. Through analysis of Table 11, we can state that in the years 2012 and 2013, Goldman Sachs registered an increase in interbank deposits significantly higher than the average for USA commercial banks, while it registered a result worse than average in 2014.

To approximate another measure for the reputation of the Bank as regards depositors and shareholders, we have estimated the percentage cost of customer deposits and the percentage cost of equity. Regarding the percentage cost of funding, it is determined as the average rate paid by Goldman Sachs for the passive collection from customers.[5] We can observe a reduction in the cost of funding from customers since 2008, which, net of cyclical phenomena, shows a gradual reduction in the risk premium demanded by depositors, indicating that the crisis and the various financial scandals that have hit the Bank have not significantly dented its reputation in the eyes of depositors (Table 12).

As regards the determination of the cost of equity (Ke), we applied the CAPM:

$$Ke = Rf + \beta^* (Rm - Rf)$$

where

- Rf is the risk-free integrated country risk factor, identified by the average annual return (December 31 of each year) of the 10-year Treasury bond issued by the US.
- β is the measure of the stock's volatility relative to the market, which is the correlation between the yield logarithmic actual share of Goldman Sachs and the overall yield of the reference market (S&P 500 Financial) compared to the variance of the total returns of the market.
- (Rm − Rf) is the risk premium required by the market, considered to be constant and, in line with some practice valuation, equal to 5 % (Mps 2013).

[5] The calculation method is based on the relationship between the annual interest expenses and the average of the last 2 years of total liabilities.

The table 13 provides changes in the cost of equity in the last 6 years, showing that, in the face of almost constant growth from 2009 to 2013, the cost of equity has been reduced over the last year (Table 13).

About the amount and impact of speculative derivatives, we analysed derivatives in the financial statements in relation to the assets and liabilities measured at fair value. As we can see from the table 14, the impact of derivative positions active over the past 3 years on the activities ranged between 17.49 % and 11.58 %. The incidence of liabilities derivatives instead fluctuates between 39.82 % and 21.60 % over the last 3 years (Table 14).

Table 13 Cost of equity

2014	2013	2012	2011	2010	2009
5.43 %	7.31 %	6.56 %	5.38 %	5.64 %	1.86 %

Source: Author calculations based on corporate data

Table 14 Incidence of derivatives in the financial statements (values in millions $)

	Active derivatives	% incidence on assets (fair value)		Liabilities derivatives	% incidence on liabilities (fair value)
2014	63,279,000	11.58	2014	63,016,000	21.60
Δ % 2014–2013	9.33 %		Δ % 2014–2013	26.74 %	
Δ 2014–2013	5,400,000		Δ 2014–2013	13,294,000	
2013	57,879,000	17.07	2013	49,722,000	39.02
Δ % 2013–2012	−18.68 %		Δ % 2013–2012	−1.40 %	
Δ 2013–2012	−13,297,000		Δ 2013–2012	−705,000	
2012	71,176,000	17.49	2012	50,427,000	39.82
Δ % 2012–2011	−11.06 %		Δ % 2012–2011	−13.73 %	
Δ 2012–2011	−8,852,000		Δ 2012–2011	−8,026,000	
2011	80,028,000	21.97	2011	58,453,000	40.31
Δ % 2011–2010	9.19 %		Δ % 2011–2010	6.80 %	
Δ 2011–2010	6,735,000		Δ 2011–2010	3,723,000	
2010	73,293,000	20.53	2010	54,730,000	38.89
Δ % 2010–2009	−2.60 %		Δ % 2010–2009	−2.28 %	
Δ 2010–2009	−1,960,000		Δ 2010–2009	−1,279,000	
2009	75,253,000	21.98	2009	56,009,000	43.41

Source: Author calculations based on corporate data

In relation to the liquidity of the Bank, two indicators were calculated: the *current ratio*,[6] the ratio of current assets and current liabilities, and the *quick ratio*, the ratio between the sum of immediate and deferred liquidity on total current liabilities. In recent years, these indicators have remained fairly constant, indicating the Bank's stable condition in terms of liquidity (Table 15).

For assets, we note an inversion of the trend and a decrease in total assets over the last 2 years, as shown in the following table (Table 16).

Regarding the bank's capitalization, estimated by the indicators Tier 1 Ratio and Total Capital Ratio, we can observe that these are constant over the years for Goldman Sachs, although in 2011 there was a sharp decline that was immediately recovered in 2012 (Table 17).

Table 15 Liquidity ratios

	2014	2013	2012	2011	2010	2009	2008
Current ratio	1.38	1.06	0.99	1.14	1.09	1.10	1.19
Quick ratio	0.38	0.54	0.42	0.35	0.37	0.41	0.78

Source: Author calculations based on corporate data

Table 16 Total assets (values in millions $)

	Total assets
2014	856,240,000
Δ % 2014–2013	−6.06 %
Δ 2014–2013	−55,267,000
2013	911,507,000
Δ % 2013–2012	−2.88 %
Δ 2013–2012	−27,048,000
2012	938,555,000
Δ % 2012–2011	1.66 %
Δ 2012–2011	15,330,000
2011	923,225,000
Δ % 2011–2010	1.31 %
Δ 2011–2010	11,893,000
2010	911,332,000
Δ % 2010–2009	7.35 %
Δ 2010–2009	62,390,000
2009	848,942,000

Source: Author calculations based on corporate data

[6] In current assets, we consider cash, cash equivalents, and securities purchased with resale agreements, while in current liabilities, we consider securities sold under repurchase agreements, and short-term loans, including the current portion of long-term pre-loans and installments due immediately.

Table 17 The evolution of *Tier 1 Ratio* and *Total Capital Ratio*

	2014	2013	2012	2011	2010	2009	2008
Tier 1 Ratio	13.80 %	16.70 %	16.70 %	13.80 %	16.00 %	15.00 %	15.60 %
Total Capital Ratio	16.00 %	19.90 %	20.10 %	16.90 %	19.10 %	18.20 %	18.90 %

Source: Author calculations based on corporate data

Table 18 Debt to banks

	2014	2013	2012	2011	2010
$\frac{\text{Debts to banks}}{\text{Total Asset}}$	14.86 %	15.02 %	12.71 %	14.76 %	10.27 %

Source: Author calculations based on corporate data

The US investment bank has also adhered to public support programs. In detail, on October 2008, Goldman Sachs agreed to accept $10 billion in TARP funds, which was returned with interest in June of 2009, when the US government allowed the refund. Also on July 22, 2009, Goldman Sachs regained the warrants in the Treasury portfolio for $1.1 billion.

Concluding the analysis of financial statement indicators, we analysed the index of indebtedness to banks compared to total assets. This index increased from year to year, with the exception of 2012, as shown in the table 18.

5 Conclusions

The analysis of the business case of Goldman Sachs appears to be a clear example of how a loss of reputation in terms of the public opinion may not necessarily cause reputational damage in the markets. The multidimensional nature of a bank's reputation may, in fact, mean that a bank suffers reputational loss with a particular stakeholder but that this does not have negative effect on the bank's relations with other stakeholders.

After the financial tsunami of 2007–2009, which affected Goldman's reputation as well as that of the other US investment banks, many other unpopular events further undermined the Goldman's reputation in the public opinion. We refer to Goldman's complicity in concealing the Greek public deficit and in the AIG crisis, the flourishing emoluments for management during a period of general crisis, the obscure relationship with the US government and the SEC's inquiries, such as ABACUS.

These unpopular events undermined Goldman's reputation in the public opinion, but not in the markets or financial authorities, as Goldman Sachs has successfully faced several financial scandals, preserving and even strengthening its image as an unbreakable financial giant. Furthermore, Goldman Sachs gave the impression that it exited before others from the financial crisis emerging even stronger, as it predicted, also betting, making a great profit, and, because the financial tsunami of 2007–2009 reduced the number of its competitors, even increasing its market power.

So the empirical evidence of the Goldman's case study teaches us that a good reputation in the markets or with the financial authorities represents a barrier protection essential for minimizing the negative consequences of adverse events that may affect both the company and the system in which it is inserted. Unlike Lehman Brothers, the case of Goldman Sachs shows us how it was possible for Goldman to manage events harmful to its reputation in terms of public opinion, preserving its market share and consolidating its image as an unbreakable financial giant in the eyes of the markets, investors and financial authorities.

References

Goldman Sachs (2012) The Goldman Sachs anti-money laundering program, April

Goldman Sachs (2013a) Annual report

Goldman Sachs (2013b) Compensation Committee Charter, April

Goldman Sachs (2014) Corporate Governance and compensation practices at Goldman Sachs, April

Goldman Sachs (2015a) Code of business conduct and ethics

Goldman Sachs (2015b) Compensation principles

McCoy PA, Morrison AD, Wilhelm WJ Jr (2010) Computerization and the ABACUS: reputation, trust, and fiduciary responsibility. Investment banking. Working Papers Series 10(301). University of Oxford

Mps (2013) Half-yearly financial report

Pacelli V (2014) Consulenza finanziaria e ottimizzazione di portafoglio. Bancaria editrice, Rome

Vincenzo Pacelli is a Tenured Assistant Professor of "Banking and Finance" at University of Foggia (since November 2008), where he is also Academic Senator (since October 2010). He holds a PhD in "Banking and Finance" from the University of Roma "Sapienza" (Italy). Currently, he teaches the courses "Financial Portfolio Management" and "Economics of Financial Intermediaries—Advanced Course" at the Department of Economics of University of Foggia. In addition, he taught the course "Banking and Finance" at the Department of Economics of University of Bari.

He is a member of the Council of PhD School in "Management and Finance" at University of Foggia, member of the organizing committee and chair of different International Conference, ordinary member of the "Italian Association of Professors of Economics of Financial Intermediaries and Markets" and member of the scientific committee of "CeSAC". He is also a member of the Editorial Board of the *Journal of Intelligent Learning Systems and Applications*, published by Scientific Research Publishing, Inc. USA, and he was an editor or reviewer for the following journals: *Applied Economics, Journal of Intelligent Learning Systems and Applications, Lecture Notes in Computer Sciences, Entropy, British Journal of Economics, Management & Trade.*

Since 2005, he has authored (or co-authored) more than 40 scientific publications. His major areas of research are as follows: Governance, Performance and Risks in Banks; Forecasting in Financial Markets; Intangibles in Banks; Credit Risk Management; Reputational Risk Management; Artificial Intelligence in Banking and Finance; Asset Allocation.

The Case Study of Lehman Brothers

Vincenzo Pacelli

Abstract This chapter analyzes the case study of Lehman Brothers, highlighting the internal and environmental determinants of reputational crisis. In particular, the chapter focuses on corporate social responsibility, corporate governance, remuneration policies, stakeholder engagement, quantitative indicators of the bank's financial statements, dynamics of the share price and deepens the impact of administrative or judicial inquiries and the dissemination of negative news through the media on the credit ratings and reputation of Lehman Brothers.

1 Introduction

Lehman Brothers Holdings Inc. was founded in 1850 by two brothers Henry, Emanuel and Mayer Lehman, as a specialized company in the brokering and trading of raw materials, particularly cotton. During its early life, the company began operating in the territory of New York, where it then established its headquarters and added offices in London and Tokyo, strengthening its growth prospects with its official entry in the New York Stock Exchange in 1887.

In 1973, Peter G. Peterson headed the company during its first crisis period that reached its peak with the establishment of Lehman Brothers Kuhn, Loeb Inc., which became, over time, the fourth largest investment bank in the USA until its spin-off in 1994, Lehman Brothers Holdings Inc., under the leadership of CEO Richard S. Fuld, Jr.

However, beginning in August 2007, Lehman Brothers entered its most serious crisis, which culminated on 15 September 2008, following a few weeks of anguish and vain hopes of either a public or a private rescue, with the company's failure and its filing for bankruptcy. Upon default, Lehman Brothers became the fourth American investment bank to experience international turnover, and thus exposure in the financial services sector. At the time of its bankruptcy, Lehman Brothers had an

V. Pacelli (✉)
University of Foggia, Foggia, Italy
e-mail: vincenzo.pacelli@unifg.it

S. Dell'Atti, A. Trotta (eds.), *Managing Reputation in The Banking Industry*,
DOI 10.1007/978-3-319-28256-5_5

annual turnover of approximately 640 billion of dollars in assets, as evaluated in the financial statement. Although these assets were certified by rating, they were disclosed at a low value on the market. In fact, many analysts (such as Einhorn, trader, chairman and co-founder of *Greenlight Capital*) criticized the valuation policies of illiquid assets adopted by Lehman Brothers, considering that the policies did not respect the FAS 157, which is the accounting rule introduced in 2007 in the USA that imposed time to review asset value, including illiquid assets such as a real estate asset, and thus reflect in the financial statement the fair value (re-evaluating and devaluing it on market trends) rather than the cost at liquidation. This uncertainty regarding the real value of the assets in the portfolio has been one of the main causes of the collapse of securities of many financial intermediaries as well as the bankruptcy of Lehman Brothers, which was quite possibly the largest bankruptcy of all time. In the months before the bankruptcy, Lehman Brothers, led by CEO Dick Fuld, desperately attempted to raise capital by issuing its own debt or equity securities or by selling packages more or less relevant to its shares or assets to re-capitalize, raise liquidity, lower the leverage ratio and thus reduce the risk perceived by the markets. However, the results of these efforts were negligible, and the collapse of the institution continued and became the target of speculators and short sellers. Moreover, the lack of investor confidence in the accounts of the Bank—according to the market, Lehman Brothers had not properly evaluated or reported all assets in the portfolio—resulted in Lehman Brothers becoming a toxic asset that no longer generated trust. Thus, in a climate of generalized distrust, many negative rumours, credible or not, were circulated by competitors or short sellers and found fertile ground in the investing public, while the official statements of the Bank were no longer considered reliable or plausible.

2 The Analysis of the Internal Qualitative Determinants of Reputational Risk: Corporate Social Responsibility, Corporate Governance, Remuneration Policies and Stakeholder Engagement

We conduct a brief analysis of the possible internal determinants of reputational risk with respect to Lehman Brothers, focusing attention on corporate social responsibility, corporate governance, remuneration policies and stakeholder engagement.

Based on the company's documents, it is clear that Lehman Brothers was aware that the business and its reputation could be affected negatively by the legal proceedings and sanctions arising from legislative violations related to its operations and, in particular, to the company's inability to deal appropriately with conflicts of interest (Lehman Brothers 2007a).

Bank management was aware that, even in the absence of a contraction of the market, the company's return on investment was exposed to a significant volatility that could result in significant losses and damages to its image and to the value of its brand, thus having a significant bearing on the ability to attract new investors. To this end, Lehman Brothers acknowledged in its annual reports that to maintain its reputation among customers, investors, supervisory authorities and all other stakeholders, it was important, in particular, for the company to minimize legal risks and improve operations.

The strategy for preventing and managing reputational risk for Lehman Brothers depended on a number of factors, including the assessment, the choice of potential customers and the conducting of its activities in compliance with high moral standards. Potential customers were assessed using a rigorous and complex multi-stage process that began with individual business units and extended to product groups. In assessing the customer, these groups underwent a comprehensive examination of their past, their business activities and their proposed transaction when determining whether these customers posed potential risks to the reputation of Lehman Brothers. The proposed transactions were screened by independent committees within Lehman Brothers. These committees were composed of senior members from various divisions of the Bank, including members from the Bank's risk division.

Another aspect that Lehman Brothers considered particularly relevant in the management of its reputation involved any misuse or disclosure of confidential information by its employees.

In general, the Bank had established a specific policy for the evaluation, management and monitoring of risks to its reputation, and the policy resulted in the following operational principles:

- to establish policies for internal and external communication of the main risk factors as well as the relative levels of tolerance;
- to monitor and enforce risk policies at all levels;
- to measure quantifiable risks using methods and models based on tested hypotheses;
- to identify emerging risks through the monitoring of portfolios, the development of new activities, the development of unusual or complex external events and the influence of the market;
- to develop periodic reports on individual risks for all relevant stakeholders.

By analysing the official documentation of Lehman Brothers with respect to corporate social responsibility (CSR), it is found that, in the last years before its bankruptcy, the Bank did not prepare social budgets or reports on issues of corporate social responsibility (CSR). Such neglect is perceived as a sign of a lack of interest on the part of the Bank with respect to its CSR. It is noted, however, the publication on its website regarding its code of ethics expresses the company's commitment to conduct all activities in accordance with the law and the highest ethical standards.

Regarding the issue of CSR, while there is the presence of Lehman Brothers in some ethical indices, this presence in the US Index, US 100 Index and Global Index of FTSE4Good[1] ended after March 12, 2004.

With respect to anti-money laundering, Lehman Brothers, in accordance with the USA PATRIOT Act, which includes regulations regarding money-laundering and terrorism, as well as other laws and regulations enforced in the United Kingdom, the European Union and Japan, had established policies, procedures and internal controls designed to comply with all such laws and regulations, including:

- verification of customer identity when opening an account;
- conducting due diligence;
- strengthening and monitoring of customer transactions and the reporting of suspicious activity;
- staff training;
- results reports.

With respect to reputational rankings, Lehman Brothers is not included in the rankings and evaluations of corporate reputation. However, this is due to the lack of data related to the pre-bankruptcy period. Nonetheless, it is emphasized in the annual report that the Bank does not include information regarding its reputational rankings or its awards for CSR, with the exception of the Guangming Corporate Social Responsibility Award, China 2007.[2] The award, which honours significant contributions by companies operating in China, was conferred on Lehman Brothers for its commitment to helping people with disabilities through the sponsoring of a contest for the design a software program for the blind and for its contribution to helping disadvantaged children through the support of health care programmes and the reconstruction of primary schools.

A recent study (Stevens and Buechler 2013) revealed that Lehman Brothers established a fundamental work of protection against illegal actions by employees, but it has done little to promote a sustainable ethical culture that substantiates, from every perspective, the importance of such a culture to the Bank. This is demonstrated by the findings of this study, which emphasize that the ethical culture of Lehman Brothers was not, in any way, the result of its code of ethics.

Moreover, the code of ethics of Lehman Brothers indicates that if an employee was aware of any conduct or activities that violated the specific code or a law or applicable regulation, it was the responsibility of the employee to promptly report the violation to the senior director, the Director of Human Resources, or an appropriate representative of the legal, compliance or internal audit department. However, it is further noted that it was the express authority of the Board of

---

[1] This index, created in 2001 by the FTSE Group, was designed and managed by the Ethical Investment Research Services (EIRIS) to measure the performance of companies that meet the standards of globally recognized corporate responsibility, such as the transparency and the applicability of sustainability criteria.

[2] It is an award presented by the Chinese government and the Guangming Daily, a leading publication of news distributed in China.

Directors or its internal committee to authorize, in specific situations, individual employees or administrators to waive the adherence to the code of ethics, but only in accordance with company policy. Lehman Brothers, however, ensured immediate communication with its shareholders regarding any waivers to applicable laws and regulations granted to its executive officers or directors. In addition, there is a failure to provide a clear cut penalty procedure for employees or directors who violate the company's code of ethics (Lehman Brothers 2004).

With regard to the corporate governance of the Bank, the presence of CEO-duality is emphasizes, as the Chairman of the Board of Directors, Richard Fuld, served simultaneously for 14 years as the Chief Executive Officer (Lehman Brothers 2007b).

However, on the date of Lehman Brothers' bankruptcy (September 15, 2008) and for the 4 years prior to its bankruptcy, the Board of Directors, was composed of ten members, eight of whom are independent. The members of the committees formed within the Board were also exclusively all independent directors. A low percentage of female representatives on the Board is noted, however, as there were only two female board members before April 5, 2006, i.e., 20 % of the Board, after which there was only one female representative on the Board, i.e., 10 % of the Board.

Furthermore, Lehman Brothers never established a specific company policy of approval regarding new products within its organization, and in recent years, it never developed an ethics or CSR committee.

A key element in the philosophy of Lehman Brothers as it concerns the remuneration policy was to more closely align the interests of directors with those of the shareholders of the Bank, thus bestowing a significant part of the total remuneration of top managers in the form of ordinary shares and/or restricted stock units (RSU) of the company and, in some select cases, stock options. The policy of Lehman Brothers provided that every administrator should maintain ownership of at least 6000 common shares and/or RSUs in the Bank at any time during their tenure on the Council of Directors, thought they were not expressly provided the same treatments and benefits as directors in the event of termination of office (golden parachute) (Lehman Brothers 2007b).

The variable for the fixed part of the salary regarding the total remuneration of top management was generally exceptionally high in the last 3 years of the Bank's activities in that it constantly surpassed 96 % (Table 1). This, although usual for an American investment bank, can be perceived as an element of risk, as it can represent an incentive for management to take high risks. In this sense, there is also the absence of procedures for the deferral of the variable component of the total remuneration, which emphasizes a high propensity for short-termism of executive pay and, consequently, encourages top management to take more risks.

Table 1 Incidence of the variable on the fixed part of the salary of the total remuneration of top management

Cluster	2007	2006	2005
Top management	97.53 %	96.62 %	96.11 %

Source: Author calculations based on corporate data

Table 2 Number of employees

2007	Δ 2007–2006	2006	Δ 2006–2005	2005	Δ 2005–2004	2004	Δ 2004–2003	2003
28,600	+2700 (+10.42 %)	25,900	+3000 (+13.10 %)	22,900	+3300 (+16.84 %)	19,600	+3400 (+20.99 %)	16,200

Source: Author calculations based on corporate data

In this respect, it is significant to note that when the Bank quoted, the employees were owners of only 4 % of the shares of the company, for a value corresponding to approximately \$60 million. In 2007, however, the employees owned approximately 30 % of the shares, or approximately \$11 billion.

Regarding the establishment of a remuneration committee, Lehman Brothers established the Compensation and Benefits Committee and assigned to it the following functions:

- annually establish policies, principles and procedures for the evaluation of the CEO and senior management based on objective criteria, such as the performance of the business, the realization of long-term strategic objectives and the development of management;
- oversee compensation programs, long-term incentives and bonuses for top management (Lehman Brothers 2008).

With regard to employee relations, we noticed a fairly constant increase in the number of employees of Lehman Brothers over the last few years prior to the bankruptcy. In fact, as presented in Table 2, the number of employees over the past 5 years of activity systematically increased by approximately 3000 units per year, although there is noted degressivity in percentages over the years.

The policies of stakeholder engagement in Lehman Brothers tended to more closely identify with volunteer activities and non-profit services performed by employees for the support of the different communities in which the Bank operated. Lehman Brothers boasted, in fact, a proud history of altruism and social investment, especially in healthcare, the arts and the education of youth (Lehman Brothers 2007a).

Diversity has always been at the centre of the cultures and values of Lehman Brothers. To this end, Lehman Brothers emphasized policies to build an environment that favoured talent, integrity and respect and where each individual was able to reach the pinnacle of his career and contribute to better results for Bank customers, thus enhancing the specific talents of the employees.

3 The Influence of the Administrative and Judicial Inquiries and *Media* on Rating and Reputation

We analysed the impact on the ratings and reputation of Lehman Brothers due to the sanctioning of administrative and judicial procedures and disseminating news via media.

Table 3 Ratings of Lehman Brothers

		Fitch judgment	Outlook
June 2008	Short-term debt	F−1	Stable
	Long-term debt	A+	
November 2007	Short-term debt	F−1 +	Negative
	Long-term debt	AA−	
November 2005	Short-term debt	F−1 +	Positive
	Long-term debt	A+	
June 2001	Short-term debt	F−1	Stable
	Long-term debt	A+	

		Moody's judgment	Outlook
November 2006	Short-term debt	P−1	Positive
	Long-term debt	A1	
October 2003	Short-term debt	P−1	Stable
	Long-term debt	A1	

		S&P judgement	Outlook
June 2008	Short-term debt	A	Stable
	Long-term debt	A+	
November 2005	Short-term debt	A−1	Stable
	Long-term debt	A+	
September 2004	Short-term debt	A−1	Positive
	Long-term debt	A	

Lehman Brothers, even until a few months pre-bankruptcy, maintained high ratings by the major international agencies (Moody's, Standard & Poor's and Fitch) (Table 3). Table 3 indicates evidence of the changes in ratings by the major international agencies (Moody's, Standard & Poor's and Fitch) in the final years preceding the default of Lehman Brothers.

This was despite the recent rumours about the poor condition of the Bank's financial stability and despite the different administrative sanctions received by the supervisory authorities. Among the latter, in 2003, the Bank, together with nine other companies, found itself in the crosshairs of the Securities and Exchange Commission (SEC), the Attorney General of New York and several other regulatory authorities for the undue influence they exercised on divisions within investment banking against analysts who were valuing securities to make distorted judgements and artificially reorient the options of customers. Lehman Brothers finalized a transaction, known as a global settlement, that established financial sanctions totalling $1.4 billion, of which $80 million was held by Lehman Brothers, and imposed structural reforms, including the complete separation of the investment banking business from research, the prohibition of establishing remuneration of analysts linked—directly or indirectly—to the revenues in investment banking and the obligation to provide its customers with free and independent research conducted by third parties. In August of 2003, the SEC condemned Lehman Brothers and the investment company SG Cowen and ordered them to pay a total of $7.5 million for not having verified the operations of their broker, Frank Gruttadauria, who had unduly subtracted from the customers of both companies a total of $115 million.

Focusing on media coverage, we analysed the diffusion of news on Lehman Brothers using the databases of the Wall Street Journal, Class CNBC and the Il Sole 24 Ore from January 1, 2007 to September 15, 2008—the date of the Lehman Brothers declaration of bankruptcy.

In particular, analysing the database of the Il Sole 24 Ore[3] from January 1, 2007 to September 15, 2008, we analysed all articles that had as their subject Lehman Brothers, excluding repeated news stories and those that did not have a neutral connotation. Accordingly, we discretely analysed 19 articles and found that 84.2 % of the articles had a negative connotation. This percentage is not surprising, however, given that the Bank was in the midst of a particularly negative period and given the tendency of the media to focus on negative news.

We present herein five news articles selected by the media and analyse their impact on the share price of the Bank compared to that of the S&P 500 index, 3 days before and 5 days after the news (Table 4).

To analyse the dynamics of the stock price, i.e., the net of cyclical and sectoral phenomena, we conducted a technical analysis in which we compared the trend of the share price of Lehman Brothers with the S&P 500 Index. It was noted that since August 1, 2008, which was the last period of great volatility and the collapse of the title, and more specifically, since the news regarding the will (need) of the Bank to sell its riskier assets, the other analysed events failed to cause reputational damage to stock prices.

4 The Analysis of the Share Price and Quantitative Indicators

Finally, we analyse the dynamics of share price and quantitative indicators with respect to Lehman Brothers.

In Fig. 1, the significant increase in sales volume of the title in the last months preceding the bankruptcy and the correspondence of the collapse of the stock price (shown on the ordinate) are presented. The title of Lehman Brothers then recorded a lower volatility relative to the US financial sector of reference up to the weeks immediately preceding the default, at which time the title became the target of analysts, speculators and short sellers. Many analysts (such as Einhorn, trader, chairman and co-founder of the financial Greenlight Capital) criticized the political assessment of illiquid assets taken by Lehman Brothers, contending that the assessment does not conform to the FAS 157—the accounting rule introduced in the US in 2007 that required time to review the value of its assets (including illiquid assets such as real estate) and record their fair value on the balance sheet (re-evaluating

[3] See: http://www.ricerca24.ilsole24ore.com

Table 4 Analysis of news

Date news	Source	Summary
14 March 2007	Wall Street Journal	The finance director Christopher O'Meara claims that the business of Lehman Brothers in the subprime mortgage sector amounts to only 3 % of the revenue of the Bank.

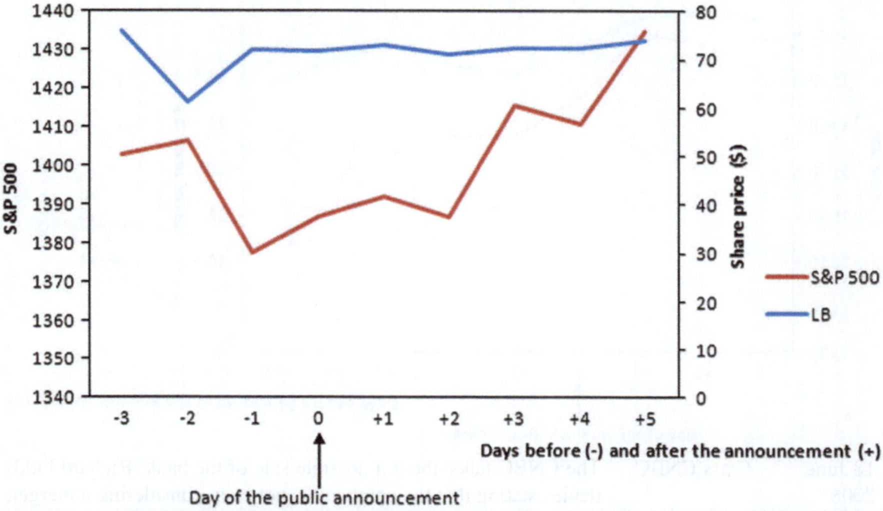

Date news	Source	Summary
19 July 2007	Wall Street Journal	Lehman Brothers under the lens of the tax authorities. The Internal Revenue Service (IRS), the authority responsible for American tax revenue, has requested bank information on some complex transactions involving derivatives to verify if these transactions have allowed investors offshore to evade taxes when inserting share dividends.

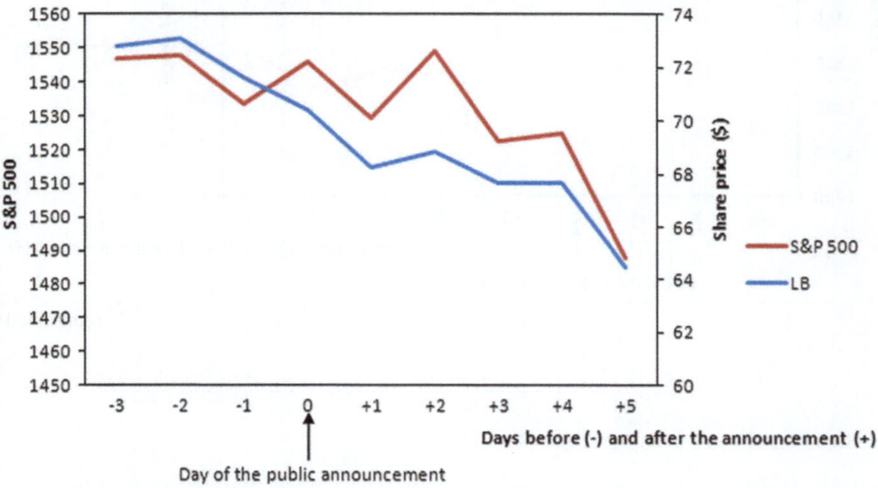

(continued)

Table 4 (continued)

Date news	Source	Summary
2 June 2008	Wall Street Italia	The agency Standard & Poor's lowered the rating of Lehman Brothers from AA+ to A−

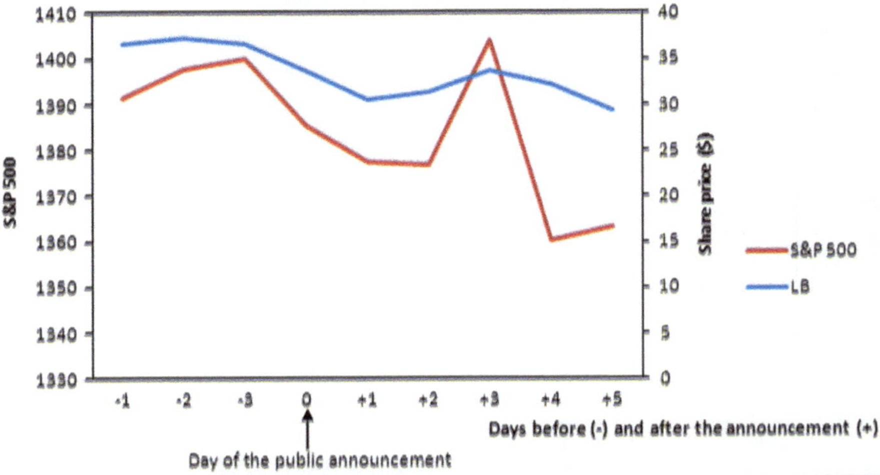

Date news	Source	Summary
18 June 2008	Class CNBC	The CNBC talks about a possible sale of the bank. Richard Fuld denies stating that the company is not even considering a merger.

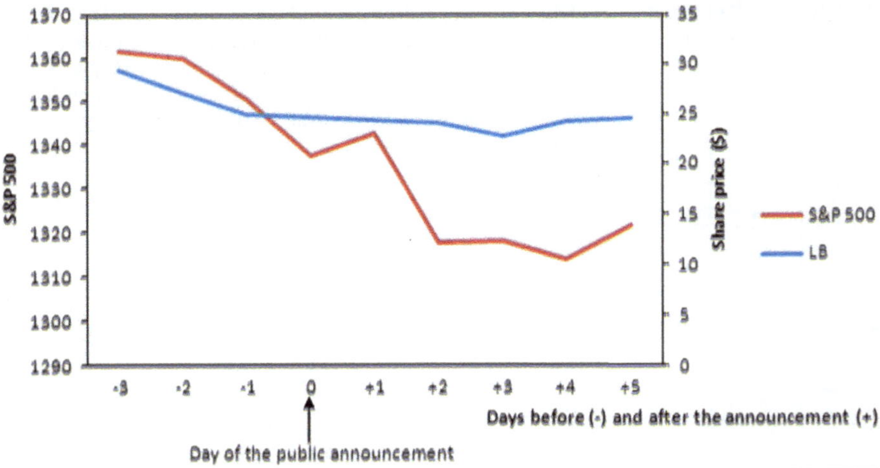

(continued)

Table 4 (continued)

Date news	Source	Summary
1 August 2008	Wall Street Italia	The media report the news on the will of the Bank to sell its riskier assets to regain credibility in the markets after the collapse of the stock.

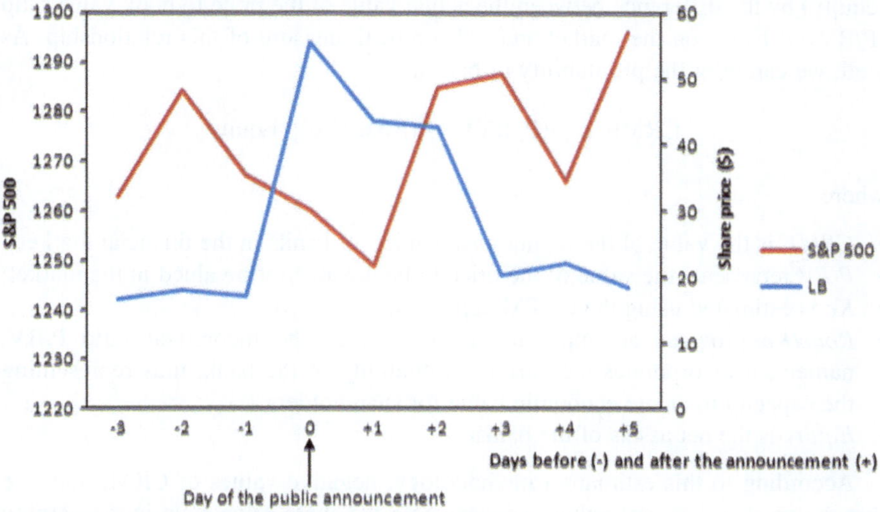

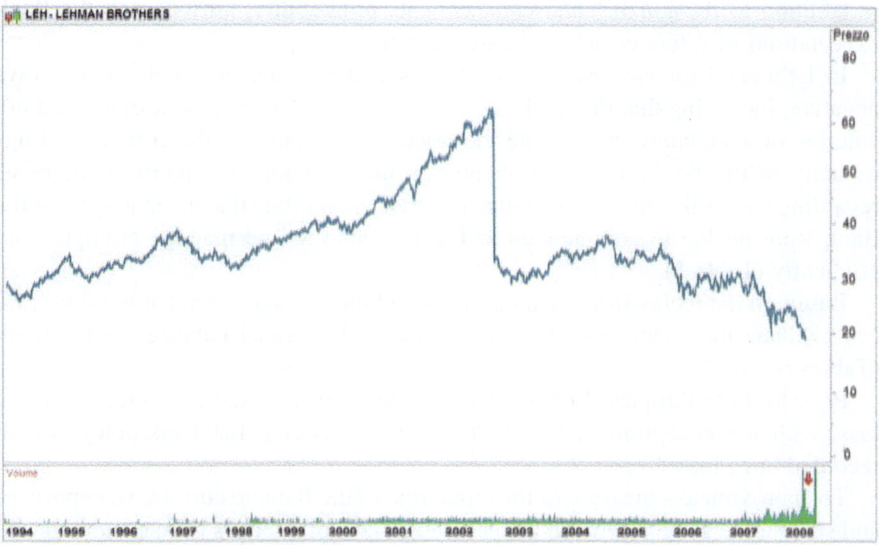

Source: Author calculations on Bloomberg data

Fig. 1 Analysis of share price and volume of sales

and devaluing them according to market dynamics) rather than reporting their cost at acquisition. This uncertainty regarding the real value of the assets in the portfolio was one of the main causes of the collapse of the stock of Lehman Brothers.

To estimate a monetary value representing the reputation of banks in the financial markets, it is possible to multiply the value of the net assets of the banks (equity) by the difference between the actual value of the price to book value ratio (P/BV) of banks on the market and a theoretical measure of this relationship. As well, we can infer the profitability of banks:

$$\text{CRMF} = [(\text{P/BV}) - (\text{Roae/Ke})]^{*}\text{Equity}$$

where

- *CRMF* is the value of the reputational capital of banks in the financial markets;
- *P/BV* represents the value of the price to book value ratio valued in the market;
- *Ke* is estimated using the CAPM approach;
- *Roae/Ke* provides an approximate estimate of the theoretical ratio P/BV, namely, it incorporates the current profitability of the bank, thus representing the capacity to create economic value for shareholders.
- *Equity* is the net assets of the banks.

According to this estimation methodology, negative values of CRMF indicate that the market does not value or incorporate the share price even in the earning capacity of the Bank. Positive values of CRMF indicate, however, that the market, in addition to recognizing and enhancing its profitability, attributes to the Bank expectations of future economic value creation.

In Lehman Brothers last 5 years, the estimated value of CRMF was always negative, indicating that the market, for the 5 years before the bankruptcy, did not valorize or adequately incorporate the price of the shares or the current earnings capacity of the Bank. This is probably the most obvious symptom of the crisis regarding the Bank's reputation in the markets, and it is one that the managers of the Bank were unable to comprehend and thus unable to and manage promptly and efficiently (Table 5).

Based on the reclassified balance sheets and income statements of the Bank, we can evaluate the conditions of the economic and financial balances of the Bank (Tables 6 and 7).

Prior to its bankruptcy, Lehman Brothers had never closed a balance sheet at a loss, with the exception of the 2008 quarter preceding the bankruptcy, which recorded huge losses.

To approximate a measure of the reputation of the Bank to customers, depositors and shareholders, we estimated the percentage cost of deposits from customers and the cost of equity. Cost of debt by the customers is determined by the average rate paid by Lehman Brothers to customers.[4] A steady increase in the cost of customer

[4] It is calculated by the ratio of interest expenses and the average of the last 2 years of the total liabilities.

Table 5 Performance of reputation capital on financial markets

	2007	2006	2005	2004	2003
CRMF (data in millions $)	−41,691.24	−19,643.87	−89,294.07	−25,539.43	−23,029.46

Source: Author calculations

Table 6 Reclassified balance sheets

Values in millions $	2007	2006	2005	2004
Assets				
Current assets				
Cash and equivalents	20,029	12,078	15,619	14,274
Trade receivables	43,277	27,971	21,643	18,763
Inventories	313,129	226,596	177,438	144,468
Other current assets	301,234	225,156	184,664	169,829
Total current assets	677,669	491,801	399,364	347,334
Fixed assets				
Property, equipment and leasehold improvements	3861	3269	2885	2988
Identifiable intangible assets and goodwill	4127	3362	3256	3284
Other assets	5406	5113	4558	3562
Total non-current assets	13,394	11,744	10,699	9834
Total assets	691,063	503,545	410,063	357,168
Liabilities and equity				
Trade and other payables	517,357	382,538	323,044	278,156
Short-term borrowings	28,066	20,638	2941	2857
Obligation to return securities received as collateral	–	–	4975	4749
Total current liabilities	545,423	403,176	330,960	285,762
Long-term liabilities				
Long-term debt	123,150	81,178	62,309	56,486
Total non-current liabilities	123,150	81,178	62,309	56,486
Total liabilities	668,573	484,354	393,269	342,248
Stockholder equity				
Preferred stock	1095	1095	1095	1345
Total common stockholder equity	21,395	18,096	15,699	13,575
Total stockholder equity	22,490	19,191	16,794	14,920
Total liabilities and stockholder equity	691,063	503,545	410,063	357,168

Source: Author calculations based on corporate data

deposits since 2004 is observed, though according to the last available budget, which indicates a net cyclic phenomena, a progressive increase in the risk premium demanded by depositors is evidenced (Table 8).

However, with respect to the determination of the cost of equity (Ke), we applied the formula of the CAPM:

Table 7 Reclassified income statements

Values in millions $	2007	2006	2005	2004
Total revenues	59,003	46,709	32,420	21,250
Interest expenses	39,746	29,126	17,790	9674
Net revenues	19,257	17,583	14,630	11,576
Non-interest expenses				
Compensation and benefits	9494	8669	7213	5730
Non-personnel expenses	3750	3009	2588	2328
Total non-interest expense	13,244	11,678	9801	8058
Income before taxes and dividends on trust preferred securities	6013	5905	4829	3518
Provisions for income taxes	1821	1945	1569	1125
Dividends on trust preferred securities	–	–	–	24
Income before cumulative effect of accounting change	4192	3960	3260	2369
Cumulative effect of accounting change	–	47	–	–
Net income	4192	4007	3260	2369
Net income applicable to common stock	4125	3941	3191	2297

Source: Author calculations based on corporate data

Table 8 Percentage cost of debt by the customers

2007	2006	2005	2004	2003
6.89 %	6.64 %	4.84 %	3.02 %	5.81 %

Source: Author calculations

Table 9 Cost of equity

2007	2006	2005	2004	2003
5.98 %	7.04 %	2.87 %	5.13 %	5.20 %

Source: Author calculations

$$Ke = Rf + \beta^* (Rm - Rf)$$

where

- Rf is the risk-free integrated country risk factor, identified in the average annual return (December 31 of each year) of the 10 year Treasury bond issued by the US state.
- β is the measure of the volatility of a stock relative to the market, which is the correlation factor between the logarithmic yield of the actual title of Lehman Brothers and the overall yield of the reference market (S&P 500) compared to the variance in the total returns of the market.
- (Rm − Rf) is the risk premium required by the market, considered constant and consistent with some practice valuation, equal to 5 % (Mps 2013).

Table 9 shows the changes in the cost of equity capital over the last 5 years.

Table 10 Incidence of derivatives in the financial statements (values in millions $)

	Active derivatives	% incidence on assets (fair value)		Liabilities derivatives	% incidence on liabilities (fair value)
2007	44,595,000	14.24	2007	31,621,000	21.13
Δ % 2007–2006	96.49 %		Δ % 2007–2006	75.51 %	
Δ 2007–2006	21,899,000		Δ 2007–2006	13,604,000	
2006	22,696,000	10.02	2006	18,017,000	14.30
Δ % 2006–2005	25.77 %		Δ % 2006–2005	15.79 %	
Δ 2006–2005	4,651,000		Δ 2006–2005	2,457,000	
2005	18,045,000	10.17	2005	15,560,000	14.07
Δ % 2005–2004	3.36 %		Δ % 2005–2004	2.09 %	
Δ 2005–2004	586,000		Δ 2005–2004	318,000	
2004	17,459,000	12.09	2004	15,242,000	15.83

Source: Author calculations based on corporate data

In reference to the indicator of the amount and impact of speculative derivatives, we analysed derivatives in the financial statements in relation to the assets and liabilities measured at fair value.

As evidenced by Table 10, the percentage of positions in active derivatives in recent years on the activities at fair value ranged between 10.02 % and 14.24 %, while the ratio of passive derivatives on liabilities at fair value ranges between 14.07 % and 21.13 %. In both cases, we notice a substantial increase that amounts to more than double, with respect to the previous year, the value of derivatives on the balance sheet in the last year prior to bankruptcy. Thus, the net increase in the incidence of derivatives on the financial statement of Lehman Brothers in 2007 exceeds that of any previous year.

In relation to the liquidity of the Bank, two indicators were calculated: the current ratio,[5] which is the ratio of current assets and current liabilities, and the quick ratio, which is the ratio between the sum of immediate and deferred liquidity on the total current liabilities.

In recent years, these indicators have remained constant, but always less than a unit, thereby indicating a critical liquidity situation, which suggests that the future income from the selling of most liquid current assets was not sufficient to cover

[5] In current assets, we consider cash and cash equivalents and securities purchased with resale agreements, while in current liabilities, we consider securities sold under repurchase agreements, short-term loans, including the current portion of long-term pre-loans and installments due immediately.

Table 11 Liquidity ratios

	2007	2006	2005	2004	2003
Current ratio	0.67	0.65	0.72	0.74	0.70
Quick ratio	0.82	0.80	0.86	0.88	0.80

Source: Author calculations based on corporate data

Table 12 Total assets (values in millions $)

	Total assets
2007	691,063,000
Δ % 2007–2006	+37.24 %
Δ 2007–2006	+187,518,000
2006	503,545,000
Δ % 2006–2005	+22.80 %
Δ 2006–2005	+93,482,000
2005	410,063,000
Δ % 2005–2004	+14.81 %
Δ 2005–2004	+52,895,000
2004	357,168,000

Source: Bankscope

Table 13 The evolution of the *Tier 1 Ratio* and the *Total Capital Ratio*

	2008	2007
Tier 1 Ratio	10.70 %	7.10 %
Total Capital Ratio	16.10 %	10.70 %

Source: Author calculations based on corporate data

future releases resulting from the extinction of current liabilities. In the months preceding the bankruptcy, Lehman Brothers, led by its CEO Dick Fuld, desperately attempted to raise capital by issuing its own debt or equity securities or by selling packages more or less relevant to its shares or assets to recapitalize, raise liquidity, lower the advantage ratio and reduce the risk felt by markets. However, the efforts resulted in only minimal results, as evidenced by the continuing collapse of title, thus causing it to become the target of speculators and short sellers. Moreover, it caused investors to have little confidence in the accounts of the Bank—according to the market, Lehman had not properly evaluated and he then devalued all assets in the portfolio—causing Lehman Brothers to become a toxic asset that no one trusted (Table 11).

With respect to the assets, we note a significant increase of total assets in the last 3 years of Lehman Brothers, as presented in Table 12.

Regarding the Bank's capitalization, it was possible to recover data from only the last 2 years. As a representative example, however, we compare, in Table 13, the evolution of the Tier 1 Ratio and the Total Capital Ratio over the last 2 years. The comparison indicates that, even until a few months prior to the bankruptcy, Lehman Brothers had excellent capital ratios that were consistent with the current requirements of Basel III.

Table 14 Debt to banks

	2007	2006	2005	2004	2003
$\frac{\text{Debt to banks}}{\text{Total assets}}$	4.25 %	4.25 %	3.67 %	3.28 %	1.09 %

Source: Author calculations based on corporate data

The US investment bank did not benefit from support programs, even in the final months of difficulty before its failure. Thus, the lack of public funds has often been regarded as one of the determining causes that led to the bankruptcy of Lehman Brothers.

Concluding the analysis on indicators of the financial statement, we analysed the index of indebtedness to banks compared to total assets. This index increased year-to-year until 2007, when it remained constant compared to the previous year. These findings are presented in Table 14.

5 Conclusions

The analysis of the Lehman Brothers case is a clear example of a corporate crisis induced solely by the progressive and rapidly increasing reputational crisis of the company in general and of its management in particular. Until the last financial year before its default, in fact, the Bank had never signed a financial loss and had solid capital ratios that even in 2007 were consistent with the current standards imposed by the financial authorities. Until the weeks immediately preceding its default, the title of Lehman Brothers had never recorded a lower volatility relative to the American financial sectorial reference index. Nothing, therefore, before the perfect storm of the summer of 2008, could have portended the default of the Bank, although the estimated value of the CRMF of the Bank was always negative in its last 5 years, indicating that the market, for 5 years before the Bank's bankruptcy, did not valorize adequately or incorporated in the stock price even the current earnings capacity of the Bank. While this point is probably the most obvious symptom of the crisis of the Bank's reputation in the markets, the management of the Bank was not able to respond effectively and promptly to prevent failure.

In August 2007, the Lehman Brothers faced its most serious crisis with respect to its reputation. This period culminated on 15 September 2008 when, after a few weeks of agony and vain hopes of public or private redemption, the company declared bankruptcy. Upon default, Lehman was the fourth US investment bank with a global operation (and exposure) in the financial services industry. At the time of the bankruptcy, Lehman Brothers had a turnover of approximately $640 billion in assets as valued in the financial statements at that value, but which, although certified by rating, were of little value in the market. Many analysts (such as Einhorn, trader, chairman and co-founder of the financial undertaking Greenlight Capital) criticized the political assessment of illiquid assets taken by Lehman Brothers, believing that such assessment not respect FAS 157, that is, the accounting rule introduced in the US in 2007 that requires time to review the value of illiquid assets, including those such as real estate, and account for them in the financial statements at fair value rather than at the cost of acquisition. This uncertainty regarding the real value of the assets in the portfolio was one of the main causes of the crisis of reputation faced by the Bank, which then led to the collapse of its share price. In the months preceding its bankruptcy, Lehman Brothers, led by CEO Dick Fuld, tried desperately to raise capital by issuing its own debt or equity securities or by selling packages more or less relevant its shares or its assets to recapitalize, raise liquidity, lower the leverage ratio and reduce the risk perceived by the markets. However, these efforts met with limited success due to the continuing collapse of the title, which caused it to become the target of speculators and short sellers and to lose the confidence of the Bank's investors Such events caused Lehman Brothers to become a toxic asset that no one trusted. According to the market, Lehman Brothers had first not evaluated and it then devalued all assets in its portfolio. In a climate of generalized distrust with respect to the Bank's accounts and its stock, the negative rumours, credible or not, put into circulation by competitors and short sellers found fertile ground in the investors and no longer had any effect on the official statements of the Bank (Pacelli 2014).

Another important aspect in the crisis of the Bank's reputation is represented by the excessive weight of the variable component of the total management remuneration. From our analysis, it appears that the percentage of the variable component of the total remuneration was extremely high in the last 3 years of the Bank's activities. This situation, although usual for an American investment bank, was likely considered by the markets as an additional risk factor, as such high percentages tend to encourage management to take high risks. In this sense, there is the absence of procedures for the deferral of the variable component of total remuneration. Additionally, a high propensity for short-termism of executive remuneration and, consequently, the encouragement for management to engage in more risk is, again, evidenced.

References

Lehman Brothers (2004) Code of ethics
Lehman Brothers (2007a) Global philanthropy
Lehman Brothers (2007b) Corporate governance guidelines
Lehman Brothers (2008) Compensation and Benefits Committee of the Board of Directors
Mps (2013) Half-yearly financial report
Pacelli V (2014) Consulenza finanziaria e ottimizzazione di portafoglio. Bancaria editrice, Rome
Stevens B, Buechler S (2013) An analysis of the Lehman Brothers code of ethics and the role it played in the firm. J Leadership Account Ethic 10(1):43–57

Vincenzo Pacelli is a Tenured Assistant Professor of "Banking and Finance" at University of Foggia (since November 2008), where he is also Academic Senator (since October 2010). He holds a PhD in "Banking and Finance" from the University of Roma "Sapienza" (Italy). Currently, he teaches the courses "Financial Portfolio Management" and "Economics of Financial

Intermediaries—Advanced Course" at the Department of Economics of University of Foggia. In addition, he taught the course "Banking and Finance" at the Department of Economics of University of Bari.

He is a member of the Council of PhD School in "Management and Finance" at University of Foggia, member of the organizing committee and chair of different International Conference, ordinary member of the "Italian Association of Professors of Economics of Financial Intermediaries and Markets" and member of the scientific committee of "CeSAC". He is also a member of the Editorial Board of the *Journal of Intelligent Learning Systems and Applications*, published by Scientific Research Publishing, Inc. USA, and he was an editor or reviewer for the following journals: *Applied Economics, Journal of Intelligent Learning Systems and Applications, Lecture Notes in Computer Sciences, Entropy, British Journal of Economics, Management & Trade.*

Since 2005, he has authored (or co-authored) more than 40 scientific publications. His major areas of research are as follows: Governance, Performance and Risks in Banks; Forecasting in Financial Markets; Intangibles in Banks; Credit Risk Management; Reputational Risk Management; Artificial Intelligence in Banking and Finance; Asset Allocation.

UniCredit and Reputation: A Journey Integrating Stakeholders' Perceptions into Business Planning and Strategies

Antonino d'Eugenio

Abstract The chapter aims to describe how UniCredit has developed a competitive advantage model based on its Reputation Management System. The case presents the solutions adopted by UniCredit to measure and improve stakeholders' perceptions, starting from the foundation studies, based on qualitative and quantitative survey researches, the extensive analysis conducted to identify reputation factors for competitive advantage, and the statistical tests carried out to show the correlation between the Bank's practices, its Reputation and its business success. The case also describes the challenges encountered when entering new markets occupied by well positioned international players: how does UniCredit use its reputation monitoring findings to steer stakeholders' opinions to its favour, to build trust and gain market share? Finally, the case study offers a glimpse of the solutions that UniCredit is implementing in order to respond to the increasing relevance of new media channels and the Internet, which offer previously unimagined opportunities for personal expression and communication, in the belief that in the near future, the current stakeholder listening methods will be devoid of interpretative utility.

1 UniCredit Highlights

UniCredit is a leading European commercial bank operating in 17 countries with more than 147,000 employees, over 8500 branches and an international network spanning some 50 markets (Fig. 1).

UniCredit benefits from a strong European identity, its extensive international presence and a broad customer base (Fig. 2).

A. d'Eugenio (✉)
Group Stakeholder Insight, UniCredit, Milan, Italy
e-mail: antonino.deugenio@unicredit.eu

S. Dell'Atti, A. Trotta (eds.), *Managing Reputation in The Banking Industry*,
DOI 10.1007/978-3-319-28256-5_6

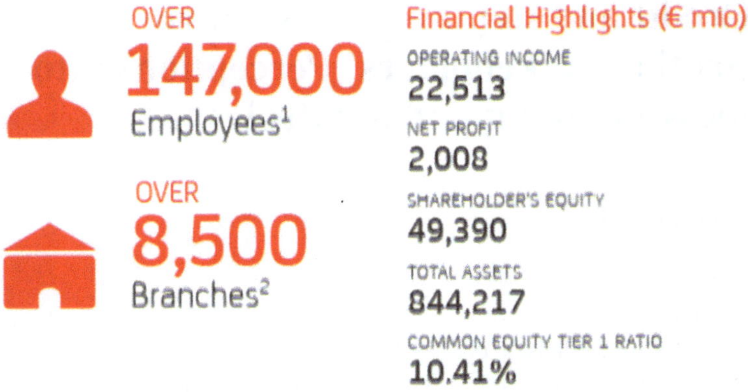

Fig. 1 UniCredit financial highlights. (1) Data as for 31st December 2014. FTE = "Full Time Equivalent": number of employees counted per rate of presence. Figures include all employees of YapiKredi Group (Turkey). (2) Data as for 31st December, 2014. Figures include all branches of YapiKredi Group (Turkey). *Source*: UniCredit Financial Highlights 2014

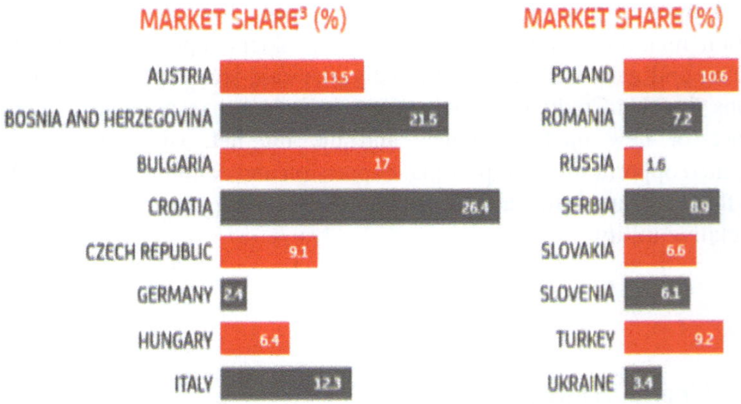

Fig. 2 UniCredit market shares. (3) Market share in terms of total assets as of 31st December 2014 in EC Countries. Market Shares in terms of Total Customer Loans as of 31st December 2014 for Italy, Germany and Austria. *Data as of 30th November 2014. *Source*: UniCredit National Centre Banks, UniCredit Research, UniCredit EC Strategic Analysis. Data as of 30th September 2014, except for Bosnia and Herzegovina, Slovenia (2nd Q, 2014), Romania (1st Q, 2014), Hungary (FY 2013) and Bulgaria (3rd Q, 2014)

2 The Business Model

The restructuring process that began at the start of 2012 has resulted in a major simplification of UniCredit operating processes. For example, in order to bring the bank closer to our customers, national offices now possess greater decision-making powers. The aim of this change is to simplify the business by implementing a more streamlined chain of command, a more efficient commercial network, and a greater

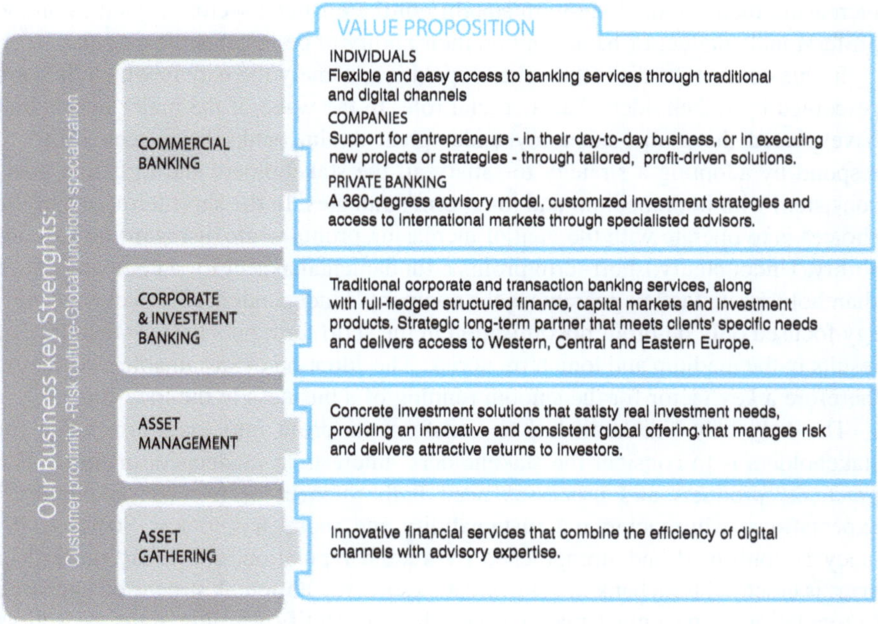

Fig. 3 UniCredit business model. *Source*: UniCredit Internal Papers

ability to create personalised solutions. Additionally, it enables the bank's national offices to be more effective at developing the markets they serve (Fig. 3).

Corporate reputation refers to the overall assessment of a firm's 'good name' from the perspective of its stakeholders. Researchers and practitioners identify corporate reputation as the most important intangible asset of a firm, and maintain that it is positively associated with reduced transaction costs, as well as financial (i.e., customer spending) and non-financial (i.e., word-of-mouth) outcomes.

The evaluation given by a firm's stakeholders is crucial for building and retaining a good corporate reputation. Arguably, customers are the most important stakeholder group. However, multiple stakeholders–such as investors, competitors, suppliers and society at large—also have an interest in a focal firm's reputation, and emit signals that shape the focal firm's reputation. Thus, adequately capturing multiple stakeholders' perceptions toward the focal firm is critically important.

Over the last few years, the reputation of the banking system has been badly hit. The end of the last decade was marked by the subprime mortgage crisis and the insolvency of many banks, which entailed an unprecedented global recession. The subsequent European sovereign debt crisis, coupled with the erosion of the reputation of the financial sector, has undermined public confidence in banks' ability to support the real economy.

The financial crisis has turned the spotlight onto the issue of trust and has shown how important it is for a bank to operate in a sustainable manner. This has led to an increasing focus on the long-term stability of the financial sector, as well as on the professional conduct of banks and on their ability to be responsible citizens.

In this context, banks' established reputation, namely the way in which they are perceived by stakeholders, has a crucial role. In the wake of the major events that have placed the global economy under great strain, banks have been asked to respond by adopting a strategy to satisfy all the stakeholders and to define goals consistent with both medium and long-term strategies. In the short term, one of the choices is to operate with the goal of increasing profits while disregarding sustainability. Undoubtedly, short-term profits a fundamental aspect for a company, since shareholder satisfaction guarantees the company's independence. However, a strategy focused only on profit maximisation in the short term puts the sustainability of results in the medium and long term at risk. The adoption of sustainable practices is therefore a key factor for the smooth running of a business in the long run.

The only way UniCredit has to transform its profit into long-term value for stakeholders is to consider the stakeholders' interests in its decision-making. The practices, products and processes need both to meet or exceed stakeholders' expectations, while achieving sustainability and social legitimacy. Social legitimacy is confirmed and strengthened by a solid reputation, and today more than ever, is essential for a bank to act to create a solid reputation. A structured approach to reputation management makes it possible to identify warning signs as well as stakeholders' needs and expectations.

3 Reputation Assessment in UniCredit

The interest in reputation dates back to 2009. The 2008 Sustainability Report stated: "Reputation and value mean profit sustainability and lead to social legitimacy for our customers, employees and shareholders. Creating value means responding at best to the needs of all these subjects. That hardly seems like an outdated concept. Indeed, it seems even more relevant today."

This underlying belief was the starting point around which the Group started to build a connection with its main stakeholders. This approach, defined as stakeholder engagement' by UniCredit, increases awareness of the main stakeholders in order to improve the bank's ability to manage risks and resolve conflicts. Only by focusing on stakeholders' interests at the decision-making stage and implementing practices and products that meet or exceed expectations with the bank can the bank strengthen its reputation.

Reputation is thus of crucial importance, becoming one of the key pillars of the sustainability model, along with profitability and legitimacy. A strong reputation is based on financial performance, management skills, commitment to the community, and bringing home what has been promised.

In order to analyse and evaluate stakeholders' perceptions, UniCredit implemented a Reputation Monitoring programme in 2009 with the following objectives:

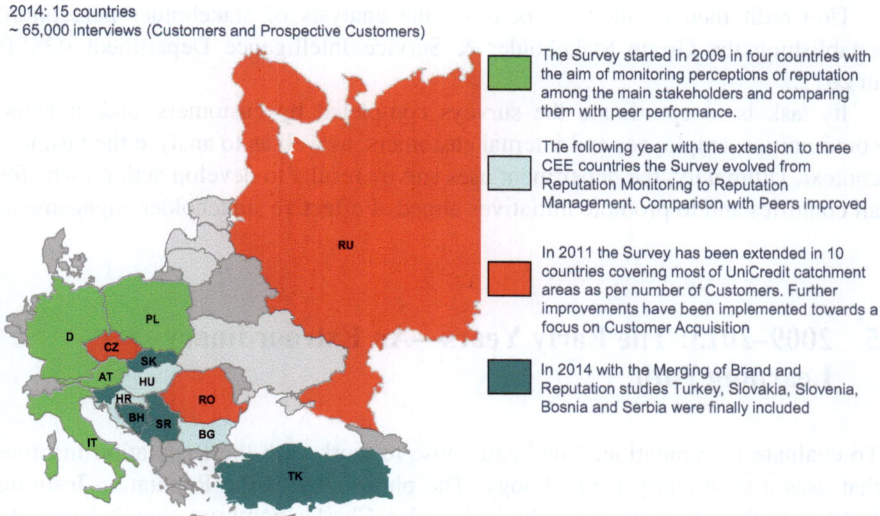

Fig. 4 UniCredit reputation journey. *Source*: UniCredit Internal Papers—Reputation Presentation

- to identify and continuously monitor key aspects of stakeholder groups in countries where UniCredit operates;
- to assess the bank's activities and its ability to meet the needs and expectations of its stakeholders;

Reputation monitoring, achieved through a series of interviews, thereby helps to identify the factors that most affect reputation.

The Reputation Assessment first focused on four countries (Italy, Germany, Austria and Poland), which accounted for approximately 80 % of the bank's revenue. The process was then extended a year later to three other EC countries: Bulgaria, Croatia and Hungary. Starting from 2011, the survey added the Czech Republic, Russia, Romania giving a total of 10 countries. In 2014, the Bank decided to merge Brand and Reputation studies, and the Survey was thus extended to 15 countries (Fig. 4).

4 Organisational Change

Up until 2011, reputation assessment within UniCredit had been managed through the Identity & Communications department.

2011 was a real watershed: reputation began to play a major role. Simply put, a bank's reputation is one of the key factors that influence a customer's decision to approach a given company. Along with the need for Customer Acquisition, due to the global economic crisis, this assumption led UniCredit to adapt a more strategic approach towards monitoring and evaluating reputation.

UniCredit then decided to focus on the analysis of stakeholder perception, establishing the Group Stakeholder & Service Intelligence Department (GSSI) in 2011.

Its task is to coordinate the surveys completed by customers, stakeholders, communities, employees and internal customers, as well as to analyse the business context. Ultimately, the department uses survey results to develop action plans for all countries and to promote initiatives aimed at effective stakeholder engagement.

5 2009–2013: The Early Years—An Extraordinary Learning Path

To evaluate its reputation, UniCredit chose to work with the Reputation Institute that uses a proprietary methodology. The philosophy of the Reputation Institute focuses on the notion promoted by its founder, Charles Fombrun, that "a corporate reputation is a perceptual representation of a company's past actions and future prospects that describe the firm's overall appeal to all of its key constituents when compared with other leading rivals" (Fombrun 1996).

According to this approach, the corporate reputation is the result of a mixture of three components: direct experience of the brand (purchase of products, services, experience in points of sale, financial investments, job offered by the company, suppliers); what the brand says about itself through marketing, communication, advertising; and what is said about the brand (by media, opinion leaders and experts, friends and families) (Fig. 5).

The RepTrak Pulse model developed by the Reputation Institute is based on this concept. RepTrakPulse measures the degree of admiration and trust that stakeholders express toward the company, and assesses the strength of the emotional bond. This index is measured on a scale from 0 to 100 and gives the chance to benchmark outcomes against results obtained by major competitors.

The seven key dimensions of Corporate Reputation are: Performance, Products and Services, Innovation, Citizenship, Leadership, Working Environment and Governance. Each of these dimensions contributes to the stakeholders' perception of the company.

The RepTrak Pulse system evaluates the emotional bonds between the company and the public, and determines which dimensions have a greater impact on the support and recommendation expressed by the stakeholders.

6 The Survey Method

Until 2014, the process of reputation monitoring was based on an annual survey carried out in the main countries of the Group across all categories of stakeholders.

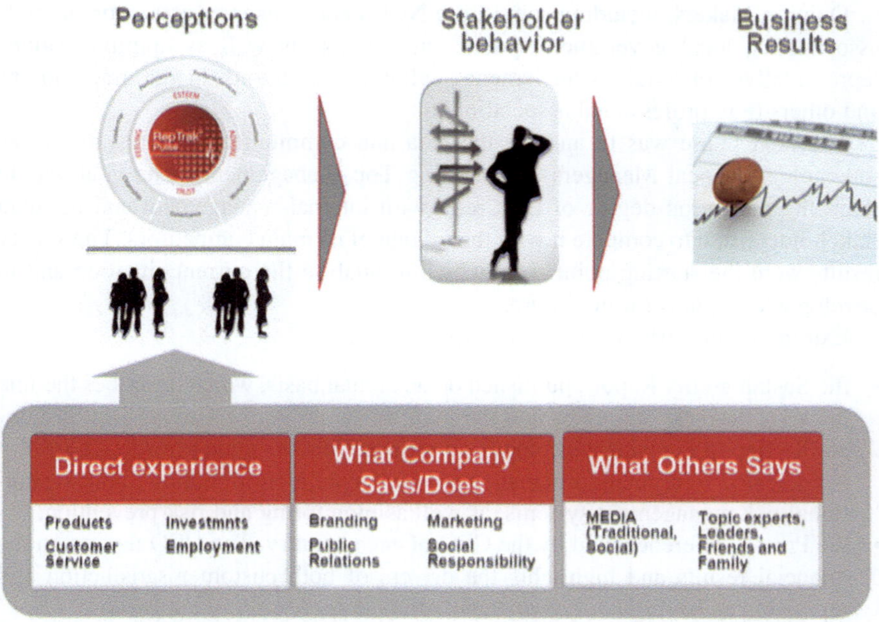

Fig. 5 The reputation system. Corporate Reputation originates in the emotional bonds of key stakeholders affecting the company's business, and ensuring their support and trust. *Source*: UniCredit Internal Papers—Reputation Presentation

The questionnaires were based on the CATI system (Computer-Assisted Telephone Interviewing), with telephone interviews lasting about 25 min. In 2012 in Italy and in the Czech Republic, the CATI system was flanked by the CAWI system (Computer-Assisted Web Interviewing), i.e. an online questionnaire. The use of the two systems together reduced errors in measurement and increased the response rate among young professionals. The survey was carried out on an annual basis over a period of 4–6 weeks (in September and October).

The target of the questionnaire was broad, and included different types of stakeholders. Respondents were divided into three major groups: customers, non-customers and opinion makers. Customers were segmented by income threshold, commonly classified into:

- Mass market
- Affluent
- Private banking customers

Companies were segmented on the basis of total revenue into:

- Small Businesses
- Medium Enterprises
- Corporate Companies
- Large Multinationals

Opinion Makers, including some from NGOs and consumer associations, trade associations, local government, public institutions, as well as opinion leaders, representatives of religious movements, cultural associations, media, trade unions and others (e.g. professional associations).

The next phase was to analyse the data and communicate the results to key stakeholders (Local Managers and Holding Top Management). The goal was to share the reputation degree of UniCredit with internal management and its main stakeholders, and to compare it with that of one of its main competitors. The survey results were the starting point from which to analyse the current situation and to develop action plans for the future.

Externally, the survey results are explained in:

- the Sustainability Report, published on an annual basis, which describes the link between business strategies and the main activities of the Group. The Sustainability Report explains the company's approach and its main priorities; part of it is dedicated to reputation management and contains information about reputational risk management systems, as well as monitoring and risk prevention;
- the Press Conference held by the CEO of each country. The CEO reports on the financial results and highlights the drivers of both customer satisfaction and reputation as having both *contributed to the achievement of the results*.

7 Building an Effective Call to Action

The results of the reputation assessment are a starting point for examining areas that need to be improved and for helping to implement an action plan. Each function, after analysing the data, formulates an action plan with the main activities for the following business year.

Each action plan is divided into four parts:

1. Key drivers, or areas for improvement emerging from the survey.
2. Key actions, activities and initiatives planned for each area.
3. KPI, indicators that measure the degree of implementation of a particular action.
4. Time plan, the time frame within which the action will be implemented.

Group Stakeholder & Service Intelligence is responsible for collecting the action plans of the various functions and monitoring results. All the Action Plans give rise to the priorities the Group commits to work on over the following year.

8 2014: The Paradigm Shift Driving a Clear-Cut Quantum Leap

The global financial crisis pushed the already complementary disciplines of Brand Management and Reputation Management closer together, linking Identity, Reputation and the Brand. Thus UniCredit began exploring an Extended Perception Model that incorporates Brand and Reputation more holistically.

Until 2013 UniCredit observed and monitored the Brand Awareness and Brand Identity content and the Reputation Perception through two separate surveys (Brand Equity Survey and Reputation Survey). Brand Equity KPIs measure Brand Prominence, Image and Propensity, while the Reputation Survey measures the general esteem in which the Bank is held by the public. Both Surveys serve the scope of comparing UniCredit's performance with that of its main competitors.

According to recent studies, there has been a paradigm shift in the way companies assess their performances. During the early phase, companies evaluated their processes, i.e. any indicator testing the efficiency of internal operations. During the second phase, companies started to evaluate performance measurement, i.e. the contribution of communication to business through KRIs (Key Results Indicators) and KPIs (Key Performances Indicators), the former being more related to past and what the organisation has achieved, and the latter more oriented to future organisational performance (Parmenter 2007). In this second phase, reputation assessment goes beyond mere measurement indexes of performance. According to experts (Bititci et al. 2012; Kaplan and Norton 2001; Johnson and Broms 2000) this second type of assessment does not allow companies to manage their performance in turbulent times, in terms of tangible and intangible resources, as they do not allow for the assessment and management of performance on the basis of the specific situation the company is going through.

For UniCredit, a third phase of integrated performance management was needed. In this phase, it was crucial to go beyond the measurement (index) itself. The key element is the strategic knowledge that one gets from it to manage the new flexible boundaries (networks, collaborative organisations etc.) of the company. The advantage of an approach based on a network-based reputation is that it measures how reputation is co-construed with stakeholders, rather than setting predefined perceived dimensions of reputation. Also, it helps to measure how the reputation is supported by the company's reality because it acknowledges that relationships are the means by which organisations coordinate actions, create relationships and constitute or maintain their reputation over time.

In order to overcome the above-listed drawbacks of brand and reputation assessment and reach a state in which the bank may be closer to business needs and relevant stakeholders requests, we embarked on a yearlong project that engaged many functions of the bank and external stakeholders in its design phase.

9 Main Project Goals

The general aim of the project is the fusion of the Brand and Reputation surveys in order to:

- find a method to better assess and measure the indexes and drivers that contribute most strongly to the Bank's ability to create value over time;
- integrate, rationalise and simplify the design of the two surveys;
- renew and update the Indexes and Drivers to that have the greatest impact on the Image and the Reputation of the Bank;
- improve effectiveness of survey results (larger sample size, increased number of survey cycles);
- reduce costs by avoiding the duplication of complementary listening activities;

The benefits expected are:

- to face the market with one approach;
- to improve index and item monitoring. To reduce complexity in risks and the identification of opportunities;
- to obtain more understandable and communicable results and findings;
- to create drivers which are clearly linked to business value creation/strategic alignment and actionability;
- to monitor KPIs for relevant competitors (at least five per country);
- to reduce the total cost of the two research projects by 25 %.

9.1 Merging the Two Methods of Analysis: Model Selection

During this phase, all the main international providers were invited to send in their Model responding to a formal restricted request for information.

Three of them were shortlisted on the basis of their international presence, demonstrated experience on both subjects—Brand and Reputation—and possession of the necessary capabilities: IPSOS; TNS; DOXA.

The contract was awarded to IPSOS because its Model met UniCredit requirements for an appropriate service cost.

9.2 Questionnaire Redesign: Statistical Analysis and Qualitative Study

The over 50 items that formed the main drivers of the Brand and Reputation survey were statistically evaluated in order to measure their impact on the Bank's Brand and Reputation perception.

The 20 most impacting items were subjected to qualitative evaluation to find out whether they were still in line with Stakeholders' expectations and to revise their wording.

The aim of the Qualitative phase was to identify 16 very relevant items in terms of Reputation and Brand perception: Quantitative analysis on Reputation and Brand results helped to identify the most important items in each country.

9.3 *The UniCredit Ipsos Model*

After three successive runs and invitations to tender, we chose to work with Ipsos, and to develop a model with their help, suited to our needs.

The model uses a holistic approach built around the Reputation Pyramid of the most important Indicators of Brand and Reputation: Awareness (total spontaneous and prompted awareness), Familiarity (capability of expressing an opinion about the bank), Favourability (positive stance toward the bank), Trust (the linchpin of reputation) and Advocacy (one of the most important forms of supportive behaviour). Taken together, all the steps constitute the Reputation Pyramid, synthetically measured as Reputation Power (performance of the Pyramid among familiar stakeholders) and Reputation Strength (total performance of the Pyramid) (Fig. 6).

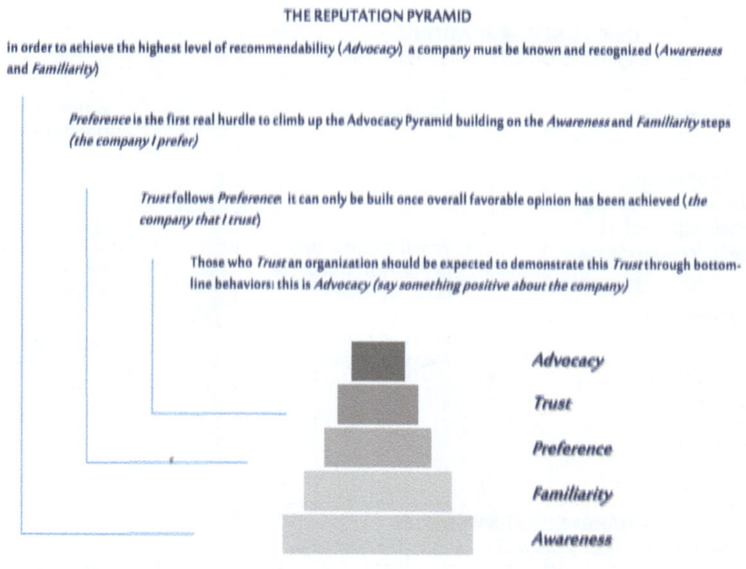

Fig. 6 The UniCredit Ipsos model. *Source*: Ipsos paper: the reputation model

9.4 Core Metrics and Drivers

The analytical part of the survey includes 23 items grouped around four main areas, the impact of which is considered when choosing which to work on.

Identifying the drivers of Advocacy tells you:

- which levers to pull/release in order to steer your reputation;
- how to identify which drivers have most impact and thus drive stakeholders up the reputation pyramid.

Drivers of Preference/Advocacy include elements of what an organisation does as well as what it stands for. Metrics specific to the bank and its sector on action are included, leading to actionable variables designed to value creation, promote buy-in and endorse Strategy alignment.

9.5 Main Goals of the Survey

The activity of Brand and Reputation Management implemented annually by UniCredit is undoubtedly a great investment in terms of time and resources.

The investment has to demonstrate its benefit for the business both in terms of results monitoring (brand investment crucial to awareness, advocacy and reputation) and goal-setting (findings, conclusions, recommendations, and call to action) (Fig. 7).

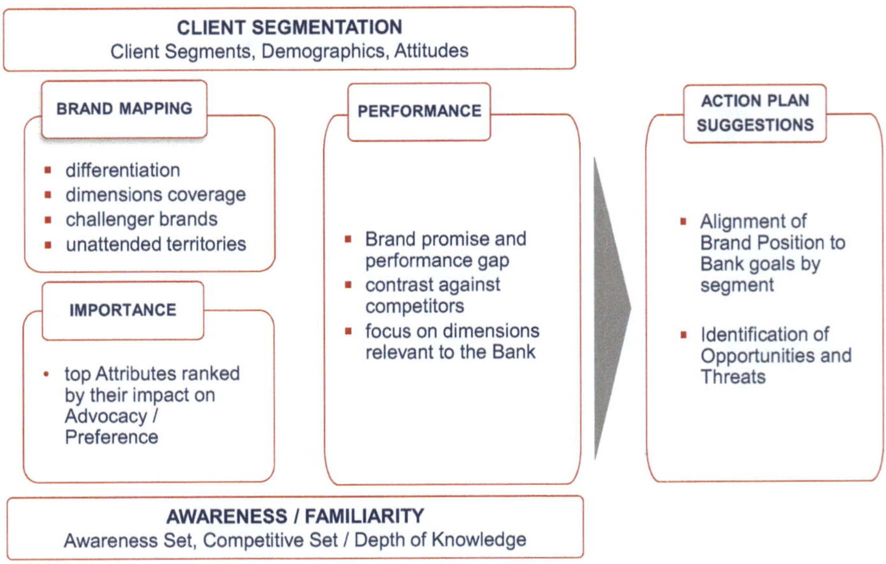

Fig. 7 The brand and reputation system revealed: measure, analyse and act. *Source*: UniCredit Internal Papers—Reputation Presentation

All the survey presentations try to make managers' decision-making easier and more efficient, in order to:

- align the Image and Positioning of the Brand to the Bank's goals: i.e. Brand recognition, increase in sales volume;
- improve Brand perception and Reputation of the Bank among stakeholders and competitors;
- identify the dimensions of Preference/Advocacy, examine their perceived importance levels and to contrast differences regarding targets (Mass, Affluent, Small Business, Corporate), demographics and attitudinal variables;
- monitor so-called supportive behaviour influenced by Brand and Reputation: Propensity to purchase and the dissemination of positive opinions of the Bank;
- identify potential opportunities and threats that may either arise from unexpected quarters or where competitors are already in the lead.

9.6 *Example of Measurements: Awareness*

UniCredit measures awareness in terms of 'Top of Mind' and 'Spontaneous Recall', i.e. "Q.1 Let's talk about the banks you know. Could you please state the names of all the banks that come to mind?", and aided recall, i.e. "Q.2 Which of the following banks/banking groups you have heard of?"

In the following chart, results for 10 countries are reported. UniCredit achieves the best results in terms of spontaneous awareness in Croatia and Italy (top of mind and spontaneous recall) (Fig. 8).

9.7 *Example of Analysis*

The Importance of Awareness In this chart, we see there is a strong correlation between Awareness and Propensity (the main measure of Prospective Customers' approval). The correlation loses strength when awareness reaches a very high level (Fig. 9).

Positioning of UniCredit in the 10 Countries Considered UniCredit banks have a very heterogeneous positioning in the 10 countries considered (Fig. 10):

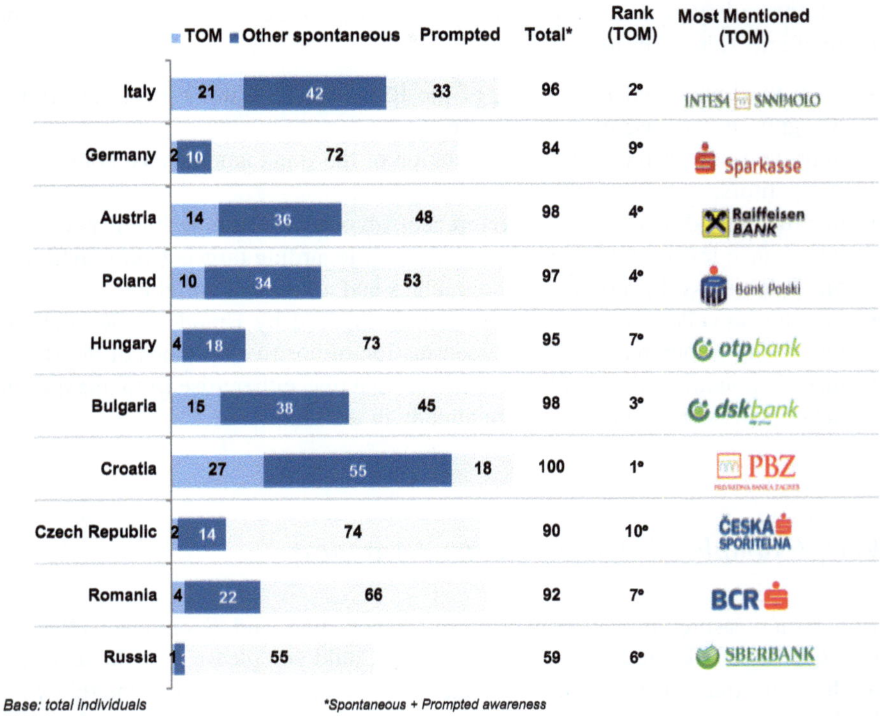

Fig. 8 Brand awareness of UniCredit and best performer in 10 countries. *Source*: UniCredit Internal Papers—Reputation Presentation

10 Future Projects and Developments

10.1 Background

We believe that all sociological discourse is now obliged to come to terms with the digital sphere, or miss investigating and theorising whole swathes of significant human activity. So many relationships are conducted partly—or completely—online that sociology which overlooks this aspect it is simply inadequate (Bauman and Lyon 2013).

The online has quickly become a basic means of communicating, of 'connecting' with others, and is now a dimension of daily life for almost all of the banking population of Europe.

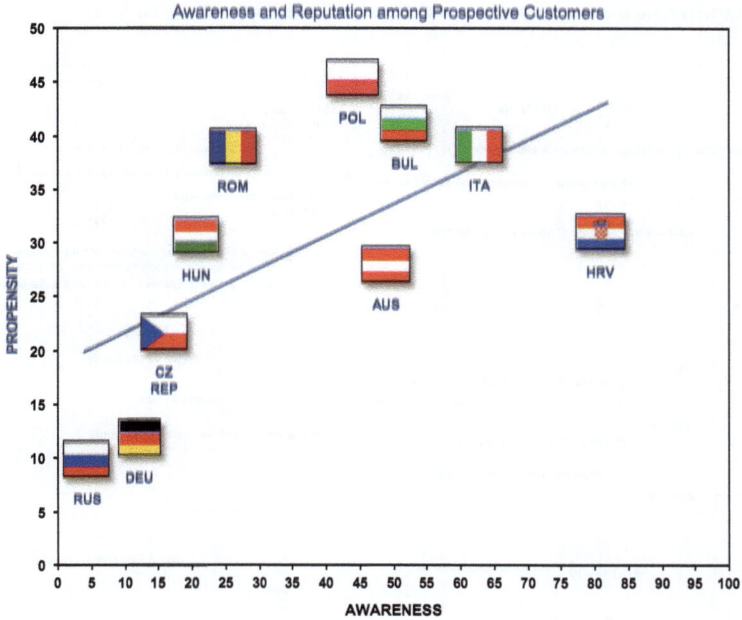

Fig. 9 Correlation between awareness and reputation among prospective customers. *Source*: UniCredit Internal Papers—Reputation Presentation

10.2 Status Quo

In the past, the stakeholders' perceptions of corporate reputation was based on media channels such as the print media, radio, and television.

From a micro-economic perspective, this may be characterised as an information oligopoly in which a limited few offered contents about the firm to many stakeholders.

The advent of the 'information age' saw the rise of the internet as a new communication channel and the perspective changed to what might be called 'polypoly', that is, multiple stakeholders (e.g., customers, market analysts, etc.) contributing information/contents regarding the bank.

In other words, with the advent of Web 2.0 technologies, stakeholders became *prosumers*, simultaneously producing and consuming contents.

It is therefore possible to distinguish between perceived and actual judgments of stakeholders concerning the Bank. Stakeholder (e.g., customer) responses to survey questions represent the perceived reputation, while their firm-related expressions online (e.g. blogs) represent the actual reputation of the firm in the eyes of stakeholders. Thus, because of the increasing number of prosumers and their impact on real (rather than perceived) corporate reputation, a comprehensive measurement of a firm's reputation needs to include this channel.

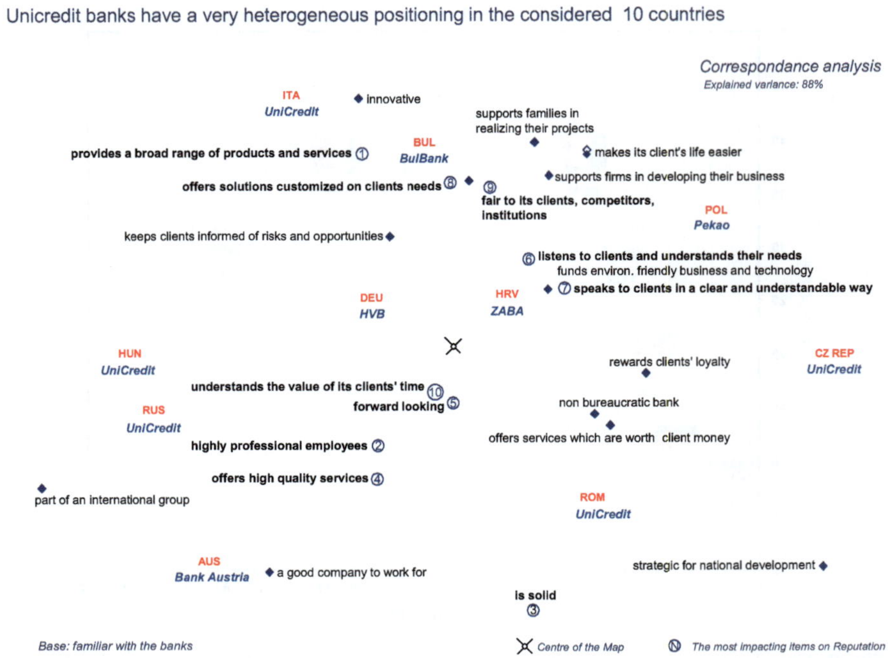

Fig. 10 Cross-country correspondence analysis. *Source*: UniCredit Internal Papers—Reputation Presentation

For an individual bank, it is therefore crucial to expand the ways in which reputation is measured in order to manage its reputation effectively. In particular, in light of the developments outlined above, the aim of the future stage is to develop a new holistic approach so as to collect, measure and scrutinise the corporate Brand Reputation of UniCredit, covering a concept of a semi-automatic collection of reputation-relevant data. Not only does the intended measurement approach include the perception of key stakeholders (i.e. customers, competitors and investors), but is scalable to several other stakeholder groups (e.g., employees, suppliers, society) combined with manifest data (e.g., forum posts and social media activities).

Thus, the underlying idea is to develop a reputation measure that shifts the focus from a single channel (i.e. interviews) and a single stakeholder group (i.e. the general public) to a holistic, multi-channel and multi-stakeholder approach. The approach has to be designed to include conventional survey-based data (as is currently used), coupled with methods and sources of measurement which will:

- reduce the amount of cost-intensive CATI//CAWI interviews;
- help to obtain a picture of corporate reputation that "closes the gap between perception and reality."

10.3 Methodology

The holistic measurement approach links the perception of multiple stakeholder groups with manifest data while 'listening' to multiple channels. Corporate reputation is a reflective construct, measured on stakeholder perceptions. For this reason, our measurement approach cannot completely overlook a questionnaire survey of key stakeholders. In addition, the measurement approach utilises manifest data while listening to customers across multiple channels and involves analyses of the information gathered (e.g., search robots and web crawlers).This approach may be scaled up to include other stakeholder groups.

Corporate reputation can be conceptualised as an attitude-like judgment, a stakeholder's evaluation arising from either or both his/her personal interaction with the bank, as well as from reputation-relevant information received about the bank. In other words, how other stakeholders' articulations about the focal firm influence a stakeholder's evaluation.

Although reputation is a perception (because it is built in person's mind and not objectively measureable), we distinguish between the perception of corporate reputation (as captured by interviews and standardised questionnaires) and manifest corporate reputation (as indicated by various uses of language, including signalling words and emoticons in Web 2.0 environments).

The advantages of the approach are as follows:

- Through the use of manifest data, the need for interviews decreases/fades out.
- Thanks to the ability to potentially include all stakeholder groups beyond customers, a more realistic and complete picture of UniCredit's reputation can be drawn.

11 Foundation Research Project

11.1 The Impact of Twitter Conversations on UniCredit's Reputation and Its Corporate Repercussions

11.1.1 Starting Point of the Project

In 2013–2014, the University of Madrid assessed the status of UniCredit's reputation online from May 2013 to April 2014. During the project, the research team measured the online sentiment toward UniCredit (i.e. voice of Twitter users) and how much this sentiment influenced other conversations on the web and, ultimately, corporate outcomes (i.e. the opening and closing of accounts).

One of the main results was that Twitter users mainly express a negative sentiment toward UniCredit. They also found that the negative sentiment of top conversations toward UniCredit is linked to negative corporate outcomes. Specifically, they found that conversations with a negative sentiment toward UniCredit had a negative effect on corporate outcomes for a up to 2 weeks after the conversations became highly reputed online (meaning after they became speechmakers, that is, retweeted or mentioned many times).

As a follow up to the project, the team will further analyse the conversations for a longer period of time, i.e. 2008–2014. This analysis will show what they think it is the most important yet still unanswered question about online reputation: whether social media have an impact on the bottom line of businesses and whether this impact is permanent or temporary. By analysing whether the sentiment over the years toward UniCredit online is a constant or just a temporary trend, they will be able to assess whether or not a negative sentiment online really constitutes a reputational risk for the bank.

11.1.2 Main Advantages of the Project

The team will cross online data (sentiment online), offline perception data (corporate reputation surveys data) and offline real data (opening-closing of accounts) through a Machine Learning approach, and they will assess the impact of top online conversations on reputation and outcomes.

Research questions and data cross-analysed:

- Can it be confirmed that the negative sentiment toward UniCredit has a negative effect on corporate outcomes for a period of time lasting up to 2 weeks after the conversations become well reputed online?
- Is the negative sentiment toward UniCredit (and toward the industry) a trend? If so, is it risky?
- When negative sentiment explodes, does it have momentary impact on UniCredit Reputation or a long term one to the point to change UniCredit's Reputation (for the worst)?
- Can the impact of negative sentiment toward UniCredit be predicted? And its impact on corporate reputation or outcomes?

To answer the above questions, three sets of data will be used:

- Twitter conversations on UniCredit from 2008 to 2014 (daily);
- opening-closing of accounts 2008–2014 (daily);
- Twitter conversations concerning UniCredit and its competitors 2008–2014 (daily);
- UniCredit's reputation data, 2008–2014 surveys (yearly);
- UniCredit Brand Awareness data, 2008–2014 (weekly)

12 Conclusions

A bank that wants to build a solid reputation has to focus on interactions with its stakeholders. Paying attention to one form of narrative at a time doesn't help: in order to manage a system effectively, we might focus on the interaction of various parts rather than their behaviour taken separately.

Globalisation and the ever-connected present world are increasingly blurring the lines that once separated different media channels (broadcast and social networks).

In the past, the media were portrayed as a monolithic collective entity churning out narratives that refracted and amplified organisational projections. The rise of social networks makes that representation obsolete because the motivational drivers, contextual conditions and patterns of diffusion that characterise narratives in traditional media and social network are converging. Failure to acknowledge this may limit our theoretical understanding of the formation of people's perceptions and companies' reputations.

As a matter of fact, the spread of web-based technologies and the rise of social networks have significantly changed the social processes that shape organisational perceptions (reputation). As a consequence, a shift in theoretical understandings and methodological practices to account for these changes is required. The processes underpinning the online phenomenon have transformed many—if not all—aspects of the traditional modern social world.

First of all, national and local borders have become immaterial, as power and organisations move into the *space of flows*. Business without boundaries is the catchphrase of the day: as a consequence, it means that in no sector, no remote place exists where the company can hide and nurture its market niche. Any competitor, from wherever and from whatever business sector, has access to it and the right to exploit it.

A methodological cosmopolitanism is required that takes these new processes into account and does not "mischaracterise developments by situating them in an arbitrarily bounded context" (Beck 2005). From the customer's point of view, is the mobile banking experience different in Munich, Vienna or Milan?

Time is ever more declined as present tense. Nowism, access to services 24/7, is becoming the only thing that matters in the business arena, thereby doing away with all the former features of duration (Bauman 2000).

Social networking portends more, easier and looser connections. Increased competition means that customers are continuously allured by new offers, new and improved services. Shorter product lifetimes drive customers to embrace the 'new' and reject the 'old'(obliged in a sense by the threat of digital exclusion). Cutting connections is all too easy in the virtual mobile world: we can always press the delete key, switch from one app to another, whenever we want, on the spur of the moment, instantly and without having to go through the rigmarole of meeting with an individual in flesh and blood to negotiate decisions (Bauman 2007). And since the grass is always greener in the other side, customers become used to foregoing the relationship at the very first sign of dissatisfaction in the hope of better and improved customer services elsewhere. Brand loyalty, identification with a brand, thus becomes an ever rarer phenomenon, an irrational attitude from the utilitarian point of view of today's customer, fraught with the risks of loading trust unnecessarily and thus limiting her/his degree of freedom. For this reason, as much empirical research shows, greater customer satisfaction is not a guarantee of a future loyal customer base.

Business scope is also under threat in all fields (Uber is merely the epitome of this trend). For example, telecommunication companies today are capable of providing banking services, gathering detailed knowledge of customer behaviour (geo-localisation, detailed and real-time knowledge of customers' spending patterns), and may become disruptive in the sector of mobile payments, deposits and personal loans. So the very notion of who the peers companies and competitors are should be rethought.

The segmentation of customers has to be rethought as well. Needs, wants and desires cannot be identified using averages drawn from survey statistics based on erstwhile valid ideal types; instead, extra effort should go towards a better knowledge of the behaviour of the individual client (as Google and Amazon have already put in practice).

We believe that in the near future, current methods of stakeholder listening will be devoid of interpretative capacity, and for this reason, the future state we are striving to bring about foresees an interactive, integrated and personalised method of stakeholder management driven by the use of business analytics from many different sources.

References

Bauman Z (2000) Liquid time. Polity Press, Cambridge

Bauman Z (2007) Consuming life. Polity Press, Cambridge

Bauman Z, Lyon D (2013) Liquid surveillance. Polity Press, Cambridge

Beck U (2005) Power in the global age: a new global political economy. Polity Press, Cambridge

Bititci U, Garengo P, Dörfler V et al (2012) Performance measurement: challenges for tomorrow. Int J Manage Rev 14(3):305–327

Fombrun C (1996) Reputation: realizing value from the corporate image. Harvard Business School Press, Boston, MA

Johnson HT, Broms A (2000) Profit beyond measure: extraordinary results through attention to work and people. The Free Press, New York, NY

Kaplan R, Norton D (2001) The strategy focused organization. Harvard Business Press, Boston, MA

Parmenter D (2007) Key performance indicators. Wiley, Hoboken, NJ

Antonino d'Eugenio is currently responsible for the Brand and Reputation Study at UniCredit, Milan, and a member of the EMEA Reputation Leaders Network RI. Prior to this, he was a corporate professional for more than 20 years, with a career in Process Improvement and Marketing Roles. As a team leader, he pioneered the UniCredit online Brand and Reputation assessment. Before joining UniCredit, he spent 12 years as a Business Lean Six Sigma professional in large corporations across Europe, such as Ferrari, Tetra Pak and Nortel Networks.

He holds a degree in Political Science from Pisa University and a Master Degree in Lean Operations. He currently cooperates with IE Madrid in the field of Social Media Sentiment Analysis in the banking sector.

Intesa Sanpaolo: A Case Study on Reputation Management and Its Relationship to Corporate Social Responsibility

Cristina Laura Paltrinieri, Daniela Fraire, and Rosella Carè

Abstract This chapter explores and interprets the dynamics and major characteristics of the reputation management process of Intesa Sanpaolo, with a focus on its relationship to corporate social responsibility. The case highlights the role of reputational risk management in banks and offers useful suggestions for putting knowledge into practice.

1 Company Profile

The Intesa Sanpaolo Group (ISP) was formed on 1 January 2007 by the merger of Banca Intesa and Sanpaolo IMI. With more than 11 million customers[1] and approximately 4500 branches in Italy, ISP is the largest banking group in Italy and the leader in all segments (retail, corporate and wealth management) in that country. It is also one of the foremost banks in the eurozone based on market capitalization (all data, figures and information provided in this section are as of 31 December 2014).

ISP also has a selective presence in the international retail market, with subsidiary banks in 12 countries in Central and Eastern Europe, the Middle East and North Africa that account for approximately 1400 branches and more than eight million customers. The strength of the group in areas outside of Italy is derived from banks

This chapter is the result of a collaboration between the authors. In particular, Paltrinieri and Fraire contributed to paragraphs 1, 2, and 3; Carè contributed to paragraph 4.

[1] The figures in this paragraph are correct as of 31 December 2014.

C.L. Paltrinieri (✉)
Intesa Sanpaolo – External Relations Department – Researches and Surveys, Milan, Italy
e-mail: cristina.paltrinieri@intesasanpaolo.com

D. Fraire (✉)
Intesa Sanpaolo – External Relations Department – Researches and Surveys, Turin, Italy
e-mail: daniela.fraire@intesasanpaolo.com

R. Carè
University Magna Graecia, Catanzaro, Italy
e-mail: care@unicz.it

S. Dell'Atti, A. Trotta (eds.), *Managing Reputation in The Banking Industry*,
DOI 10.1007/978-3-319-28256-5_7

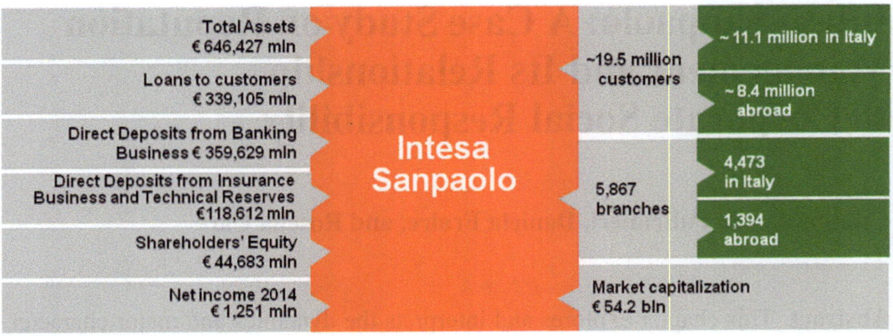

Source: Intesa Sanpaolo

Fig. 1 The Group at a glance: results (All data are as of 31 December 2014 except for market capitalization that is as of 30 June 2015. The shareholders' equity includes net income)

with strong local ties and significant market shares, most of which are the leading banks in their respective countries based on total assets.

In addition, to serve its corporate clients, Intesa Sanpaolo has a specialized international network that covers 29 countries.

Figure 1 summarizes the Group's main results as of 31 December 2014 (market capitalization as of 30 June 2015).

Intesa Sanpaolo's governance model comprises a Supervisory Board whose members are appointed at the Shareholders' Meeting and a Management Board whose members are appointed by the Supervisory Board.[2] The Management Board appoints the Managing Director, who is the Group's sole CEO and has full powers, from among its members. There are a number of Committees within the Supervisory Board, including the **Internal Control Committee** (responsible for overseeing corporate administrative liability), the **Nomination Committee** (which provides advice and recommendations for the appointment of the Management Board and the General Managers), the **Remuneration Committee** and the **Risk Committee**. The Managing Director and CEO is assisted by a number of Head Office Departments, some of which are grouped into Governance Areas.

From an operational standpoint, the Group's work is divided into seven business units (Fig. 2) that collectively comprise approximately 40 different specialist companies and banks:

- *Banca dei Territori Division* is active in the Italian household and business market and includes Banca Prossima, the first European bank dedicated exclusively to social enterprises and non-profit organizations.
- *The Corporate and Investment Banking Division* has 43 branches in Italy serving 16,000 clients that include medium-to-large companies, public administrative agencies and financial institutions. This division includes Banca IMI, which is

[2] While this book is under the process of being published, the governance model has been revised in favour of the adoption of the one-tier governance system.

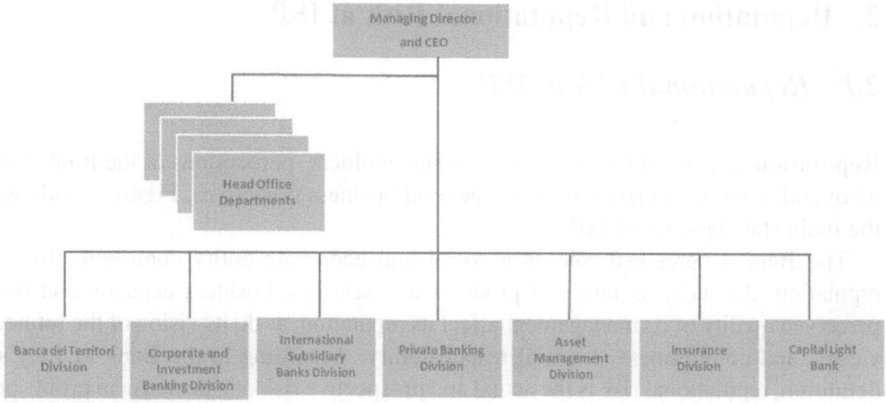

Source: Intesa Sanpaolo

Fig. 2 Business structure

Italy's leading operator in investment banking, structured finance, merchant banking and capital markets.

This division also has branches, representative offices and subsidiaries in 29 other countries to assist Group customers with international activities and is connected to a network of thousands of correspondent banks;

- *The International Subsidiary Banks Division* includes the Group's retail subsidiaries in 12 foreign countries;
- *The Private Banking Division* comprises banks and other companies that collectively account for over 230 branches and more than 5700 private bankers serving 79,000 private clients;
- *The Asset Management Division* offers asset management solutions for the Group's customers, third-party sales networks and institutional clients and manages approximately 203 billion euros in assets;
- *The Insurance Division* provides insurance and pension products for the Group's customers and has a total of approximately 112 billion euros in technical provisions and approximately 27 billion euros of premiums;
- *Capital Light Bank* is dedicated to extracting value from the Group's non-core assets. The responsibilities of this division include managing non-performing loans and mortgaged properties that the Group has repossessed, disposing of non-strategic equity investments, extracting value from other non-core assets, etc.

2 Reputation and Reputational Risk at ISP

2.1 Reputational Risk at ISP

Reputation can be defined as the sum of stakeholders' perceptions of the Bank and its overall conduct, performance and general business objectives. Figure 3 outlines the main stakeholders of ISP.

The Bank's perceived role as a social and economic entity contributes to its reputation. As such, its range of products and services, business capacity and the perceived quality of its management affect its reputation, as do its vision of the future, values, and commitment to social responsibility. According to the Bank of Italy's definition, reputational risk is the actual and prospective risk of a decrease in profits or capital due to a negative perception of a bank in the areas described above. ISP is affected by the **intrinsic risks of banking**, specifically, credit risk, market risk, liquidity risk, insurance-related risk and strategic risk. Reputational risk is generally seen as a secondary risk, not in the sense that it is less important but because it can derive from a primary risk event (operating, compliance, credit, liquidity, etc.). Certain types of primary risk have greater negative consequences on company reputation relative to other types of risk because they undermine fundamental aspects such as stakeholder **trust** and **image**. As a general rule, reputational risks generated by credit risk and market risk are tolerated more, whereas risks derived from operating risks relating to losses incurred by customers, inefficiency, poor internal controls and improper conduct are tolerated less. These tolerance thresholds/margins must be assessed by setting suitable limits within the Risk Appetite Framework

COLLABORATORS:
- Branch personnel
- Staff
- Junior collaborators
- Senior collaborators
- Personnel in roles of responsibility
- Top management
- Trade unions

SUPPLIERS:
- Large suppliers
- Small suppliers
- Commercial partners
- Sub-suppliers

CUSTOMERS:
- Private individuals and households
- Financially vulnerable private individuals and households
- Small- and medium-sized enterprises
- Large enterprises
- Start-ups
- Consumer associations,
- Public entities and the public administration
- Third sector
- Trade associations

ENVIRONMENT:
- Environmental associations
- Future generations
- Scientific community

SHAREHOLDERS:
- Small investors
- Foundations
- Institutional investors
- Socially responsible investors
- Shareholders' associations

COMMUNITY:
- Associations representing community interests
- Regulatory authorities
- National and international public institutions
- Media

Source: Intesa Sanpaolo

Fig. 3 Map of Intesa Sanpaolo stakeholders

(RAF), which ensures consistency among risk objectives (the maximum risk that can be assumed), the business model and strategic guidelines. This consistency is essential to establishing a governance policy and to the implementation of risk management processes. The Intesa Sanpaolo Group ascribes significant importance to risk management and monitoring, both of which are considered essential to the reliable and sustainable generation of value in a scenario of controlled risk. For this reason, a report on risks and associated hedging policies is periodically prepared and is available to all stakeholders. The policies on risk appetite are defined by the Bank's **statutory bodies** (the Supervisory Board and Management Board) with the support of other governing bodies, including the Internal Control Committee and Risk Committee, as well as the **Chief Risk Officer**, who reports directly to the CEO. The **Risk Committee** assists the Supervisory Board with strategic supervision of risk and the internal control system. The Chief Risk Officer is responsible for compliance with current national and international regulations, risk management, credit quality monitoring, anti-money-laundering policies and internal validation. The responsibilities of the **Risk Management** function, performed together with the competent corporate functions, include the following:

- measuring and monitoring Group exposure to different types of risk, including reputational risk
- monitoring capital absorption
- providing the supervisory bodies with the information required under current law
- managing risk measurement and control systems in accordance with international regulations

In contrast to other types of risk, it is difficult to directly and immediately quantify reputational risk. Management of reputational risk is based mainly on preventing and containing negative effects on reputation through strong and sustainable growth that creates value for all stakeholders while simultaneously minimizing possible adverse events through rigorous and detailed governance, control and guidance performed at the various service and function levels.

2.2 *Reputational Risk Management*

ISP's reputational risk management model involves systematic and comprehensive reputational protection across the various company functions, thereby covering the entire spectrum of company activities.

Systematic protection is assured by:

- specific organizational structures dedicated to relations with various stakeholders, such as Compliance, Anti-Money Laundering, External Relations, Internal Communication, Corporate Social Responsibility, International &

Regulatory Affairs, and International & Regulatory Affairs, Investor Relations and Rating Agencies

- an integrated system for the management of primary risks that can cause reputational damage;
- determining and managing customers' risk tolerance and identifying the various risk tolerance profiles with respect to the objective and subjective characteristics of the customer; and
- compliance with ethical and behavioural standards set out in a company Code of Ethics, an Internal Code of Conduct and CSR policies to guarantee transparency and professionalism in relations with stakeholders, as explained in more detail later in this document.

Overall control of reputational risk is ensured by the **Reputational Risk Management** process (Fig. 4), which is responsible for identifying and assessing the main reputational risk scenarios to which the Group is exposed and for defining areas of intervention for the management/mitigation of these risks.

This process takes place annually and is broken down as follows:

1. The main risk areas to which the Group is exposed are identified. This identification process, which is completed with the assistance of all company units directly involved in protecting the company's reputation, is based both on data regarding external scenarios (which are principally managed by the Corporate & Social Responsibility unit and the Researches and Surveys unit of the External Relations Department, as discussed below) and internal analyses of scenarios that are relevant to the bank, which are conducted primarily by the Risk Management Department in collaboration with the Compliance Department. These internal analyses also include targeted assessments of major competitors' best practices to determine any additional risk factors that could affect the Group's reputation.
2. A questionnaire is produced and distributed to a select group of top managers at the Parent Company and the main Group Companies. These managers express their views on the entire range of risks (risk assessment) and indicate, in their

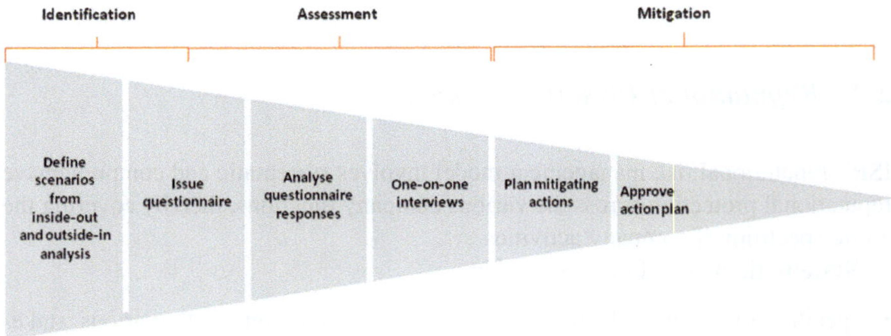

Source: Intesa Sanpaolo

Fig. 4 Reputation risk management at Intesa Sanpaolo

respective areas of competence, possible strategies to mitigate these risks. Each risk assessment also includes an estimate of the probability that the risk scenario will occur, the reputational impact that such scenario could have and the potential geographical scope of the scenario and its impact (local/global).

3. The answers are reviewed and grouped into clusters to conduct the necessary analysis, which is used as the basis for discussion in one-on-one interviews with the managers of the various Business Units/Governance Areas. These discussions lead to the selection of a small number of priority subjects for which action plans can be prepared.
4. The action plans are presented to company management—specifically, the Supervisory and Management Boards and the Risk Governance Committee—for the necessary approvals and definitive "go ahead" for the plans.

This process is coordinated by the Risk Management function in collaboration with Compliance. In 2014, the survey showed that the main primary risks that gave rise to reputational risks related to operations and compliance. In particular, top management identified scenarios in the following areas as the most critical in terms of potential harm to the company's image: credit and the economic cycle, breaches of industry regulations (e.g., AML, MIFID, embargoes) and the security of electronic transactions. Thus, the main categories of stakeholders most affected by these risks are customers, shareholders, the broader community, and regulatory/supervisory authorities.

2.3 *Image and Reputation: How They Are "Measured" at ISP*

At ISP, the state of the Group's image and reputation is assessed by the Researches and Surveys function of the External Relations Department, which reports directly to company top management. The task of the Researches and Surveys function is to determine how the Bank and its communications are perceived by various segments of the public by asking members of these segments about their attitudes and feelings regarding banking, consumer spending, technology and the socio-economic situation. The information collected through this process is used to develop and properly guide the Bank's communication strategies and to assess the effectiveness of these strategies. Communication plays a crucial role in managing a company's reputation because it is the vehicle that goes the "last mile"—to use an expression from the telecom sector—between the company and the market. Communication is the final, often decisive, part of a process (i.e., the company's business). Such process not only must have solid and robust fundamentals but also must be correctly communicated to achieve its fullest effect. The role of communication is crucial in crisis management, too. The Researches and Surveys function explores the company's reputation among customers and non-customers and how this reputation is formed, by assessing: 1) direct interactions with customers at the Bank's various touch points (which include branches, website, ATMs and customer care); 2) the Bank's communications (including advertising, media presence, sponsorship and events); and 3) public opinion as expressed through various channels, including—increasingly importantly—social media. In this regard, data from the Facebook-based customer care service and dedicated periodic "social media listening" are particularly useful. Reputation also encompasses the brand and its image, which determine the extent of the clients' "emotional" connection with the brand and the products/services that it represents. A (good) reputation creates consensus around a brand; thus, client appreciation of the products/services associated with the brand plays an important role in reputation.

A brand may be ascribed either a fixed, absolute economic value or a comparative value relative to the rest of the sector (especially competitors of the brand). ISP analyses the results of external studies conducted by companies that specialize in "brand equity" and of internal studies conducted by internal functions using various calculation methods.

The Researches and Surveys function processes and re-interprets the following information to compose a portrait of the Group as seen through the eyes of public opinion: reputational data obtained through research, surveys and focus groups conducted in cooperation with leading specialist companies; data collected through a review of the most authoritative Italian and international studies in various areas of interest; and finally, data from other studies conducted by the Group.

The results based on these data are periodically presented to management and circulated around the company through a dedicated internal newsletter.

2.4 The Outcomes of Reputation Measurement

To measure the Group's image and reputation, the Researches and Surveys function collaborates with the major Italian market research companies, using both multi-client analyses and periodic, continually updated and specially commissioned research conducted by dedicated observers.

Multi-client analyses conducted independently by the research company for multiple clients have the advantage of providing an authoritative assessment of the banking system as a whole by placing all competitors on the same level. Specially commissioned research provides greater depth regarding subject areas that are of specific and direct interest to the bank, and this form of research can therefore generate relevant recommendations for the future.

Gfk Eurisko's multi-client retail banking analysis ("Multifinanziaria Retail") shows that in 2014, ISP's image among customers improved by more than that of other banks among their own customers and by triple the banking sector average, putting the Group at the top of the league table of "traditional" banks (i.e., not exclusively online).

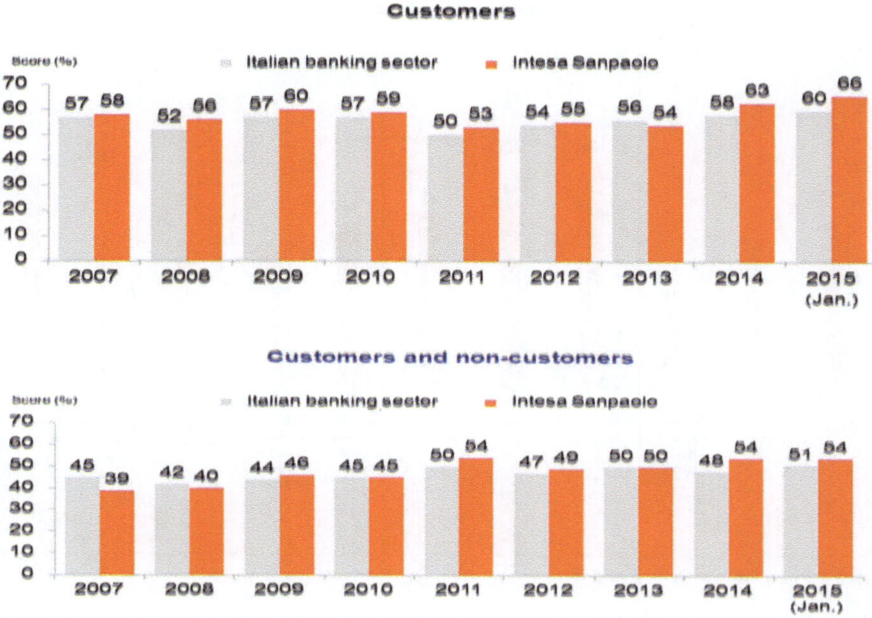

Fig. 5 Intesa Sanpaolo's image. *Source*: GFK Eurisko (2015) Multifinanziaria Retail. Document not publicly available

In addition, the Bank's image among the public in general (customers and non-customers) improved more than that of the other banks and more than the market average, albeit in the latter case the gap is lower in absolute values (Fig. 5).

This measurement was obtained by evaluating two categories of perceptions: 1) perceptions relating to objective characteristics and technical operations, such as organization, professionalism, prestige, products and services, convenience, multi-channel offering, etc.; and 2) perceptions of bank customers based on the personal relationship between the customer and the bank, such as the bank's willingness to listen, clarity and transparency, etc.

For each of these criteria, ISP achieved opinion percentages at the top of the assessment scale. In addition to these figures, Intesa Sanpaolo has for years had an Observatory focused on the Bank's image, which was created in collaboration with IPSOS.

The Observatory analysis identifies the strengths of ISP in the eyes of customers (individuals, small businesses and large companies) (Fig. 6) and shows an overall profile that is well ahead of the banking sector average.

Intesa Sanpaolo also assesses its reputation using a multi-client analysis performed annually by Doxa. The Doxa analysis is complemented by the analytical model of IPSOS, which is based on ad-hoc assessments.

The Doxa reputation analysis (Banking Reputation Monitoring 2015) is based on subjective and emotional criteria (such as credibility, trust, respect and alignment of values) and on more objective and rational criteria, such as the quality of the

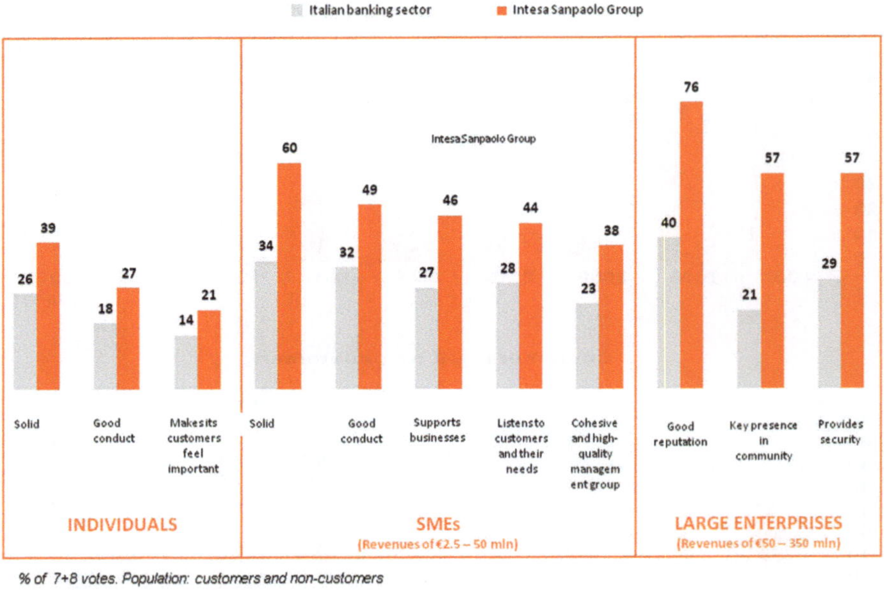

Fig. 6 Solidity, good conduct and listening: the Group's main strengths, especially among businesses. *Source*: IPSOS (2014) Osservatorio Immagine Intesa Sanpaolo. Document not publicly available

Table 1 Survey sample

Stakeholders interviewed		Total interviews by market
Mass market	Customers	2324
	Non-customers	
Affluent[a]	Customers	686
	Non-customers	
Private[b]	Customers	341
	Non-customers	
Small business	Customers	1073
	Non-customers	
Medium enterprise[c]	Customers	296
	Non-customers	
Total		4720

Source: Doxa (2015) Banking Reputation Monitoring. Document not publicly available
[a]People whose assets are not entrusted to dedicated managers
[b]People with assets in excess of 500,000 euros
[c]Companies with an annual turnover in excess of 3,000,000 euros

services offered, capacity for innovation, work environment and engagement with the community. The surveyed population includes households, small businesses, large companies and opinion leaders (Table 1).

The 2015 Doxa analysis of the banking sector shows that ISP has a better reputation than the average bank among both customers and non-customers—indeed, it is ranked first (Fig. 7).

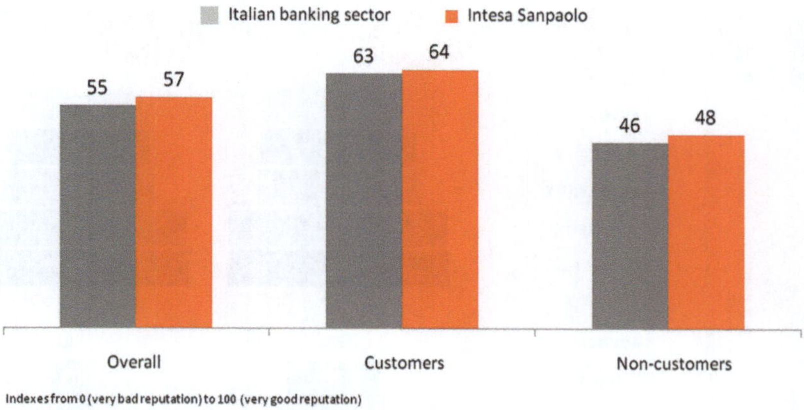

Fig. 7 Reputation. *Source*: Doxa (2015) Banking Reputation Monitoring. Document not publicly available

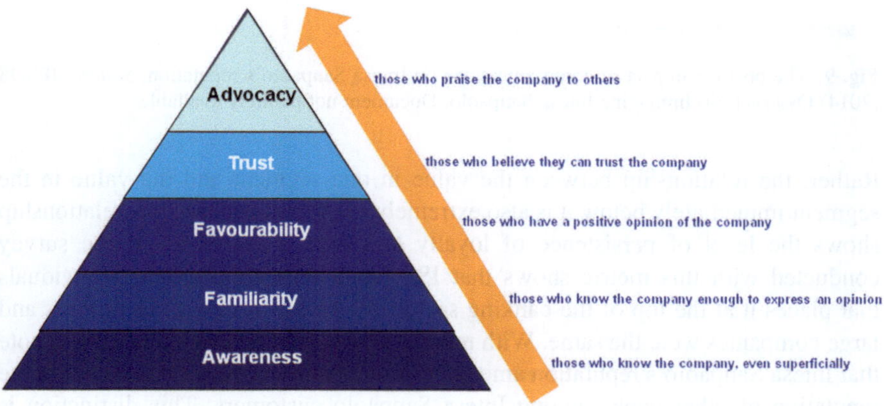

Fig. 8 The IPSOS reputation pyramid – methodology. *Source*: IPSOS (2014) Osservatorio Immagine Intesa Sanpaolo. Document not publicly available

It is interesting to note the gap between the reputation of Intesa Sanpaolo and the industry average among non-customers. Because this sample by definition does not have direct experience with the Bank, the gap must be attributed to its reputation in the market.

The research shows that ISP's good reputation has a positive influence on two aspects of consumer behaviour: 1) for customers, the inclination to stay with the bank and to recommend it to others and 2) for non-customers, the attractiveness of ISP if changing banks and the propensity to speak positively about ISP in any case.

The IPSOS model uses a scale characterized by different levels of appreciation for the Bank (Fig. 8). In ascending order, these levels are as follows: being aware of the Bank; being familiar with the Bank; having a positive opinion of the Bank; fully trusting the Bank; and the propensity to recommend the Bank to others.

Note that in this model, it is not just the absolute value of each individual segment (including the segments at the top of the pyramid) that is important.

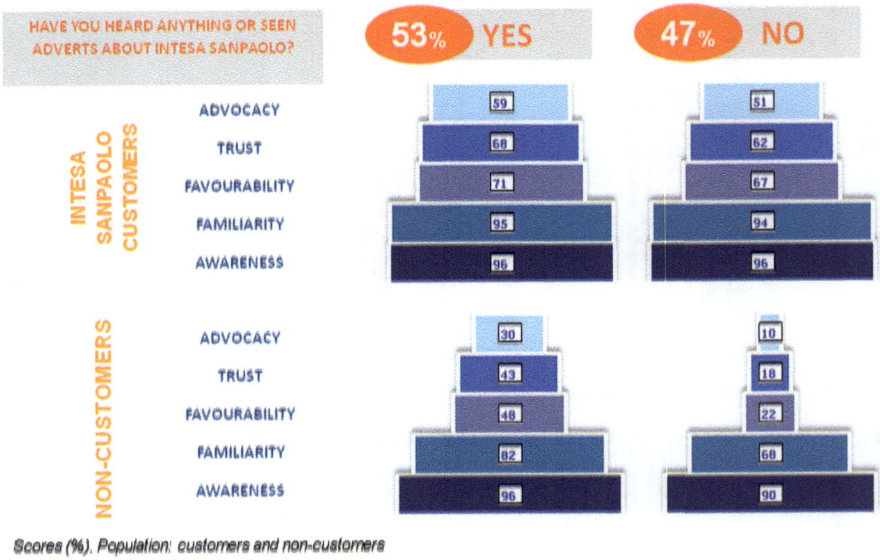

Fig. 9 The positive impact of communications on Intesa Sanpaolo's reputation. *Source*: IPSOS (2014) Osservatorio Immagine Intesa Sanpaolo. Document not publicly available

Rather, the relationship between the value in one segment and the value in the segment immediately below it is also extremely important because this relationship shows the level of persistence of loyalty and trust. The results of the survey conducted with this metric shows that ISP has a reputation among individuals that places it at the top of the banking sector; the results for small businesses and large companies were the same. With respect to individuals, it is interesting to note that Intesa Sanpaolo's reputation among customers of other banks is better than the reputation of other banks among Intesa Sanpaolo customers. This distinction is further confirmation that reputation is an important competitive advantage for ISP. The reputation pyramid model also clearly shows the value of communications in creating and maintaining reputation (Fig. 9).

Finally, it should be noted that the Researches and Surveys function of ISP has been reviewing and analysing news about the Bank in the media for a number of years.

3 The Relationship Between Corporate Social Responsibility and Reputation: A Detailed Look

3.1 ISP's Attention to Social and Environmental Issues

ISP is aware that it has a considerable impact on the social and environmental context in which it operates. It therefore perceives a responsibility to act in a manner that not only generates profit but also creates value for all stakeholders.

ISP recognizes the importance of **corporate social responsibility** as an integral part of its strategy and, based on its belief that socially and environmentally sustainable choices are also economically successful, ISP feels that it is possible to create value over time by running the business along three major trajectories—financial, social, and environmental—all of which are supported by transparent corporate governance.

Activities of ISP to support, develop and promote culture, art and learning play an important role in the various relationships between ISP and the community in which it operates.

The basis of this approach is the identification and acknowledgment of the expectations of all Bank stakeholders (see: Fig. 3). This implies a constant dialogue with stakeholders, the identification of targets for improvement, the development of initiatives to achieve these targets and, finally, the monitoring of the results according to a typical feedback process. This approach is also based on forecasting, monitoring and managing risk, including reputational risk, that emerges from the Bank's activities as well as from the activities of, e.g., customers, partners or suppliers.

Two information gathering methods in particular contribute significantly ISP's ability to monitor the attitudes of stakeholders and therefore to assess reputational risk: the Facebook-based "call centre" for customer assistance and systematic "social media listening" to collect reactions from a range of social networks.

ISP adheres to the main international initiatives to promote dialogue between companies, supranational organizations and civil society and to pursue the principles of sustainable development, respect for the environment and human rights.

3.2 The Corporate Social Responsibility Function

The task of monitoring and coordinating social responsibility issues within the Group is entrusted to a dedicated **Corporate Social Responsibility function**, which reports through the Chief Governance Officer to the Managing Director and CEO, the Chairman of the Management Board and the Chairman of the Supervisory Board.

This function collaborates with a network of liaison officers in the various structures of the Bank. These officers act as "peripheral" sensors on the subject and help to spread the culture and to promote the taking of responsibility by all company functions. Liaison officers also record the outcomes of initiatives and propose solutions to any critical situations.

The **CSR management** process is therefore a dynamic procedure that involves the entire company structure from the top management downward and entails listening, planning, implementing and monitoring. The CSR management model rests on two main pillars: the Code of Ethics and the Sustainability Report. The **Sustainability Report** records the outcomes of a CSR management process based on a virtuous cycle of engaging and listening to stakeholders, defining targets for improvement, monitoring progress through KPIs and, finally, reporting. The report is structured according to a **Materiality Matrix** that identifies the areas of greatest risk/opportunity for developing the business in a sustainable manner.

3.3 The Code of Ethics

The Code of Ethics (Fig. 10) governs and guides relationships with all stakeholders, including partners and suppliers. It was adopted in June 2007 as a **self-governance** tool that establishes voluntary commitments undertaken by the Bank in light of the expectations of various stakeholders. It is in essence a Constitutional Charter that not only guides the actions of each employee in their dealings with stakeholders according to a system of shared values but also defines the Bank and, in a sense, its identity. It is a charter of positive commitments rather than a list of behaviours to avoid.

The Code of Ethics stems from the company's mission to deliver excellence to stakeholders and to honour the pact with its stakeholders. This mission gives rise to a number of overarching values and principles, which in turn determine concrete actions, decisions, choices and working practices. Even more tangibly, the spirit of the company mission is expressed in the rules, processes, tools and products/ services of the Bank, up to and including daily Bank activities, even seemingly

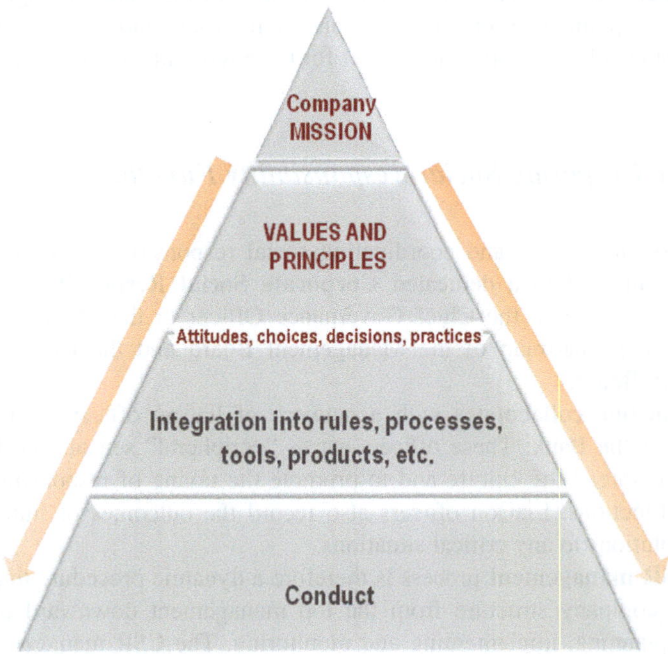

Source: Intesa Sanpaolo

Fig. 10 Code of ethics—the model

inconsequential behaviours such as switching off the light when leaving the office or using the correct recycling bins. Everything is covered by one key phrase: taking responsibility for oneself. Indeed, all company structures are encouraged to take personal responsibility at every stage of the process; there are no “commandments” issued from on high. In addition, ISP’s Code of Ethics is in line with the universal principles of the UN Global Compact on human rights, labour, the environment and combating corruption. In accordance with current laws, ISP monitors the application of its Code of Ethics through an internal control system to continuously assess the risks that could arise if the Code of Ethics is not implemented completely. Since 2014, the monitoring of operating structures and the reviews of the CSR unit has been accompanied by an annual assessment conducted by independent third-party organizations, including Bureau Veritas. Among other activities, ISP monitors the areas identified in the international standard ISO 26000 regarding the integration of social responsibility into business practices: organizational governance, human rights, protection of workers, the environment, proper management practices, customer-related issues, and the engagement and development of the community. Particular attention is paid to the subjects of money laundering and corruption, which are subjects on which all staff receive special training. The CSR presents an annual report to the Supervisory Board’s **Internal Control Committee** that addresses the implementation of the Code of Ethics, critical issues and reports from stakeholders, as well as the consequent corrective actions recommended.

3.4 The Sustainability Report

Intesa Sanpaolo’s Sustainability Report is a voluntary initiative to communicate the results of its activities on an annual basis in terms that go beyond economic and financial descriptions. The first such report was produced in 2007. The Sustainability Report can be considered a complement to the Business Plan 2014–2017, which establishes the goal of confirming Intesa Sanpaolo’s identity as the bank of the real economy that is dedicated to serving households and businesses, satisfying a healthy demand for credit and managing customers’ wealth in a responsible manner. The report is the outcome of a process centred on dialogue with stakeholders. It includes assessments of the Bank’s ability to operate in line with its stated values, thereby meeting the expectations of its stakeholders, and describes the process of identifying critical areas and how it plans to resolve them. In addition to serving as a means of communication, the Sustainability Report is a vehicle for monitoring progress and planning improvements. In preparing its Sustainability Report, Intesa Sanpaolo follows the guidelines of both the ABI (the Italian Banking Association) and the Global Reporting Initiative and in particular adheres to the international organization’s latest and most stringent standard, GRI G4. In 2013, Intesa Sanpaolo joined the London Benchmarking Group, an internationally renowned model to measure and report on a company’s contribution to the community, in terms of both the contributions made directly by the company (inputs) and the results and impacts of its investments (outputs and impact). The structure of Intesa Sanpaolo’s

Sustainability Report 2014 is also based on the framework provided by the International Integrated Reporting Council (IIRC), an international organization that aims to lead companies towards integrated reporting of economic, social and environmental aspects. Among its various recognitions, Intesa Sanpaolo has been named one of the 319 most sustainable companies in the world by the prestigious Dow Jones Sustainability Index.

3.5 *The Materiality Matrix*

The materiality matrix (Fig. 11) is an annually updated map that compares the views (expectations, requests, comments) of **stakeholders** with the key elements of the company's **business strategy**. ISP introduced this approach as far back as 2010 to establish a continuous link between stakeholder expectations and business strategy, measure any divergence between them and, if necessary, implement corrective actions.

Stakeholders' views are collected through interviews, focus groups, questionnaires, surveys and media analysis (the "stakeholder engagement" process). The CSR Unit performs these listening activities with respect to specific issues or works

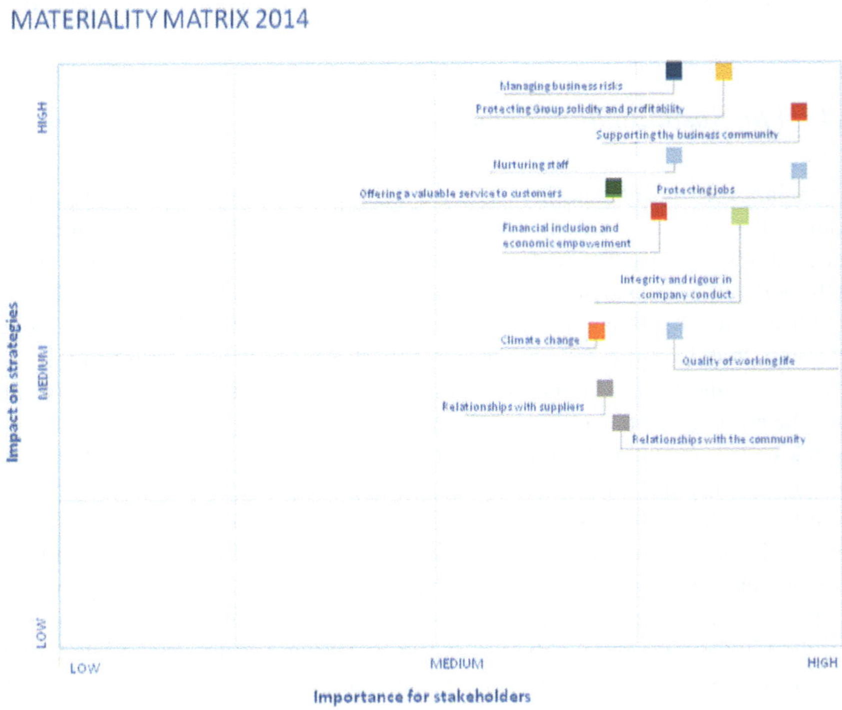

Source: Intesa Sanpaolo

Fig. 11 Materiality matrix 2014

closely with the company units responsible for stakeholder relations (e.g., Customer Satisfaction, Investor Relations, Trade Union Relations and Internal Communication).

The axis of the matrix that measures the importance of the subject areas to the business assesses the strategic goals set out in the Business Plan, public communications and other official company documents.

Cross-referencing these elements shows the areas of greatest focus, which represent a blend of business and stakeholder priorities. The results reflect the economic, social and environmental impacts of the organization and/or allow the views and decisions of stakeholders to have a substantial influence on business strategy.

Once the major areas have been identified, a **planning process** begins with the definition of targets for improvement (if necessary), execution of the relevant actions, continuous monitoring of progress, and reports and reviews of the process.

The areas identified by the materiality matrix for 2014 are:

- Protecting Group solidity and profitability (in Fig. 11, this area refers to: Protecting Group solidity and profitability)
- Managing business risks (in Fig. 11, this area refers to: Managing business risks)
- Integrity and rigor in company conduct (in Fig. 11, this area refers to: Integrity and rigor in company conduct)
- Human resource development and management (in Fig. 11, this area refers to: Protecting jobs, Nurturing staff, and Quality of working life)
- Offering a valuable service to customers (in Fig. 11, this area refers to: Offering a valuable service to customers)
- Access to credit and savings management (in Fig. 11, this area refers to: Supporting the business community and Financial inclusion and economic empowerment)
- Climate change (in Fig. 11, this area refers to: Climate change)

Relations with suppliers and the community do not qualify as material issues, but Intesa Sanpaolo recognises their high social and environmental value and therefore provides detailed disclosures on the website and in single issue notebooks.

4 Conclusions and Outlook

This Intesa Sanpaolo case study provides useful information regarding reputation and reputation management at banks. In particular, the ISP case reveals five key factors:

1) The **role of disclosure in communications with the market and customers**. The Group's reporting is based on and in line with the international requirements set out in the Global Reporting Initiative (GRI G4), which focus on materiality analysis, governance disclosure and the explicit statement of policies adopted to manage social and environmental impacts in the value chain. Note that although disclosure is a requirement for banks—consider, for example, the guidelines of the ABI

(Italian Banking Association) and the Global Reporting Initiative—it is undoubtedly an area of strength for all banks that adopt voluntary disclosures, including ISP.

2) **Dialogue with stakeholders**. At ISP, the Sustainability Report process is centred on dialogue with major stakeholders because the purpose of the report is to provide an account of the company's ability to operate in line with its stated values. In particular, the materiality matrix introduced in 2010 depicts the nexus between stakeholder expectations and company strategy, which not only shows whether the two are aligned but also (and above all) identifies any divergences and the appropriate corrective actions.
3) **Active reputation management**. A relationship of trust with customers and the markets is a primary asset of the Group, so much so that it has developed a model for the "active management" of its reputation. The values and principles of conduct that are outlined in the Code of Ethics and the Corporate Social Responsibility unit play key roles in this regard. The Code of Ethics, if viewed as a governance tool, is an integral part of ISP's approach to social and environmental responsibility, and relations with stakeholders are at its core.
4) The **connection between the concepts of Corporate Social Responsibility and Corporate Reputation**. As proof of the strong ties between the concepts of Corporate Social Responsibility (CSR) and Corporate Reputation, the CSR unit has a leading role in stakeholder dialogue, the assessment of the social, environmental, and reputational risks of bank activities and the coordination of the social and environmental reporting processes. The CSR unit supports company leadership in setting sustainability strategies and policies that are designed to generate value for stakeholders. ISP has a two-level model of reputation management: the first level is directly entrusted to individual company units and comprises "simple" defensive tasks, whereas the second level involves "comprehensive protection" that is organized through a process of "reputational risk management". In addition, the Business Plan launched by Intesa Sanpaolo for the 3-year period 2014–2017 shows the ever increasing integration of social and environmental responsibility into core business concerns.
5) **Focus on image**. The results presented in Figs. 5 and 6 show that the Group's image and perception among customers (and the public in general) have improved despite the general deterioration of trust in the banking sector stemming from the economic and financial crisis in advanced economies. However, it is among businesses that the Group achieves its best results (Fig. 6). These figures seem to confirm that the active management of ISP's image among all stakeholders is capable of preventing and containing any negative reputational effects.

The approach adopted in the Group's operations seems to be in line with the literature on the subject. The analysis of the ISP case shows that reputation management is a key element of "how to do business". Accordingly, the pursuit of sustainable profits is transmuted into the need to manage not only economic and financial variables (such as earnings, liquidity and solidity) but also variables relating to the company's environmental impact and its ability to protect the interests of people and companies. A strong reputation and initiatives to monitor and maintain this reputation are cornerstones for preserving the current and prospective profitability of ISP.

Moreover, the concepts of reputation and reputational risk seem to have fluid boundaries and have expanded to encompass new aspects such as the focus on social media and network listening. As such, continuous monitoring of reputation undoubtedly lays the foundations for reputational management in the future.

References

Doxa (2015) Banking Reputation Monitoring. Document not publicly available

GFK Eurisko (2015) Multifinanziaria Retail. Document not publicly available

IPSOS (2014) Osservatorio Immagine Intesa Sanpaolo. Document not publicly available

Cristina Laura Paltrinieri Graduated in Economics at the Cattolica University in Milan. After working for many years in Banca di Roma and Crédit Agricole, she entered Intesa Sanpaolo in 1998, where she handled the Investor Relations for a decade within the Chief Financial Officer Area. She then dealt with the Coordination of the International Communication of the Group for few years within the External Relations Department. She currently works on Researches and Market Surveys to understand the evolving scenario of communication and technology and to measure the impact of communication activities on brand image and reputation.

Daniela Fraire Gradueted in Commication Science at the University of Turin, with a specialization in advertising and communication for private enterprises. She has worked in Intesa Sanpaolo (previously Sanpaolo IMI) since 1997. After an experience as branch operator, she worked in Small Business Department, covering marketing, internal and external communication, customer management models and developing commercial and project skills. Currently, she works on research and surveys in the External Relation Department of Intesa Sanpaolo, addressing P.E.S.T. analysis, monitoring bank image and reputation analysis and evaluating the results of communication activities.

Rosella Carè received a PhD in Health Care Management and Economics from the University Magna Graecia of Catanzaro and a PhD in "Sciences de Gestion" from the Conservatoire National des Arts et Métiers of Paris in March 2014 with a dissertation that focused on the sustainability of public expenditure. During 2012 and 2013, she was a visiting PhD student at the ESCP Europe of Paris. Currently, she teaches "Problem Solving and Decision Making", "Financial Markets and Instruments", and "Economics of Financial Markets" at the University Magna Graecia of Catanzaro. Her research interests are: Social and Sustainable Finance; Impact Investing; Alternative Finance and Sustainability; Reputational risk and reputational crisis in the banking sector.

Part III
From Experience to Knowledge

Managing Reputation: Reflections and Operational Suggestions

Stefano Dell'Atti, Vincenzo Pacelli, Stefania Sylos Labini, and Annarita Trotta

Abstract Moving on from a comparison of the analysed case studies, this chapter highlights the main findings and discusses the relevant phases of reputational crisis management for banks and provides helpful suggestions and advice to scholars and practitioners. In addition, the chapter focuses on the methods and tools that are beneficial in the various phases of a reputational crisis. Finally, useful guidelines for enhancing the effectiveness of banks' reputation management are suggested.

1 Introduction

The reputation of a company has long been considered, in both the academic and professional sectors, an intangible resource of primary importance that can determine a significant improvement in financial performance over time (Weigelt and Camerer 1998; Schwaiger 2004). However, in recent years, reputation has been given further and wider support with reference to banks, as evidenced, among other factors, by the many interventions of the national and international supervisory authorities providing not only a definition of reputational risk but also an identification of its possible economic and social impact (Basel Committee on Banking Supervision 2001, 2006, 2012, 2014). The growing attention of the Supervisory Authorities with respect to the possible occurrence of reputational risks for banks is due to the recent increase in the possible sources of risk, as well as the frequency of risk in the event of reputational crisis in different financial systems. In light of the case studies analysed in this volume, this paragraph aims to draw some useful lessons by the joint vision of the several reputational crises analysed.

Although this chapter is the result of the collaboration between the authors, paragraphs 1 and 3.2 can be attributed to Stefano Dell'Atti, paragraph 2 can be attributed to Vincenzo Pacelli, paragraph 3.1 can be attributed to Stefania Sylos Labini and paragraph 4 can be attributed to Annarita Trotta.

S. Dell'Atti (✉) • V. Pacelli • S. Sylos Labini
University of Foggia, Foggia, Italy
e-mail: stefano.dellatti@unifg.it; vincenzo.pacelli@unifg.it; stefania.syloslabini@unifg.it

A. Trotta
University Magna Graecia, Catanzaro, Italy
e-mail: trotta@unicz.it

S. Dell'Atti, A. Trotta (eds.), *Managing Reputation in The Banking Industry*,
DOI 10.1007/978-3-319-28256-5_8

First of all, the joint analysis of case studies investigated in this book confirms that building a good reputation is an on-going, dynamic and multidimensional process that involves not only the management of the bank but also all its human and organizational components. In addition, the multidimensional nature of the reputation of a bank may make a bank suffer the loss of its reputation with a particular stakeholder; however, this does not have a negative effect on the bank's relations with other stakeholders. In many cases, the severity of the event may cause harmful reputational damage to spread within the bank, eroding the reputation of the bank with various stakeholders. Creating and maintaining a good reputation derive, essentially, from coherence between the signals sent by the bank to the various categories of stakeholders and its conduct over time. In other words, it is essential for a bank to realize a perfect match between the transmitted image that is perceived externally and actual behaviour. The eventual gap between these two elements can generate a negative perception by various stakeholders and, then, a potential reputational risk towards one or more counterparties. The analysis in this book therefore emphasizes the strong connection that exists between the image and the reputation of a bank. However, while the image, understood as the sum of the distinguishing characteristics of an organization, is linked to the ability to manage the short-term perceptions of its stakeholders; reputation, understood as the integration of the image with the actual behaviour of the company, is an integral part of the identity of the organization and belongs to a logic of long-term management. One aspect that instead joins the image of a bank to its reputation is the fact that both of these intangibles, especially in the financial sector, are not confined to a single enterprise, but rather have strong implications of a systemic nature, as evidenced by the reputational crises analysed in this volume. In addition to reputation at the individual level, in fact, collective reputation or the confidence in the financial system as a whole have great importance in the case of banks. Although, in fact, reputation is an intangible individual asset and its management is focused on each individual operator, the possible loss of reputation of an operator can cause negative effects for the entire economic system, creating a crisis of confidence among investors. This trust, in fact, has a systemic matrix: all depend on everyone in a financial system. In general, as the crisis of 2007 taught us, the stability of an entire economic system depends on each actor working in it.

2 A Joint Vision of Reputational Crisis: Which Lessons Can Be Drawn?

Empirical evidence also teaches us that a good reputation represents a barrier of protection essential to minimizing the negative consequences of adverse events that may affect both the company itself and the system in which it is embedded. A prime example in this regard is the case of Lehman Brothers, which, unlike other banks such as Goldman Sachs or Unicredit, failed to cope with the strong speculative pressures exerted on its own shares at the end of the summer of 2008. The analysis of the business case of Lehman Brothers seems to be a clear example of corporate crisis induced solely by progressive and rapid reputational crisis of the company in general and of its management in particular. Until the last financial year before the default, in fact, the Bank had never signed a financial loss and had solid capital ratios in line even in 2007 with the current standards imposed by Basel III. Until the weeks immediately preceding the default, the title of Lehman Brothers had ever recorded a lower volatility relative to the American financial sectorial reference index. Nothing, therefore, before the perfect storm of the summer of 2008 could have portended the crisis of Lehman Brothers, which culminated on 15 September 2008, after a few weeks of agony and vain hopes of public or private saving, with the company bankruptcy. Upon default, Lehman was the fourth US investment bank with a global operation (and then exposure) in the financial services industry. At the time of the bankruptcy, Lehman Brothers had a turnover of approximately 640 billion USD of assets (valued in the financial statements for that value), which, although of a certified rating, were of very little value in the market. In the months preceding the bankruptcy, Lehman Brothers, led by its historian CEO Dick Fuld, tried desperately to raise capital by issuing its own debt or equity securities or by selling packages more or less relevant to its shares or its assets, to recapitalize, to raise liquidity, to lower leverage ratios and to therefore reduce the risk perceived by the markets. However, these actions produced very few results because the continuing collapse of the title, which became a target of speculators and short sellers, and the very low investor confidence in the accounts of the bank had made Lehman Brothers a toxic asset that was no longer trusted. According to the market, Lehman Brothers had not correctly evaluated and devalued all the assets in the portfolio. In a climate of generalized distrust in the bank's accounts and stock, even the negative rumours more or less reliably put into circulation by competitors or short sellers found fertile ground in the investors and no longer had any effect the official statements of the Bank. The case of Lehman Brothers is a clear example of how a loss of reputation is able not only to destroy economic value but also to irremediably exclude the bank from the competitive scene, determining, in this way, final and irreparable damages.

Instead of Lehman Brothers, the cases of Goldman Sachs and Barclays teach us how it is possible to manage events that are harmful to a bank's reputation in the public's opinion, while preserving its market share and consolidating its image towards the markets and investors.

The analysis of the business case of Goldman Sachs seems, in fact, to be a clear example of how any loss of reputation in the public's opinion may not necessarily cause reputational damage towards markets. After the tsunami of 2007–2009, which affected Goldman's reputation, as well as that of other US investment banks, in fact, several unpopular events further undermined Goldman's reputation in the public's opinion. We refer to Goldman's complicity in the Greek public deficit concealment and in the AIG crisis, to the flourishing emoluments for the management in a period of general crisis, to the obscure relationship with the US government and to the inquiries of the Securities and Exchange Commission (SEC), as in the ABACUS case. These unpopular events undermined Goldman's reputation in the public's opinion but not in the markets, as Goldman Sachs has successfully faced several financial scandals, preserving and even strengthening its image of a financial unbreakable giant. Furthermore, Goldman Sachs gave the impression of emerging even stronger from the financial crisis because it predicted its arrivals, betting and making a great profit, before the others and because the financial tsunami of 2007–2009 reduced the number of its competitors, even increasing its market power.

With regard to Barclays, after the Libor turmoil, the British international bank understood the preliminary need to admit its responsibilities immediately in order to minimize the negative impact on stakeholders and the need to change its way of doing business, restructuring its reputation and focusing essentially on structural and cultural change, the resignation of people strictly related to the investigations, the sustainability of reorganization programs, new strategies of risk management and social and financial reporting.

The study of the business cases analysed in this volume also highlights how, for the purpose of building and maintaining a good reputation, preventive response actions are decisive. Reputation risk, in fact, unlike other types of financial risk, is not characterized by a minimum level of tolerability connected with the possibility of achieving a higher profit. It, however, is a type of risk that needs to be avoided because of the huge (and often difficult to manage) economic and social effects resulting from its manifestation.

The analysis of the case studies highlights how the following managerial drivers are essential for the effective prevention of a reputational crisis in the bank:

- To respect the financial equilibrium by maintaining constant adequate liquidity conditions;
- To maintain an adequate level of capitalization in line at least with the supervisory framework;
- To maintain relations with the various stakeholders and, in particular, to pay attention to the social dimension of bank activities;
- To adequately manage the potential critical issues related to corporate governance, namely, the adoption of appropriate management models aimed at making transparent the allocation of responsibilities, the implementation of processes of decision-making and risk-taking. In particular, among the main underlying causes of the reputational crisis analysed, it is not an exaggeration to claim that an important role has been assumed by the inadequacy of their governance systems, guilty of having encouraged, among other things, the development of management and remuneration policies, achieving profits in the short term (shorterism) rather than focusing on the long-term sustainability of economic performance;
- To pay attention to the compliance function, which should pursue the aim of preventing the application of legal or administrative penalties for breaches of laws and regulations or self-regulation.

In combination with the precautionary approach, another element that is essential for reducing the risk of events of reputational crisis is the corporate culture. Given the pervasiveness of reputational risk, something that makes this risk potentially originable at all levels of the organization, the presence of a recognized corporate culture that permeates across the whole structure of the bank can be a factor of prevention and mitigation of the reputational risk and thus contribute to the generation of a solid reputation. Relevant in this regard is, therefore, the role of disclosure in the processes of communication within the bank and externally in order to share their reputational drivers with the market, customers and supervisors. Corporate disclosure and, more generally, corporate communication assume significance both as means of prevention as means of managing a reputational crisis. Once a crisis reputation was has manifested and the bank has found the need to contain its adverse effects, in addition to eliminating the cause using the appropriate managerial and operational tools, the bank should, in fact, place emphasis on the processes of communication both with the market and internally. This is to make known to all stakeholders the attention given to the particular moment in the business's life, as well as taking direct responsibility, which are prerequisites in order to restore the trust compromised by the reputational event. In addition, the activation of appropriate communication processes allows banks to take an active part in the process of regaining the lost reputation rather than being passive, waiting for the general sentiment to change with the passage of time.

Unlike the management drivers active only in the presence of an endogenous reputational event, communicational drivers also assume importance in the absence of a direct responsibility of the bank. Investments in communication, in fact, can create a flow of information in which the bank is an active part and can neutralize the negative news that, for various reasons, can circulate in the system and therefore also affect the bank's reputation. In any case, so that the communicational driver really allows the lost reputation to be reconstructed, it must always be timely, transparent and truthful. These three characteristics seem essential if we re-establish the relationship of trust with all stakeholders and improve the credibility of the intermediary.

Alongside the undeniable internal responsibilities of individual banks and their management of different reputational crises that have occurred in recent years in international financial systems, for completeness of analysis, the analysis of several case studies does not allow us to ignore the external responsibilities of the financial authorities, policy makers and rating agencies, which have, among other things, variously favoured the uncontrolled development of financial engineering, which greatly increased the exposure of banks to potential damaging events of the reputational matrix.

With the help of supervisors and policy makers, in the last 15 years, the financial markets were, in fact, invaded by a flood of financial products often incomprehensible by investors and even by experts. This refers to structured and highly complex financial instruments that would not be circulated in the markets if they were not accompanied by the often-reassuring "hallmark" of the rating agencies. The rating agencies, which should play the key role of controllers and certifiers of the quality of these securities to investors, often find themselves working in conditions of conflict of interest (as often they perceive commissions for their assessment activities by the same subjects assessed) and with a budget of information and tools inadequate for accurate evaluations. However, the problem goes beyond the dubious "good faith" and expertise of the rating agencies and more generally concerns the inadequacy and ineffectiveness of the complex system of the valuation of assets traded on financial markets. This fundamental gap (lacuna) in international financial systems, which was never remedied by accounting legislation that is incomplete and inhomogeneous among countries, is amplified in the case of financial intermediaries of a high dimension, incorporating in their balance sheet activities a multitude of assets and financial products that are often complex to evaluate, generating doubts about the real value of the intermediary and therefore about its solvency. An example of this is the failure of Lehman Brothers, which, despite having a volume of activities, certified by rating, at the time of default amounting to approximately 640 billion USD, was considered by the market almost as an empty box.

By the analysis of business cases it emerges, banks have now clearly become aware of the centrality of its relational capital in determining the development of a truly sustainable competitive advantage over time. By reading social documents, in fact, the idea that the very foundation of the value's creation for a bank is given by the ability to develop stable and lasting relationships with all stakeholders, both internal and external to the organization, is increasingly shared. Establishing effective relationships of dynamic interactions with the various categories of stakeholders not only facilitates the access to the variegated information capital necessary to the efficient management of a bank but also allows the consolidation of the mechanisms of development and protection of that information capital by the same bank. Thus, continuously feeding its information and relationship capital, the bank increases its intangible heritage (in terms of trust, exclusivity, membership, an the sharing of corporate objectives) essential for obtaining the strategic and income credibility, which is the basis for the generation and dissemination of economic value over time. Therefore, the case studies analysed show us that reputation, the synthesis of all the relationships carried out by the bank and, at the same time, input for the development of new relationships, demonstrates its importance as it integrates the economic size of the company's success with its social size (Fombrun and Van Riel 1997). Moreover, the reputation's value, as a strategic asset, is increased as a result of being a resource difficult to imitate by competitors because, based on exclusive and symmetrical relationships between the company and its stakeholders, they are therefore not replicable in different contexts (Roberts and Dowling 2002).

3 The Manifestation of Reputational Crisis: Organizational and Managerial Implications

The present paragraph intends to explore the changes at the organizational and management levels of financial intermediaries after there has been a reputational crisis. It is a still underdeveloped trend, unexplored certainly more than the subject of the management of the potential reputational risk (Antonicelli 2009). The analysis is conducted from a dual perspective: it starts from the examination of the process of management of reputational crisis before moving to a deepening of the functions involved.

3.1 The Process of Reputational Crisis Management

The first aspect to clarify is the distinction between the definitions of simple reputational risk and reputational crisis. The crisis is characterized by the effect of surprise, urgency of intervention, external pressures from the media, social networks and opinion leaders and, finally, by a strong potential for damage in terms of image and reputation (ABI work group 2010). These are the characteristics that make it necessary to establish a unit of reputational crisis management within the larger process of reputational risk management that occurs through the activation of a predetermined reputational crisis plan.[1] An adequate reputational risk management process should contemplate a dual strategy: the first of the ordinary type, tasked with the mitigation and elimination, where possible, of sources of reputational risk, the second of the extraordinary type aimed at the management of a full-blown crisis. The objective of ordinary management is therefore to minimize reputational risk, while the objective of extraordinary management is to minimize reputational damage when the risk event has already occurred and, then, the construction of a new reputation. The ordinary management process involves the identification of types of risk and the estimation of the impact that could result from their manifestation. It includes a whole series of preventive activities such as, for example, control over the processes most exposed to reputational risks, staff training, the establishment of committees for the quality that attempts to verify the membership and sharing of behavioural codes and quality standards, the monitoring of complaints, and the study of customers' perceptions.

The following considerations relate to the second type of strategy, which is the central object of this paragraph. The aspect that should not be ignored is that it is a structured process that would allow the bank to implement systematically all necessary measures to cope with a crisis when it occurs. Timeliness of answers is crucial in order to limit the damage resulting from the crisis. You cannot risk that the passage of time exacerbate the effects on those involved and/or on the bank

[1] Like other 'contingency plans', the reputational crisis plan is a document that identifies within it more or less detailed guidelines for the actions that each of the parties that must execute the plan must implement upon the occurrence of a risk event. It is a planning tool fundamental to the management process of reputational risk, whose contents range from defining notions to the subjects and skills that should be involved, depending on the different types of risk events and, finally, to the actions to be taken.

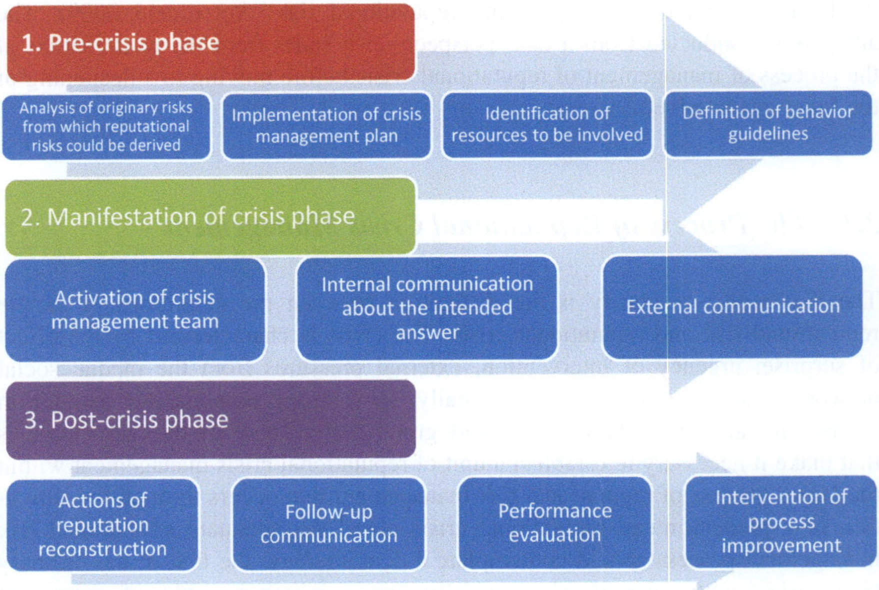

Source: own elaboration

Fig. 1 The reputational crisis management process

itself. A process of reputational crisis management can be marked temporally into three phases: the first phase is the pre-crisis phase; the second phase is the manifestation and acute phase of the crisis; the third phase is the post-crisis phase, after the acute phase is over. Each phase involves the implementation of different activities. The Figure 1 summarizes the different phases and sub-phases of the process.

In the pre-crisis phase, a definition of crisis that is more detailed than the one previously known must be created and made known to all levels of the organization involved in the process. Each bank will have a different definition of crisis according to the type of organization, market and channel in which it operates and the characteristics of the stakeholders with which it relates. In this phase, it is appropriate to distinguish between three different types of crises: a reputational crisis confined to a specific area that we can define as 'isolated', a general crisis that involves the entire bank and a systemic crisis that concerns all companies belonging to the sector or that have taken a common position or have adopted the same conduct. It must be determined in advance the level of gravity that should be reached to call upon the intervention of the Crisis Committee.

Second, an emergency plan must be defined, and it must contain the necessary information to be able to react immediately. This means identifying the issues to be presided in the case of a manifestation of a crisis; the key roles responsible for each aspect within the bank; subjects external to the bank, for example, those active in communication and in consultation and their contacts. In this way, banks should shorten the activation times of the process.

Third, the management team for a reputational crisis must be identified. Organizational choices can be variegated: one can assume an independent organizational unit dedicated to the management of reputational risk and crises; a second solution is to entrust the existing structures that address other risks in the task of monitoring the reputational risks; a specific nucleus of reputational crisis management can also enter into the process of crisis management. Depending on whether it is an isolated or a generalized crisis, the possibility to insert into the team people specialized in certain areas—those affected by the crisis—rather than enlarging the number of parties involved can be expected. Regardless of the organizational solution chosen, it is important that the 'crisis committee' is composed of figures with decision-making power appropriate to take action on a cross-strategy for the control and management of the crisis. The resources involved are numerous, and a team's skills must be equally variegated. It is important to assign the leadership of the team to a figure recognizable by the public who portrays the uniqueness of the answer implemented by the bank. The chosen organizational solution will consider clearly the size and complexity of the financial intermediary in accordance with the principle of proportionality.

Among the skills required by the figures involved in the team are the ability to exactly identify the causes that led to the crisis, the ability to make decisions quickly with little available information, the ability to address the media and the ability to work with people other than those with whom they normally work.

After setting up the organizational structure assigned to manage the reputational crisis, the lines of conduct must be defined to be consistent with the values underpinning the company culture, the so-called 'rules of intervention'.

After the moment the crisis occurs, in the second phase, the bank must react in the shortest time possible. This is the real stage of 'crisis management' in which the bank must conduct a dynamic management of action-reaction mitigation of reputational damage. In essence, the bank must be able to react quickly in response to every action of the stakeholders involved, being able, therefore, to study the moves of the "enemy" and to develop the most appropriate countermoves.[2]

The first step is to identify the nature and severity of the risk. The severity of the crisis increases with the number of persons directly affected by the event and the amounts involved—the loss to the bank or the pecuniary damage to customers—. The main sign of the severity of the crisis is the information spread by the media, which places the event in the public domain. Any repetition of the event, the start of actions in civil or criminal proceedings against the bank or its representatives and the imposition of sanctions by the supervisory authorities are factors that heighten

[2] In case of crisis of maximum severity, the Committee may be called upon to intervene, even within 24 h after the event. The use of technology, including the use of technical tools such as video-conferencing systems and/or the Wi-Fi/GSM can increase the performance of the committee in terms of efficiency and enhance their availability.

the degree of criticality of the crisis. Once the type of risk is identified clearly, the bank should publicly acknowledge its mistake. To this end, the use of social media can be an immediate and appropriate instrument if used in the proper way. While technological innovation and the increasing use of digital communication techniques for banks amplify the damage arising from the event of reputational risks, giving visibility to facts and events to a wide audience of individuals, it is also true that these techniques represent a useful means of defence for the banks themselves. Social media, if used well, in fact, constitute a strategic tool through which a bank can remedy the present crisis of reputation. Providing answers through social media is certainly better than not providing any answer, as it demonstrates the willingness of the bank to initiate an open and honest dialogue with its stakeholders (Cafarotti 2012).[3]

After the admission of guilt, which always occurs during the second phase of the process, the main managerial and organizational interventions put in place by the bank's management are implemented. This phase then can be identified as of 'reputation repairing', during which investigations are conducted and corrective actions, actions for compensation and internal restructurings are realized.

Although it is not possible to draw up an exhaustive list of measures to be implemented because they are closely related to the specific individual event of reputational crisis, its nature and the causes that determine it, as well as the strategic choices of each financial intermediary, it is, however, considered useful to recall some of the activities that are most popular and tested in practice.

First, among these, includes the replacement of the subjects that have been found guilty of legally or ethically questionable conduct.

A frequent hypothesis is that of fraud committed by an employee. In that case, it goes without saying that the bank should arrange the immediate dismissal of the responsible party and report it to the police, as well as communicating it to the print media when it becomes necessary. There is, in fact, every reason to intervene. An example is the scandal that involved Société Général in 2008, which was hit by a loss of approximately 5 billion euro because of ill-considered transactions in derivatives at the hands of a trader, Jerome Kervier. The chairman of Société Générale, Daniel Bouton, promptly dismissed the trader and filed a complaint against him. After announcing the loss, the bank's president apologized to shareholders and submitted his resignation, which was, however, rejected by the board (Dell'Atti et al. 2012a, b).

A different hypothesis is one in which behaviours that are not only 'ethically' but also 'legally' questionable are realized. In this hypothesis, it may be more difficult to conduct assessments regarding the most appropriate actions to be taken. Although lacking legal assumptions, depending on the severity of the cases, it

[3] If resorting to social media, one needs to pay attention to the language used because it is specific and differs from other traditional communication tools. It is particularly important to identify the persons whose opinion can influence a large number of people (e.g., experts in the area) and monitor their behavior. In this phase, the communication department of the bank plays a central role.

may be particularly appropriate to decide to dismiss the staff who is guilty of the affair. Even in this case, the bank can move away from the behaviour of single individual, denounce it to the authorities and inform the press, up to the implementation of extraordinary solutions regarding corporate governance, which, to a certain extend, lead to mergers and acquisition or the replacement of directors. Simply the criticality of the role of managers to represent and embody the company requires strong and responsible reactions by the company when they are guilty of ethically and legally unsuitable conduct. This also applies to the internal personnel, but with the exception that these are people who are not custodians of strong responsibility attributed to top management, even when the management extraneous to the fact is still guilty of not checking and therefore for failing to prevent the event from occurring. A familiar example of change management is represented by Italease, which was hit by a serious reputational crisis in 2007. The bank, after inspection by the Bank of Italy, put into place a series of measures, some of which were directly requested by the Supervisory Authority and others hired independently. In both cases, the actions taken were of great importance, united by the need to recover the bank's lost reputation and restore a relationship of trust with all stakeholders. The bank then appointed new directors and auditors and defined a new organizational model consisting of five different departments, aimed at maximizing the centralization of control in the Chief Executive Officer.

The manifestation of a reputational crisis often undermines the confidence of customers and other stakeholders in the bank, as well as questioning the principles and orientations on which it bases its business. It can be necessary to revise and reaffirm the value system of the bank and declare and make public the new scale of values.

Sometimes, overcoming the crisis occurs through policy change management interventions, such as the diversification of the brands made by the spin-off of the business unit involved in the scandal. When the damages are more limited, banks can resort to more targeted measures. For example, if the reputational crisis stems from the sale of a financial product that has caused pecuniary damage to the customers and for which the involvement of the bank is obvious and the fault of the bank recognized, one can intervene by withdrawing the product. This kind of action has strong signalling value marks and would certainly be appreciated by the market. In this regard, one can cite the BBVA case. During the financial crisis that erupted in 2007, BBVA, like other banks, possessed investment products with underlying Lehman securities or shares. While most financial intermediaries had assumed responsibility by merely replacing products whose value was reset with synthetic products developed ad hoc with much longer maturity and smaller returns, BBVA offered its retail customers a choice between a refund for cash and replacement with other products (Maino and Zaini 2011). Thus, BBVA has proven to its customers an increasingly high sense of responsibility for its credibility and its reputation level in the worst period of the crisis. An ad hoc advertising campaign on this initiative helped to strengthen the bank's reputation. This example demonstrates how a good management strategy, accompanied by proper communication systems, can turn an error into an advantage.

A further example of remedial action is represented by interventions of remuneration policies and incentive changes.

A policy that is oriented toward the containment and reduction of remuneration and incentive systems of the managers is certainly always appreciated by the audience. This is especially true when it represents a voluntary choice by the bank and is not imposed by supervisory authorities or subsequent to a scandal that concerns the remuneration policies themselves. It is very different; in fact, it is a reflection of the effect a remedial action can have on the reputation of a bank, depending on whether it arises from an intervention of the supervisory authority, rather than a representation of an action implemented by the company independently. In the second case, the reflection will certainly be more positive with respect to the first hypothesis. For instance, the scaling of the salaries, bonuses and benefits of managers in striking cases such as JP Morgan and Citigroup, was implemented only after serious scandals and was perceived as a 'choice' in an obliged sense and an inevitable action to put in place for the survival of the institution. JP Morgan cut salaries for four former executives involved in a deficit of several billion dollars recorded in 2012. In the Citigroup case, shareholders opposed the remuneration policy proposed, voting against salaries for managers because they were considered too high compared with the performance of the company. In both cases, the public perception with respect to these interventions was that they were remedial actions. A bank that has been guilty of having bestowed 'gold' salaries on its managers must make the necessary adjustments and change its remuneration policy. When, however, the occurrence of an event affecting the reputation and then the trust that the public places in the bank does not relate directly to remuneration but consequently involves a decrease in income or a loss of economic value of the company, it is still necessary to intervene with actions that restore profitability. In these conditions, a cut in executive pay or an intervention on managers' bonuses could represent a strategic choice and become even more agreeable to stakeholders. An intervention in this direction would have two effects: the first is remedial action, as it could have a positive impact on future profitability; the second is an improvement of the reputation of the bank. Restraining executive pay is a positive signal that affirms the willingness of the bank to safeguard the assets of the company. The perception from the outside would surely be very favourable. Being a recent issue of great interest, an intervention in this direction could enjoy a great media impact and have a positive impact in terms of regaining the confidence of stakeholders. The rigor adopted in the implementation of the intervention activities depends on the understanding that directors and top management have of the importance of the problem (Gabbi 2005).[4]

---

[4] The previously cited Société Général case is emblematic of the great opportunity that can derivate from reputational crisis of a certain relevance to the banks that are able to acknowledge their own limits and own deficiencies and to remedy them. In the case of fraud committed by the trader Jerome Kervier, it is amazing that a single entity without full power could operate without authorization, bypassing the control system of a bank, and that other colleagues acted in the same way, albeit at a lower level, according to the declaration of the trader. This testifies to serious

In the third phase, post-crisis, which coincides with the return to a normal situation in which the interest of the public and the media fades, some reputation recovery actions taken at the height of the crisis should be continued, and monitoring activity must be initiated. The effectiveness of the process of crisis management—which occurred in the previous phase—affects the time required to restore the original level of reputation enjoyed by the bank before the negative event occurs. Moreover, it would be highly inappropriate to interrupt communication with all stakeholders involved in the crisis, who, however, expect to receive the information promised to them during the manifestation of the crisis. It is therefore necessary to update stakeholders on the progress of the actions taken to combat the crisis.

In addition, the beginning of a crisis highlights a risk that has not been properly evaluated and managed ex ante in order to reduce the probability of occurrence. This means that the ordinary process of management has failed and that it is necessary to make corrections for the future. In this last phase, it is also crucial to assess the performance of the unit that handled the reputational crisis. In particular, the evaluation would concern both the people who have been part of the team and the effectiveness of the tools and actions taken. In this way, the bank can see the weaknesses of the strategies implemented and improve them and will be able to better focus the training activities addressed to the staff.

The manifestation of a crisis may highlight that the reputation enjoyed by a bank is different from the real situation. The objective of the bank should be to correctly assess the gap and cancel it, ensuring the independence of deputy bodies from reputation and correlated risk management (Cafarotti 2011). This is often hindered by an attitude of resistance by management that does not want to acknowledge the real worst performance compared with the reputation achieved and thus tends to have an optimistic view that deviates from reality. Such circumstances should push the organization to enhance its performance, but this is not always possible to achieve.

Another aspect to be considered as part of the evaluation of the crisis management is represented by the direct and indirect costs incurred to recover the reputation 'lost' or 'compromised'. Over time, the bank should aim for the restraint and the compression of these costs without affecting the effectiveness of the management process.

3.2 *The Organizational Aspects*

Moving on to examining what resources are available within the organization to be involved in the process of reputational crisis management and what skills should be

deficiencies in the organizational structure of the bank, in the information system and in staff recruitment (Bianchi 2008), as well as the urgency of conducting a structural revision.

possessed, we cannot be exempt from a general consideration of the connection existing between reputational risk and human factors that are undeniably and widely accepted in the literature concept. Although the technological factor greatly affects and changes the balance of the different components (number of resources, skills and knowledge requested, etc.) over time, the quality of the operators in terms of competence and capacity remains a key variable on which the reputation of the bank rests (Gabbi and Matthias 2009).

The departments involved in the front line to address a reputational crisis, in addition to the top management, include risk management, the compliance function, internal auditing, the communication area and the area of human resources. Other operating functions that are directly affected by the event are added from time to time.

The top management is responsible for the effectiveness of self-regulation and helps to strengthen it with consistent behaviours or to weaken it with choices and behaviours in contrast with the stated values (Zaini 2009). Through effective self-regulation, banks should mitigate the reputational risk arising from people's inappropriate behaviour. The definition of a system of values shared by senior management and all levels of the organization inspired by the principles of ethics and fairness would limit the occurrence of ethically or legally questionable conduct. In the moment in which a reputational crisis occurs, the definition of these values has not found its optimal manifestation, or the structure was not sufficiently empowered. Therefore, the self-regulation system must be revised, or the process of involvement of the people working inside the bank needs to be improved.

To this end, the role of the compliance function that operates as an internal defence to ensure the respect and implementation of the principles of self-regulation is crucial. The involvement of the compliance function is justified by the same definition of reputational risk. Reputational risk is, in fact, one of the two components of the risk of non-compliance with operational risk (D'Apolito 2008; Limentani and Tresoldi 2012). The compliance function then plays an active part in the activities of implementing the reputational risk-management process and its progressive refinement (Limentani and Tresoldi 2012). It follows that within the compliance function reside the knowledge and skills necessary to provide assistance and aid to both the top management and other departments involved in the management of reputational crisis. It is also the hub for safeguarding the culture of the bank, and it performs a central role in compelling the management towards greater ethicality.

The internal audit function, together with the compliance function, contribute to the formation and consolidation of reputation. Internal auditing, as a control function of the third level, also has the task of verifying that the compliance function performs all the tasks entrusted to it. Internal auditing must test, for example, that the compliance function has correctly reported to senior management regarding the evaluation of reputational risk. It must also ensure the smooth running of the evolution of risks.

The function of risk management is instead to serve as the repository of the necessary knowledge and skills in the field of risk management and quantification in order to evaluate the nature and severity of the risky event that occurs.

The communication area has the task of identifying the means, the language, and the best means through which to transmit the message that the company intends to send to the public in response to the event of a reputational crisis.

Finally, the area of human resources intervenes in redesigning the organizational chart and in reviewing roles and responsibilities. This intervention is necessary in the event that it is necessary to replace personnel who have been involved in the event detrimental to the bank to improve processes in which gaps and malfunctions have emerged. This function is called to support the top management in the possible revision of the remuneration policies and staff incentives.

The intervention of other operational areas is closely linked to the nature of the event that generated the reputational crisis. For example, if the damaging event concerns the trading of securities, in the process of crisis management, the finance area of the bank will certainly be involved. If the crisis is the result of an event regarding a financial instrument (a rate structure unfavourable to customers or disadvantageous to customers), the credit area will be involved. In the case of malfunctions, delays or omissions due to problems in computer systems, the intervention of the IT area of the bank will be appropriate.

The framework described shows some final considerations that affect primarily the versatility of the reputational crisis management process: the many and varied skills that need to be involved require accuracy and a high capacity of coordination and collaboration in the choice of the team of resources to be activated; the efficiency and good performance in managing the crisis depend largely on the level of education and awareness of reputation that permeates the entire company. A crucial element resides in the capability and level of professionalism of the human resources involved, whereby the adoption of internal policies for staff training also becomes crucial for the proper management of the relationship with stakeholders. The large number of determinant variables for the purpose of protecting the reputation of a bank makes the process aimed at the construction, ex ante, and re-building, ex post (after the crisis), complex. This should not discourage operators, but rather urge them to do better.

In fact, a reputational crisis, if well handled, can be an opportunity for reflection by the top management and act as a real incentive to improve. In this sense, a moment of difficulty can even result in opportunities for growth and renewal by the bank.

4 Guidelines for Enhancing the Effectiveness of Bank Reputation Management

We have investigated the theories and practices of bank reputation and the reputational crisis in banking industry. Our analysis suggests that a bank's reputation is a precious intangible asset and emphasizes the need to preserve it.

Accordingly, reputational crisis management for banks is an issue of critical importance.

Because of the significant ecosystem changes and increasingly strict regulation and enforcement of the rules of conduct, banks must pay close attention to reputation, reputational risk and potential reputational crises, which are characterized by specific features and peculiarities ad hoc. In particular, reputational crisis management should adopt a very flexible approach (ABI 2010) due to the uncertainty surrounding the various determinants and effects of reputational crisis phenomena. For this reason, reputational crises can vary from case to case (and from time to time).

A flexible process of reputational crisis management must be developed by each bank based on that bank's history and specific characteristics. The reputational crisis management approach essentially comprises three phases. The first phase—which we call the "routine" phase—requires the development of a set of actions to build and enhance reputational value. During this phase, the bank should pay attention to stakeholder groups. In addition, it is essential to identify the most important determinants of reputation and the drivers of reputational risk. Stakeholder relationships must be enhanced by building customer satisfaction and trust. In this phase, best practices, processes, protocols and plans suggested by academics, practitioners and supervisory authorities can support top management in developing a plan of action to manage reputation. It is essential that this process involves all departments and functions in the organization.

If the primary goal is to avoid reputational crises through an effective process of reputational risk management, the second goal is to strengthen the value of the bank's reputation as an intangible asset. In addition, it is useful at this stage to monitor reputational indices and reputational alarm variables. Our Model (see Chap. 1) contributes information about these indices and variables.

Communication strategies are particularly important to the construction and preservation of a bank's reputation. However, in practice, determination of the most efficient mix of methods and tools of communication is complicated and depends on relationships with each specific group of stakeholders. Voluntary disclosure by banks through official reports and formal and informal means of communication (including websites and/or social media) strengthens the bank's relationships with stakeholders and enhances the trust between them.

The case studies analysis presented in this book contributes to the identification of several key success factors in the reputation management process, including communication strategies. In particular, the cases of Intesa Sanpaolo (ISP) and Unicredit indicate that an active reputational management process should focus on communication to and dialogue with stakeholders. The ISP case study underlines the links between reputation management and CSR. Additionally, the Unicredit case shows the relevance of developing reputation through the use of new channels such as social networks. Both cases highlight the importance of measuring reputation.

Many banks attach great importance to reputation and social responsibility. Such banks use advanced models to manage reputational risk and have established special business units dedicated to the issue of reputation. Nonetheless, there remain numerous banks that should pay significantly more attention to the issue of reputation as it relates to the need to adapt capital according to the new supervisory rules.

Other cases suggest that the reputational crises have prompted banks to place much greater importance on the risk and impact of reputational damage. The lessons learnt highlight the critical importance of a flexible and monitored reputational crisis management process.

In the first phase of such processes, a bank must consolidate its reputation in the market over time; it is essential that the bank spreads the economic value generated internally (by the firm) by adopting appropriate communication tools. Note that communication processes can also backfire and destroy value if they unintentionally convey negative information that damages the company's image. Thus, it is clear that reputation is mediated by communication and that the two concepts are inextricably linked (Gabbi 2004). Established reputational capital can be helpful in situations of reputational crisis. Scholars and practitioners have previously discussed if and when a favourable pre-crisis reputation can protect a company from reputational damages (Coombs and Holladay 2006; Romenti 2006).

A timely and well-thought-out communication process is crucial in the second phase, which begins when a reputational crisis has occurred. We call this phase the "storm" phase.

Regarding the storm phase, scholars emphasize that the final impact (in terms of both economic and non-economic losses) depends on complex interactions of several factors, including the initial level of the bank's reputation, the event that triggered the reputational crisis, management's response to the crisis and stakeholders' reaction to the crisis.

Therefore, the focus during this phase is on solving problems quickly. Communication strategies must be implemented to influence stakeholders' perceptions (Coombs 1999). Several studies identify different types of reputation repair actions and communicative strategies aimed at minimizing the severity of reputational damage and at restoring firm reputation (Benoit 1997; Coombs 1995, 1999; Coombs and Holladay 2002; Sims 2009; Burke et al. 2011; Barnett and Pollock 2012).

An increased focus by stakeholders on the ethical responsibilities of a company during a crisis is evident in extant studies. Stakeholder perception that a bank has a higher level of responsibility requires a more vigorous response. In addition, stronger efforts to achieve change and accommodation are essential to influencing stakeholder perceptions (Benoit 1995; Coombs and Holladay 2002; Coombs 2007).

At this stage, the communication must focus clearly on the implementation of appropriate steps to repair and manage this exceptional situation.

At this stage, the main goal is to promptly and effectively implement a set of actions that will convince stakeholders of the bank's trustworthiness and that the crisis will not recur in the future, thereby minimizing the reputational damage (Stephens et al. 2005). The Barclays case study notes that the company's awareness of the need for effective change and its implementation of several corrective actions after a prompt admission of responsibility was the best possible response to this reputational crisis.

To be effective, actions to recover reputation must be targeted and designed based on the expectations and specific needs of every category of stakeholders. It is not improper to assume that reputational drivers that are effective for certain stakeholders may be ineffective for others. Therefore, when a bank intervenes in a crisis because its reputation has suffered a significant loss of value, it must necessarily adopt a differentiated approach that considers the various stakeholders, the appropriate tools, the timing of the intervention, the degree of articulation and the incisiveness of the actions to be undertaken (Walker and Dyck 2014).

The third phase encompasses post-crisis actions, which aim to continue the reputation repair activities and to facilitate the gradual return to normality. The major goal of this phase—which we call "post-collapse"—is to restore the bank's damaged reputation by convincing stakeholders that the bank deserves another chance. This phase has two major purposes: to determine how much the bank should invest in reputational capital and to take corrective actions. Achieving these goals enhances the results of steps taken during the first phase of reputational crisis management. Indeed, a reputational crisis should be a learning experience (Coombs 2006, 2007). Reputation repair activities may continue to be improved in ways that promise to increase awareness and efficiency. Note that the third phase will not occur in cases in which the reputational damages are so severe that they cause the bank to fail.

The duration of the third phase and the appropriate response depend on the extent of reputational damage, which can range from minimal to extremely serious. The virtue (or moral character) and "ethos" of the company may affect its ability to repair its reputation, especially in the post-crisis management phase (Shanahan and Seele 2015). Accordingly, it would seem reasonable to attribute a significant role to the complex linkages between ethics and reputation. As stated by Shanahan and Seele (2015:47): "being short on ethos can not only cause an ethical crisis and reputational damage, it can have a material impact on a corporation's ability to recover from reputational damage".

Analysis of these three phases reveals a number of similarities and differences that merit consideration. The main aspects of each phase of the reputational crisis management process (i.e., name, maxim, questions, core activities and pillars) are summarized in Table 1.

Table 1 Guidelines for a reputational crisis management process

	Phase I	Phase II	Phase III
Name	Routine	The storm	Post-collapse
Maxim	Prevention is better than cure	How we react to events is more important than the events themselves	It will not happen again; give me another chance
Key-questions	*How to build and improve the Bank's reputation?*	*How to respond to the reputational crisis?*	*How to rebuild lost or damaged reputation?*
Core activities	– Identify relevant stakeholders – Build and improve reputation – Monitor: drivers of reputational risk; reputational indices; reputational alarm variables – Design a plan	– Understand the reputational crisis – Search for solutions – Decide on a set of actions, line of conduct and style of responsiveness – Conduct reputation repair activities	– Restore the damaged reputation by implementing reputation repair activities – Invest in reputational capital – Learn from the crisis
Pillars	• Excellent relationships with stakeholders • Effective communication strategies • Bank behaviour based on ethics, values and responsibility		

Source: Our elaboration

The process of reputational crisis management–which in the view adopted here appears strictly interrelated to the process of reputation management—aims to build, protect and repair reputation, and the goals of this process must be linked to corporate strategy. Each phase focuses on specific goals. The activities that characterize the first phase could be integrated into a risk management process and improved over time. As stated by Helm (2011:17), reputational goals must be linked to corporate strategy. The second and third phases are temporary phases in the long-term process of reputation management. Therefore, the respective durations of these phases depend on the time required for complete recovery and a return to normality. In the second and third phases, banks may strive to implement effective reputation repair activities based on in-depth analyses of the causes of the immediate reputational crisis. In this context, the bank recognizes the problem, searches for solutions and responds accordingly (Rhee and Kim 2012).

The bank must pay attention to ethics and values and to the design, implementation and communication of the rules of conduct. Ethics, values and responsibility are the first pillar of the management process of the reputational crisis. Public relations and communications play a keyrole in reputation management (Fombrun 2012; Doorley and Garcia 2011). Indeed, the communication process is another main pillar of the reputational crisis management process; however, the process differs at different stages. Additionally, transparency and truthfulness are key components of communications with stakeholders (Gainess-Ross 2008). It is important to note that stakeholder relationships are the basis for the success of the reputational crisis management.

Finally, it should be noted that social media have posed new challenges, opportunities and threats to reputational crisis communications (Phillips and Young 2009). This issue is just one of the priorities on the research agendas for reputation repair (Rhee and Hadwick 2011) and reputation management.

In the banking literature, the bodies of research discussed above are a work in progress. We hope that our book not only serves as a compass for understanding this complex and multidisciplinary field of research but also inspires more discussions to develop the stream of inquiry regarding reputational crisis management.

References

ABI Gruppo di Lavoro sulla Funzione Compliance (2010) Reputational crisis management: a proposal. Bancaria 9:58–64

Antonicelli MA (2009) La gestione del rischio di reputazione nelle banche. MK 5

Barnett ML, Pollock TG (eds) (2012) The Oxford handbook of corporate reputation. Oxford University Press, Oxford

BCBS—Basel Committee on Banking Supervision (2001) Customer due diligence for banks. October

BCBS—Basel Committee on Banking Supervision (2006) International convergence of capital measurement and capital standards. June

BCBS—Basel Committee on Banking Supervision (2012) Core principles for effective banking supervision. September

BCBS—Basel Committee on Banking Supervision (2014) Consultative document Guidelines Corporate governance principles for banks. October

Benoit WL (1995) Accounts, excuses and apologies: a theory of image restoration strategies. State University of New York Press, Albany, NY

Benoit WL (1997) Image repair discourse and crisis communication. Pub Rel Rev 23(2):177–180

Bianchi T (2008) Il caso Société Générale. Bancaria 1

Burke RJ, Martin G, Cooper CL (eds) (2011) Corporate reputation. Managing opportunities and threats. Gower Publishing Limited, Farnham, UK

Cafarotti R (2011) La reputazione aziendale: modelli di gestione. Speech at the ABI Conference – Compliance in banks 2011. Stato dell'arte e prospettive di evoluzione, Rome, 10–11 November

Cafarotti R (2012) Social media e rischio reputazionale: pericolo o opportunità. MK 4

Coombs WT (1995) Choosing the right words: the development of guidelines for the selection of the "appropriate" response strategies. Manage Comm Quart 8(4):447–475

Coombs WT (1999) Ongoing crisis communication: planning, managing and responding. Sage, Thousand Oaks, CA

Coombs WT (2006) Code red in the boardroom: crisis management as organizational DNA. Praeger, Westport, CN

Coombs WT (2007) Ongoing crisis communication: planning, Managing and responding. Sage, Los Angels, CA

Coombs WT, Holladay SJ (2002) Helping crisis managers protect reputational assets. Manage Comm Quart 16(2):165–186

Coombs WT, Holladay SJ (2006) Halo or reputational capital: reputation and crisis management. J Comm Manage 10(2):123–137

D'Apolito E (2008) Il rischio reputazionale in banca: valutazione e controllo. Edizioni Scientiche Italiane, Napoli

Dell'Atti S, Iannuzzi A, Pacelli V (2012a) La gestione del rischio di reputazione nelle banche. In: Dell'Atti S (ed) Le risorse invisibili negli intermediari finanziari. Edizioni Scientifiche Italiane – ESI, Napoli

Dell'Atti S, Iannuzzi A, Cavallaro G, Trotta A (2012b) Understanding reputational crisis: evidence from the European banking sector. J Mod Account Audit 8(2):247–266

Doorley J, Garcia HF (2011) Reputation management. The key to successful public relations and corporate communications. Routledge, London

Fombrun CJ (2012) The building blocks of corporate reputation: definitions, antecedents, consequences. In: Barnett ML, Pollock TG (eds) The Oxford handbook of corporate reputation. Oxford University Press, Oxford, pp 94–113

Fombrun CJ, Van Riel CBM (1997) The reputational landscape. Corp Rep Rev 1(1-2):5–13

Gabbi G (2004) Definizione, misurazione e gestione del rischio reputazionale degli intermediari bancari. Banca Impr Soc 1:51–78

Gabbi G (2005) Il rischio operativo e il rischio reputazionale. Una possibile integrazione. In: Gabbi G, Marsella M, Massacesi M (eds) Il rischio operativo nelle banche. Aspetti teorici ed esperienze aziendali. Misurazione e gestione. Egea, Milano

Gabbi G, Matthias M (2009) Il valore della reputazione bancaria nel pensiero di Tancredi Bianchi. Banche e banchieri 4

Gainess-Ross L (2008) Corporate reputation: 12 steps to safeguarding and recovering reputation. Wiley, Hoboken, NJ

Helm S (2011) Corporate reputation: an introduction to a complex construct. In: Helm S, Lierh-Gobbers K, Storck C (eds) Reputation management. Springer, Heidelberg, pp 3–16

Limentani RN, Tresoldi N (2012) Compliance handbook. La funzione di Compliance secondo le nuove disposizioni normative: indicazioni operative. Bancaria Editrice, Roma

Maino R, Zaini F (2011) Banche e corporate governance: un passaggio critico verso Basilea 3. Bancaria 11

Phillips D, Young P (2009) Online public relations: a practical guide to developing an online strategy in the world of social media. Kogan Page, Philadelphia, PA

Rhee M, Hadwick RJ (2011) Repairing damaged to reputations: a relational and behavioural perspective. In: Burke RJ, Martin G, Cooper CL (Eds) Corporate Reputation: Managing opportunities and threats. Gower publishing Limited, UK, pp 305–325

Rhee M, Kim T (2012) After the collapse: a behavioral theory of reputation repair. In: Barnett ML, Pollock TG (eds) The Oxford handbook of corporate reputation. Oxford University Press, Oxford, pp 447–465

Roberts P, Dowling GR (2002) Corporate reputation and sustained superior financial performance. Strategic Manage J 23:1077–1093

Romenti S (2006) Corporate reputation, crisis management and stakeholder partnerships. An Italian case study. Paper presented at Iran 3rd International Conference on Public Relations, Teheran, 16–17 November

Schwaiger M (2004) Components and parameters of corporate reputation – an empirical study. Schmalenbach Bus Rev 56:46–71

Shanahan F, Seele P (2015) Shorting Ethos: exploring the relationship between Aristotle's Ethos and Reputation Management. Corp Rep Rev 18(1):37–49

Sims R (2009) Toward a better understanding of organizational efforts to rebuild reputation following an ethical scandal. J Bus Ethics 90(4):453–472

Stephens KK, Malone PC, Bailey CM (2005) Communicating with stakeholders during a crisis. J Bus Commun 42(4):390–419

Walker K, Dyck B (2014) The primary importance of corporate social responsibility and ethicality in corporate reputation: an empirical study. Bus Soc Rev 119(1):147–174

Weigelt K, Camerer C (1998) Reputation and corporate strategy: a review of recent theory and application. Strategic Manage J 9(5):443–454

Zaini F (2009) L'autoregolamentazione: dalla prevenzione dei rischi reputazionali alla compliance. Bancaria 3

Stefano Dell'Atti is a Professor of Banking and Finance at University of Foggia (Italy). He holds a PhD in Business Administration and Governance from the University Parthenope of Naples (Italy). He was an Assistant Professor in Banking and Finance at Faculty of Economics University of Foggia (from 1997 to 2000). From 2000 to 2003, he was an Associate Professor at University of Foggia. He is currently a Full Professor in Banking and Finance at University of Foggia (since 2003), where he teaches Banking and Finance and Strategy and Organization of Financial Intermediaries.

He is a member of the Council of PhD in Management and Finance at University of Foggia and Director of the Research Center Interuniversity on the Guarantee Institutions (CeSAC) of University of Foggia and University of Bari "Aldo Moro".

He is also a Member of the Editorial Board of Journal "Rivista Bancaria" and "Banche e Banchieri", and he was an editor and reviewer for a number of journals.

Over his 20-year academic career, he has authored (or co-authored) more than 50 scientific publications and 5 books. His major areas of research are as follows: Value and Intangibles in Banks; Reputational Risk; Small Banks, Guarantee Institutions; Efficiency of Financial Intermediaries, Regulation and Disclosure.

Vincenzo Pacelli is a Tenured Assistant Professor of "Banking and Finance" at University of Foggia (since November 2008), where he is also Academic Senator (since October 2010). He holds a PhD in "Banking and Finance" from the University of Roma "Sapienza" (Italy). Currently, he teaches the courses "Financial Portfolio Management" and "Economics of Financial Intermediaries—Advanced Course" at the Department of Economics of University of Foggia. In addition, he taught the course "Banking and Finance" at the Department of Economics of University of Bari.

He is a member of the Council of PhD School in "Management and Finance" at University of Foggia, member of the organizing committee and chair of different International Conference, ordinary member of the "Italian Association of Professors of Economics of Financial Intermediaries and Markets" and member of the scientific committee of "CeSAC". He is also a member of the Editorial Board of the *Journal of Intelligent Learning Systems and Applications*, published by Scientific Research Publishing, Inc. USA, and he was an editor or reviewer for the following journals: *Applied Economics, Journal of Intelligent Learning Systems and Applications, Lecture Notes in Computer Sciences, Entropy, British Journal of Economics, Management & Trade.*

Since 2005, he has authored (or co-authored) more than 40 scientific publications. His major areas of research are as follows: Governance, Performance and Risks in Banks; Forecasting in Financial Markets; Intangibles in Banks; Credit Risk Management; Reputational Risk Management; Artificial Intelligence in Banking and Finance; Asset Allocation.

Stefania Sylos Labini is a Tenured Assistant Professor of "Banking and Finance" at University of Foggia (since November 2006). She holds a PhD in "Banking and financial science" from the University of Calabria (Italy). Currently, she teaches the courses "Relationship banking" and "Economics of insurance companies" at the Department of Economics of University of Foggia.

She is a member of the Council of PhD School in "Management and Finance" at University of Foggia (XXIX cycle); member of the Council of PhD School in "Health Food Innovation and Management" at University of Foggia (XXVI cycle); ordinary member of the "Italian Association of Professors of Economics of Financial Intermediaries and Markets" and Deputy Director and member of the Council of the Interuniversity Research Center on the Guarantee Institutions (CeSAC) of University of Foggia and University of Bari "Aldo Moro".

She is a reviewer for the following journals: *Journal of Intelligent Learning Systems and Applications' special issue in Banking and Finance* and *Rivista Bancaria Minerva.*

Since 2005, she has authored (or co-authored) 25 scientific publications. Her major areas of research are as follows: Governance, Performance and Risks in Banks; Guarantee Institutions; Operational risk; Cooperative Banks; Credit Risk Management; Reputational Risk Management; Regulation and Disclosure; Management of Crisis and Debt Restructuring.

Annarita Trotta is a Professor of Banking and Finance at University "Magna Græcia" (UMG) of Catanzaro (Italy).

She holds a PhD in Business Administration from the University Federico II of Naples (Italy), where she was an assistant Professor of Banking on the Faculty of Economics from 1995 to 2001. From 2001 to 2006, she was an Associate Professor at the University of Catanzaro. Since 2006, she has been a professor of Economics and Management of Financial Institutions and Markets at UMG, where she teaches Banking, Financial Markets, and Corporate Finance.

She is currently a member of the PhD Council of the School of Theory of Law and European Legal and Economic Systems at UMG and a member of the Evaluation Unit of the LUM Jean Monnet University (Italy).

She is also a member of the Committee of Advisors of Ordines (for Interdisciplinary Research on European Institutions) and a member of the editorial boards of the following journals: "China – USA Business Review", and "Economics World".

Over her 20-year academic career, Trotta has authored (or co-authored) more than 50 scientific publications and 4 books. Her primary areas of research are Social and Sustainable Finance; Impact Investing; Alternative Finance and Sustainability; Reputational risk and reputational crisis in the banking sector; Corporate Social Responsibility in the banking sector; Subprime crisis and Credit Rating Agencies; Local banking and information asymmetries; Credit risk; Small business, Venture Capital and Informal Venture Capital; Bank-small business relationships; and Finance and Medicine.

MIX
Papier aus verantwortungsvollen Quellen
Paper from responsible sources
FSC® C105338

If you have any concerns about our products,
you can contact us on
ProductSafety@springernature.com

In case Publisher is established outside the EU,
the EU authorized representative is:
Springer Nature Customer Service Center GmbH
Europaplatz 3, 69115 Heidelberg, Germany

Printed by Libri Plureos GmbH
in Hamburg, Germany